THE WORD

A NOVEL

Praise for
The Word

"Crouch is a fine practitioner of the courtroom drama. He knows just how to bring a legal case to life without having to dress it up or dumb it down. His prose is precise and clear, pushing readers forward with an understated elegance. Characters—heroes, villains and those in between—are fully formed creatures with personal hungers, demons and large helpings of Texas personality... the pages all but turn themselves as each scene builds on the next, working outward in a spider web of connections, complications and coincidences... Inspired by news headlines, this timely novel illustrates how even the simplest seeming disputes are complex in the eyes of the law... A topical, lively legal thriller." - *Kirkus Reviews*

"Be ready for a wild ride! In The Word, real life attorney Hubert Crouch provides masterfully connected, multiple story lines that could have been ripped straight from the headlines. Corruption, greed and danger crisscross with the pursuit of honesty and truth for a page-turning, action packed story. Though this is book two in the Jace Forman series, it absolutely stands alone, though I fully intend to read book one. Crouch is in his element as the courtroom drama unfolds, writing memorable and unique characters—all with a Texas flair—for readers to love or loathe. The writing is high caliber and the story is engaging and realistic, with memorable characters. Top notch." - *Readers' Choice – 5 Star Readers' Favorite*

❖ ❖ ❖

Praise for

Cried for No One

"Readers interested in courtroom drama and fast-moving thrillers will find much to like here..." - ***Publishers Weekly***

"In the well-plotted tale, the author adeptly explores the complex interrelationships among politicos, the media and various legal and law enforcement professionals...There are a number of thriller chestnuts, too...Well-crafted with an authentic Southwestern setting..." - ***Kirkus Reviews***

"If your preference in fiction leans toward courtroom drama and mystery, you will love Hubert Crouch's Cried For No One." - ***John Seigenthaler, Founding Editorial Director of USA Today and Founder, the First Amendment Center***

"Rich with dialogue and well developed characters, the tale reveals surprising twists and turns all along the way...Grab a copy of this book and take a ride through its gripping plot, intriguing characters and shocking conclusion, all seasoned with a hearty dose of Texas flavor." - ***Dallas Bar Association***

www.hubertcrouch.com

Copyright © TXu001899601
2014 by Hubert Crouch

ISBN: 0692369007
ISBN 13: 978-0692369005
Library of Congress Control Number: 2014920504
Serpentine Books, Dallas, Texas

DEDICATION

This book is dedicated to my female law school classmates who courageously took on the "good old boy" network of the Dallas legal community and, by doing so, opened the door of opportunity for countless women lawyers in the years to follow.

ACKNOWLEDGEMENTS

Thanks to my editor, Skip Hollandsworth, whose plot suggestions and editorial revisions were invaluable in the writing process. Thanks to Amy Nettle, Paula Lovell, Brooke Floyd and Clay Small who painstakingly read the manuscript and provided me with input as to how it could be improved. And, most of all, thanks to my wife Doris, whose honest criticism and enthusiastic support were vital to the process of transforming an idea into a novel.

One man's ceiling is another man's floor.
-Paul Simon

THE WORD

A NOVEL

HUBERT CROUCH

PROLOGUE

The Tradewinds Motel was off Highway 287. It was a cheap little place, the swimming pool brown and half full, the blinking sign out front missing several bulbs. Room 8, on the back side of the motel, was sparsely furnished—unmade twin beds separated by a worn bedside table with a lone lamp on top, its shade torn and yellow from age. Gray carpet, stained in some places and in others frayed, covered the uneven floor. The walls were bare, the paint beginning to peel, cracks winding their way from the door corners to the water-marked acoustic-tiled ceiling above.

Room 8 was the classic $39.99-a-night fleabag, its usual clientele a sad collection of truckers, hookers, drifters, and addicts.

But not on this day. On this day, room 8 was a sanctuary.

Ten people were seated in a circle on the floor, eyes closed, heads bowed. After several moments of silence, one of the men raised his head and said, "Brothers and Sisters." The others looked up obediently, their eyes focused on the man who had just spoken.

"God calls us once again. And now God has called us here, to the town of Hagstrom, Texas. We must always heed his call, for as we all know, God's work is never done."

Ezekiel Shaw slowly turned his head toward a woman with waist-length gray hair and soft blue eyes. She wore no makeup, no jewelry, and no smile. A simple white dress flowed from just under her chin downward to her ankles. Her feet were bare. "Sister Rebekah, please remind us why we are here."

Without hesitation, Rebekah responded in a robotic monotone, "To follow God's instructions as laid down in the only inerrant book ever written, the Holy Bible, 1 Corinthians 11:3." Rebekah cleared her throat and recited, "'I want you to understand that the head of every man is Christ, and the head of the wife is her husband, and the head of Christ is God.'"

Ezekiel nodded approvingly. "Thank you, Sister Rebekah." His gaze shifted to another woman. Her red hair was long and curly, her eyes jade green. Likewise, she wore no makeup and no jewelry. Her dress was stark white. "Sister Naomi, why are we here?"

Naomi's response was immediate and certain: "To follow God's instructions as laid down in the only inerrant book ever written, the Holy Bible, 1 Corinthians 14:34–36, and I quote, 'The women should keep silent in the churches. For they are not permitted to speak, but should be in submission, as the law also says. If there is anything they desire to learn, let them ask their husbands at home. For it is shameful for a woman to speak in the church.'"

"Amen. Thank you, Sister Naomi, you have learned well."

Ezekiel's hypnotic stare left Naomi and settled on a petite young girl seated directly across from him. Her skin was fair, her waist-length hair almost white, and her eyes a pale blue. Just seventeen, she possessed a natural beauty that had no equal among the Sisters. As Ezekiel's gaze slowly traveled from her bare feet up her body, her lower lip began to quiver.

"Sister Mary, I am so glad you are able to be with us. This is your first crusade, is that correct?"

Mary nodded.

"Please tell us what our mission is today."

After an uncomfortably long silence, Mary finally spoke. Her voice was unsure, shaky at times. "To follow God's instructions as laid down in the only inerrant book ever written, the Holy Bible, 1 Timothy 2:11–15." Mary paused and looked down at her lap, where her fingers twitched nervously. She then raised her head, her eyes not meeting anyone's but fixing upon the lamp above Ezekiel's head. "Scripture says, 'Let a woman learn quietly with all submissiveness. I do not permit a woman to teach or . . .'" Again, an awkward silence, the words refusing to come.

Ezekiel allowed her discomfort to continue for what seemed an eternity and then finished her recitation: "'Or exercise authority over a man; rather, she is to remain quiet. For Adam was formed first, then Eve; and Adam was not deceived, but the woman was deceived and became a transgressor. Yet she will be saved through childbearing—if she continues in faith and love and holiness, with self-control.'"

Ezekiel smiled paternalistically. "That's what you forgot, isn't it, Sister Mary?"

The young girl nodded, small tears forming in the corners of her eyes.

"Well, now, it's nothing to get upset about. You just need to be more diligent in your studies. God rewards the industrious and punishes the lazy. Let us not forget that sloth is one of the cardinal sins."

Satisfied she had been humiliated enough for her transgression, Ezekiel stood while his followers remained seated. He moved to the middle of the circle, gazing around at the eyes of those beneath him.

"We are here today because we have a mission, a serious mission that we must fulfill to the best of our God-given abilities. It will not be easy, and we may be subjected to insult and scorn. Our mission is clearly laid out in God's word, found in the book of Ezekiel, Chapter 3, verses 17 through 19."

Ezekiel paused for effect. He ran his fingers through long, stringy brown hair that fell to his shoulders, and then stroked his scruffy beard. His plain white robe brushed the tops of his bare feet.

"We must warn the wicked of their evil ways. If we do not, Brothers and Sisters, their blood will be on our hands—on our hands! We cannot turn away from this solemn duty that God has entrusted to us, no matter how hard, no matter the cost. But if we follow God's call to warn those who refuse to obey his word, there is no more we can do. If the sinful then continue down their evil path, the blame will rest on their shoulders, their punishment eternal damnation."

A muttering of "amens" followed from those seated at Ezekiel's feet.

"You may now stand."

All quickly complied.

"Well, Brothers and Sisters, we have some souls to save. We have a nation to save. We have a world to save." Ezekiel glanced at his watch. "Let us proceed with haste. The service begins shortly."

In the parlor of St. Luke's Episcopal, Hagstrom's most beautiful church, the steel casket was positioned in the middle of the room, its upper half open. Visitation was scheduled to end in five minutes. The funeral director, dressed in a dark blue suit and somber tie, watched as the last of the visitors exited, leaving Janice and Eugene Hanson alone with their daughter. He nodded at the couple and then walked noiselessly out of the room, closing the door behind. Eugene took his wife's hand firmly, and they slowly made their way toward the coffin, its bottom half draped in an American flag.

Their daughter looked beautiful. Her olive skin glowed, her lips full and colored, her dark hair stylishly short. She could have been sleeping. But Eugene shuddered as his mind's eye pictured what lay under that flag. Thank God his wife didn't know. There are certain things a mother should never know—never.

Janice turned to her husband. A tear slowly began to make its way down her cheek. "To think that her life was just getting started," she murmured.

Eugene put his arm around his wife's shoulders and held her tight against him.

"Remember the heaven we were told about in vacation bible school?" Janice's eyes looked up into her husband's. "Do you think it's real?"

"Honey, you know Lauren is there right now."

Eugene felt a tap on his shoulder and looked around to see the concerned face of the funeral director.

"I'm sorry, Mr. Hanson, but you and your wife will have to say your goodbyes now. We have to close the casket. The service is scheduled to start shortly." He stepped back and turned the other way to give Eugene and Janice a final moment of privacy with their daughter.

Janice leaned over and kissed her daughter gently on the forehead. She began to say something, but the words wouldn't come. She straightened up and then turned to walk away, sobbing audibly as she made her way to the door.

Eugene took one last look at his daughter. A faint smile crossed his lips, his eyes misty. He leaned over and kissed her gently on the cheek. Unable to hold back the tears, he leaned back from the casket, saluted his fallen daughter and hero, and quietly whispered, "Second Lieutenant Lauren Hanson, you will always be my little princess. Always."

At Eugene's request, the funeral service had been brief. He and Janice just couldn't make it through a lengthy memorial as their daughter's fellow soldiers and friends solemnly paid tribute to their fallen comrade—there was way too much pain right now.

And the ultimate sacrifice she had paid for the country she loved so dearly needed no retelling, at least not today.

After the service concluded, a black hearse carrying the flag-draped casket of Second Lieutenant Hanson pulled out of the church parking lot and headed for the cemetery. Following in a limousine, Eugene and Janice huddled together in the backseat. Eugene stared straight ahead, as if in a trance. His wife wept into a handkerchief that never left her face.

As the procession slowly made its way down Main Street, the driver of the limousine turned his head over his shoulder and said, "Mr. and Mrs. Hanson, there seems to be a little disturbance just up ahead. I would suggest you close your eyes for a few moments until we get past it."

Janice still had her face buried in her handkerchief. But Eugene leaned forward. "What kind of disturbance? What are you talking about?"

He peered out the window, and his eyes suddenly widened in disbelief. A group of people—the men clad in white robes, the women in white dresses—were marching in a circle on a lot adjacent to the street, hiking placards up and down, chanting slogans and singing songs. In blood-red letters, the placards read "A WOMAN'S PLACE IS IN THE HOME, NOT ON THE BATTLEFIELD"; "WOMEN ARE FOR BEARING CHILDREN, NOT ARMS"; "THANK GOD FOR DEAD WOMEN SOLDIERS."

Eugene could feel his face flush. Janice peeked over her handkerchief to see what was happening. Both of them gasped as their eyes fixed on another of the signs, this one being hoisted up and down by a woman with long gray hair, an expression of satisfaction on her face. The sign read "GOD KILLED LAUREN HANSON BECAUSE HE HATES LESBIANS."

"Stop the car!" Eugene shouted.

"Sir, I don't think I should do that. Just ignore them. They're crazy."

But before the driver could hit the automatic door locks, Eugene had the back door open and was out on the street. He ran up to the gray-haired woman and wrested the placard from her hands, stomping on it repeatedly and yelling, "You have no right! You have no right!"

Suddenly he felt strong arms wrap around him. "Sir, sir. Calm down. Calm down." He turned around to look into the sympathetic eyes of a police officer.

"They have to be stopped!" Eugene shouted. "It's my little girl they're talking about. They have no right!" He fell to the ground, as if in shock.

The gray-haired woman sneered at him and then uttered, "We do have the right. It's called free speech. And by the way, your daughter's in hell right now, and you and your wife are to blame. You should have raised her according to Scripture. If you had, she wouldn't have come home to you in a body bag."

Eugene started crawling crazily toward the woman. At the last moment, the police officer grabbed him from behind, lifted him up, and steered him back toward the waiting limousine. As he helped Eugene back into the seat, the officer whispered, "They'll get theirs. Just leave it to God."

As the door began to close, Eugene frantically screamed, "You're not going to get away with this! I promise you that! There'll be hell to pay! I swear, you just wait . . ." The limousine resumed its journey, Eugene's muffled shouts becoming more faint as it gradually disappeared from view.

CHAPTER

1

A be Levine stroked his dark gray beard as he gazed over his reading glasses at the woman seated on the opposite side of his desk. Dressed in a wrinkled plaid shirt, worn jeans, and chukka boots, Abe looked more like an aging hippie than the executive editor of *Texas Matters,* a monthly magazine headquartered in Austin. He had been one of the first reporters hired by the fledgling publication when it opened its doors back in the Sixties, the dream of an anti-establishment group of University of Texas graduates determined to change the world—well, at least Texas. Just like its founders, *Texas Matters* had mellowed over the years but had never completely lost its liberal flair, which surfaced from time to time in editorials on the legalization of marijuana, the hypocrisy of the Religious Right, and the intellect of the state's "Tea Party" Republicans.

"Leah," he said to the young woman, "Steve isn't saying he won't run your piece. He just needs more corroboration. And I can't blame him. Hell, you're writing about Cal Connors, maybe the most feared plaintiff attorney in the state. He's threatened us with a libel suit if we print anything negative about him. That's something Steve, or any other magazine publisher, has to take seriously."

Abe looked at Leah fondly. She was only twenty-six and already one of his best reporters. It had been a little over a year since she excitedly burst into his office after covering a trial down in the Valley and told him that she had the story of a lifetime.

Leah stood and walked toward the floor-to-ceiling window in Abe's office. She turned and faced him before speaking. "But my investigation and facts are solid. I mean, what more do you want?"

"Okay, let's go over your story, brick by brick. If we can plug the holes that are troublesome, I'm sure we can get it to print."

"Okay. First, we have Cal Connors, a liar and a crook," Leah snapped.

Abe smiled and interrupted. "Without any embellishment, please."

Leah smiled back and started again. "Right. Cal Connors, a well-known plaintiff lawyer out of Fort Worth, has tried and won multimillion-dollar lawsuits throughout the country against numerous pharmaceutical companies. The drugs vary, but all the claims are similar. In every case, Mr. Connors — or the Lone Wolf, as he is sometimes called—has used an expert witness by the name of Howell Crimm." Leah paused for a moment to make sure Abe was paying attention.

"Go on," Abe said.

"Dr. Crimm has a résumé equal in length to the unabridged version of *Moby Dick* — degrees from Yale undergraduate and Harvard Med, with multiple scholastic and extracurricular honors at both institutions. But his prestigious background hasn't stopped him from submitting almost identical reports in every case in which he has testified for Cal Connors. His reports all indicate that the pharmaceutical companies manipulated test data submitted to the FDA during the drug's approval process. I've tracked down two of Crimm's lab assistants. One was involved in the testing of a drug called Fosorax, which was manufactured by Samson Pharmaceuticals and was at the heart of Connors' trial that I covered in the Valley. The drug, an antidepressant, helped millions of people before it was taken off the market as a result of the verdict he got against the company."

Abe was reading something on his computer as Leah spoke. Irritated, she sighed loudly before continuing.

"The two assistants, Dr. Sanjay Patel and Dr. Seth Coleman, are now practicing clinicians. Dr. Patel has provided me with his lab notes confirming that Dr. Crimm's testimony in the Samson trial was false. The companies hadn't manipulated any data at all about the drugs they were selling." She sighed. "Case closed, except for one detail."

"And what's that?" asked Abe.

"I promised Dr. Patel that I would not use him or his notes as a source for the story without first getting his permission."

"Leah, you've done a hell of a job on this story, better than anyone could expect. But it doesn't mean the story is ready to print. You need another source." Abe took off his glasses and rubbed his eyes. "This other research assistant, Seth Coleman. He's in Topeka, Kansas, correct?"

Leah retook her seat and crossed her legs, her front leg swinging anxiously back and forth. She couldn't believe Abe remembered where Dr. Coleman practiced. He had been listening to her after all. "Yes. But I got nowhere with him. Wouldn't give me the time of day."

"Might be worth another try," Abe responded.

"I'm listening."

"What drug did you tell me Coleman researched for Crimm?"

"Zilantin. A sleep medication made by Orpheus Pharmaceutical. Cal sued Orpheus, claiming that Zilantin caused his client to sleepwalk. His client took off in his car at two in the morning and ran into a telephone pole. Died at the scene. Connors convinced the jury to award the wife several million."

"Did he have a strong case?"

"Not when you hear all the facts. The toxicology report determined that his client had three times the legal limit of alcohol in his system. He had been drinking shots of tequila with some old college buddies all night. It was a miracle he didn't have a wreck on his way home. Before going to bed, he threw down a couple of Zilantin—who knows why."

"Ouch. How did Cal get around that?"

"The same way he did in the Samson Pharmaceuticals case. He had Dr. Crimm swear in an affidavit that Orpheus submitted flawed data to the FDA. Based on that affidavit, Connors argued that Orpheus lied to get its drug approved for a very simple reason: money, and lots of it. Zilantin sold like crazy, and Orpheus stock went through the roof. The jury bought his story."

Abe sighed. "Do you have any evidence that Crimm's report was false?"

"Nothing concrete. I did look at the reports Crimm submitted in both cases—the Samson trial and the Orpheus trial—and they were almost identical. And I know from what Dr. Patel told me off the record that Crimm lied in the Samson trial. So if Crimm lied in that case, he probably lied in the other. That's why I wanted to talk with Coleman."

"You never met with him face-to-face?"

"Nope. The moment I got him on the phone and told him who I was, he cut me off."

"Why don't you make an appointment with him under an alias? You said he practices general psychiatry?"

"Good memory."

"Okay, so give it a try. Make an appointment. Give the receptionist a fake name. When you get in to see him, maybe you can get him to open up."

Leah's brown eyes widened, and a smile creased her lips. She straightened up in her chair and re-crossed her legs. "I do have a copy of the affidavit Crimm filed in the Zilantin case. I could give that to Coleman . . ."

"And if Coleman realizes the conclusions Crimm made don't square at all with the research he did ..."

"Then he just might talk," Leah finished the sentence. "You good for the expenses?"

"Absolutely. Just send me the receipts when you get back. No five-star restaurants or expensive bottles of wine." Abe smiled.

Leah smiled back and rose from her chair. "Thanks, Abe. I hope this works."

"You never know. But let's give it a shot."

As she turned to leave, Abe said, "And Leah. Be careful. Cornered cats are dangerous."

Leah left work and arrived at her one-bedroom condo overlooking Lake Austin just after seven in the evening. She kicked off her flats, poured herself a glass of pinot noir, and nestled into one of the ultramodern swivel chairs in the sitting area adjoining her kitchen. She picked up the universal remote and pointed it in the direction of the flat screen on the wall above a credenza that housed her iPod cradle and receiver. The flat screen lit up, and she selected the "Playlist" option from the menu, scrolling down to a mellow mix of Coldplay, Snow Patrol, Jack Johnson, and Amy Winehouse. She leaned back in the chair and took a generous sip of wine. She picked up her iPad and replied to several emails from various friends and family members.

Twenty minutes later, she downed the last of the wine and strolled to her bedroom to change clothes. The minute she walked into the room, she took a step back. A strong, rancid odor hung in the air. "Smells like a rat died in there," she mumbled under her breath as she retreated to the living area.

For a moment she thought about shutting the bedroom door and having her landlord find out what was causing the smell the next morning. Then she said to herself, "Come on, Leah. Don't be a baby! There are worse things than a dead rat."

She entered the bedroom again slowly and turned her head in disgust. She surveyed the hardwood floors. Nothing. Leah slowly inched open the sliding mirrored door to her closet and gazed at the floor inside. Again, nothing.

She decided to take her shoes out of the closet to get a better look. She bent down and gingerly removed a pair of navy blue pumps from the corner of her closet and peered behind. She turned them upside down. Nothing fell out. She followed the same procedure with every shoe. Still nothing.

She got down on her hands and knees and lifted the bed skirt. It was too dark underneath to see anything. She opened the drawer of her bedside table and retrieved the flashlight she kept there in case of an emergency. She got down on all fours again and shined the light under the bed.

Nothing, of course.

Meanwhile, the smell had grown stronger and more nauseating. Maybe it was coming from the bathroom. She got up from the bedroom floor and walked inside the bathroom, taking the flashlight with her. She shined the light on the floor—nothing. She raised the toilet seat and cringed as she pointed the flashlight in the bowl—nothing. She looked behind the shower door and in the sink—nothing.

She shook her head. Could this be her imagination? She dismissed the thought. This was real.

She went back into her bedroom. Her eyes moved around the room, looking for something she might have missed, and settled on her bed. The bedspread was unevenly positioned, and there seemed to be a lump under the portion covering the pillow—clearly not the way she had left it. She inched toward the bed, her eyes not leaving the pillow. She took a deep breath.

Then she peeled back the bedspread.

For a moment, it was as if she could not move. She stared, frozen, at what she had uncovered. A two-foot codfish lay lifeless across her pillow, a wilting rose in its mouth. In red lipstick, the word "STOP" had been written in large letters on the pillowcase.

Suddenly all of Leah's senses came roaring back at once, and she screamed as loudly as she had ever screamed in her life. She ran out of her bedroom, slamming the door behind her. She scrambled to find her purse and raced out of her condo and down the hall to the elevator. She punched the elevator call button, pulled her cell phone out of her purse, and dialed 911.

"Has anything like this ever happened to you before?" Officer Jorge Gomez, Austin PD, was seated next to Leah at the bar that separated the kitchen from the living area in her condo.

"No, never."

"Ever been threatened by anyone? Disturbing emails, voice mails, letters—that type of thing?"

Leah shook her head no.

"And why the codfish? Any ideas?"

"None whatsoever."

"Any old boyfriends who might hold a grudge?"

"I have had some relationships that didn't end well but nothing out of the ordinary. And I haven't dated anyone seriously for a while. Too busy at work."

"And where do you work, Ms. Rosen?"

"I'm a reporter for *Texas Matters*. Went to work there right after I graduated from UT."

"And what do you do at *Texas Matters*?"

"I'm on the legal beat. I started out trolling the courthouse for leads. If I turned up something interesting, I would rough out a story and give it to one of the more seasoned writers to finish. About a year ago, I was assigned to cover a case down in the Valley—that was my big break."

"Was it a criminal or civil case?"

"Civil. Filed by a big-time plaintiff lawyer. His name is Cal Connors."

Officer Gomez wrinkled his brow. "That name rings a bell."

"Not surprising. He's from Fort Worth, and he loves seeing his name in the newspapers. He's all about publicity. Wears a bolo tie with a clasp molded in the shape of Texas, a black Stetson, and custom-made ostrich-skin cowboy boots. And get this—his boots are engraved in the front with the scales of justice and on the sides with his nickname, the Lone Wolf."

Officer Gomez smiled. "Yeah, I remember the guy. I've seen him on the news. I can't recall the case, but it's hard to forget someone like that."

"And that's the way he wants it."

"Did you write an article on him?"

"Working on one, but it hasn't been published yet."

"Flattering article?"

"No, not really. I believe in honest reporting. And based on what I learned, Connors is a scumbag."

"Do you think he might have hired someone to break into your apartment?" Gomez asked. "To scare you off the story?"

Leah hesitated as she considered her response. "I guess it's possible. I really don't know."

"Well, if this piece you are working on gets published, what would that do to him?"

"Who knows? It might end his career, and could lead to a criminal investigation."

"So how far do you think he might go to keep it under wraps?"

"I don't see him doing anything stupid. I mean, I just can't imagine him hiring some thug to do something like this—too much downside for him."

"Don't dismiss the possibility. We're talking about a man's reputation here. And don't forget, highly successful people think they can get away with things a normal person can't."

Leah nodded, her head spinning.

"Any other stories you have worked on where you might have made an enemy?"

Leah shook her head. "Not that I can recall."

"Well, if you think of anything, give me a call." Officer Gomez handed her a business card.

"What are the chances of catching whoever did this?"

"I've got to be honest with you, Ms. Rosen. We're understaffed and overworked. Homicides, rapes, car thefts, you name it. And don't be offended, but all we have here is breaking and entering - maybe criminal mischief. Even if we caught the person who did this, it would be a long road for you. I can just hear a defense attorney arguing you staged the whole thing so you could get some favorable publicity. And even if you did demand that the case be prosecuted, the prosecutor would probably cut a deal with no jail time. It's not exactly what you'd call a violent crime."

"You've got to be kidding! Someone broke into my apartment and put a dead fish on my pillow, and who knows what he might do next! I don't know if I'll ever feel safe again."

"I get it, and I'm sorry about that. But a jury could decide it was nothing more than a prank that went a little overboard." Gomez paused. "Have you got a friend you could stay with for a few days?"

Leah thought for a moment. "Maybe. I just hate to impose on anyone like that." She hesitated. "Is there anything else I can do to protect myself?"

"If I were you, I'd hire a professional to look into this, someone who can devote some real time to it. There's this private investigator who used to be on the force. Her name's Jackie McLaughlin, and she's the best in the business. I'd suggest you give her a call."

Leah pulled Officer Gomez's card out of her pants pocket and handed it to him. As he wrote McLaughlin's name and phone number on the back, he said, "In the meantime, I'll file a report and let you know if we turn up anything."

He handed his card back to Leah. "Have your locks changed and use the deadbolt while you're here. I'll alert the doorman downstairs to keep an eye out for anything suspicious. Sorry I couldn't be of more help. Goodnight, Ms. Rosen."

After Officer Gomez left, Leah reached for her cell and speed-dialed Abe.

CHAPTER

"Mr. and Mrs. Hanson are here."

At his office near Sundance Square, in the heart of downtown Fort Worth, Jace Forman glanced up from the stack of papers in front of him and smiled politely at his secretary. "Thank you, Harriett. Would you take them to the conference room and tell them I'll be there shortly?"

"I will. You need anything before the meeting?"

"No, but buzz Darrin and ask her to come to my office. I'd like to talk with her briefly before we meet with the Hansons."

"Sure."

"Thank you, Harriett."

Jace continued to review the correspondence, pleadings, and legal briefs that typically piled up on his desk, the result of a very busy and successful trial practice.

"Jace, you wanted to meet with me?"

Jace's gaze left the papers in front of him and locked on the emerald green eyes of Darrin McKenzie. For over eight years,

Darrin had been Jace's paralegal, adviser, and confidante. She had been indispensable to his law practice, but, equally important, she'd been a willing sounding board when personal problems raised their ugly heads. Jace could not have started his own firm without her. He could not have endured the untimely death of his wife without Darrin patiently listening to his confessions and self-doubts. She was more to Jace than a salaried employee—much more. And yet his feelings for her were hard to pin down. Their relationship was a work in process, slowly evolving, its future uncertain.

"Darrin, come in. I just want to pick your brain before we meet with the Hansons."

"I can't even imagine what they must be feeling right now. Losing their only child. And then having to go through what they did at the funeral." Darrin shuddered.

"Yeah, I know. It's terrible. I hate it, but I'm going to have to ask them some tough questions today."

Darrin nodded. "I know."

"We need to tell them up front that this isn't going to be easy. And we need to find out if there are any skeletons in their closet. The last thing we want to do is spend a lot of time and money if we don't have a case. And I am going to count on you to interrupt me if you think I am being a little too blunt."

"You don't need to worry about that. I'll speak up if I sense you're crossing the line."

Jace rose from the desk and grabbed a legal pad. Darrin took the cue and led the way out of his office toward the conference room down the hall.

"Mr. Hanson, I'm Jace Forman, and this is my legal assistant, Darrin McKenzie."

A short, balding man in his fifties stood and extended his hand to Jace. "Please, call me Eugene." He nodded in Darrin's direction. "Jace, I've heard a lot about you. All good, I might add."

Actually, it was hard to find anyone in Fort Worth who hadn't heard of Jace. After graduating law review and Order of the Coif from the University of Texas, Jace had accepted an offer from Hadley and Morgan, an old-line Fort Worth firm. He rose through the ranks quickly by chalking up one impressive legal victory after another before deciding to break off and start his own shop. Shunning flamboyance for humility, Jace had wooed juries with his down-home, no-frills style. A champion of understatement, he refused to promise the jury anything he couldn't deliver, knowing that a broken promise would fester in the minds of the twelve people who held his client's fate in their hands. Now in his mid-forties, his cross-examination skills were surgical and precise, causing many a witness to wilt on the stand. As a result, he had piled up numerous victories, prompting new clients to flock to the Forman Firm. His only problem had been finding enough time to handle all of the cases streaming through the door. He had been able to delegate some to other lawyers in the firm, but there were those clients who wanted his attention and his attention only. Loath to turn away business, he had relied on Darrin to keep all the balls in the air as he focused on the most pressing matters. It had turned out to be a winning combination, and a very profitable one as well.

"Well, thank you, Eugene," Jace said. He turned his gaze to Janice, who remained seated. Her gray hair was cut short, her eyes dark and ringed in red. She nodded to Jace and Darrin but said nothing. Darrin pulled out the conference room chair next to hers and gracefully slid in. "Mrs. Hanson, my deepest sympathies. I know this must be very hard for you."

Their eyes met, and Janice spoke. "You can't imagine." Tears welled up in her eyes. "She was everything to us—everything."

Darrin continued. "Do you feel like talking, Janice? If not, we can reschedule for another day."

"We need to get this over with."

Eugene took his wife's hand and looked at Darrin. "What would you like to know?"

Jace took the lead. "I'd like to start with some general issues first. Is that all right with you?"

Eugene responded, "Sure."

Jace continued. "Have either of you ever been a party to a lawsuit?"

They both shook their heads.

"Well, it's not an easy road, I can promise you that. It's going to take a heavy emotional toll on both of you. There will be nights when you won't be able to sleep. And most of your waking hours you won't be able to think about much of anything but the lawsuit. The other lawyer will try to upset you, ask you probing questions about sensitive topics, try to get you to rethink your decision to pursue the case. I'd be lying if I told you it won't get nasty and unpleasant. It will."

"We understand that," Eugene said, "but nothing could be worse than what we have just gone through. Do you have children, Jace?"

"I do. I have a son Matt. He's a junior at the University of Texas in Austin."

"How would you feel if you got a call one morning and a stranger told you your son had been killed?"

Jace had no response.

Eugene continued. "And then a bunch of religious nuts show up at your son's funeral and yell some of the worst things you can ever imagine about him and how you raised him." He tried to say something else, but no words would come. He held back, determined not to break into tears.

Darrin spoke. "Seriously, Mr. and Mrs. Hanson, it's no problem at all if we take a break."

Eugene waved her off. "No, no. I'll be okay. Just give me a minute. It's just so fresh in my mind—the hateful words, the hideous signs, all coming right after the loss of our only child, the light of our life."

Jace responded, "Why don't you tell us about Lauren? I know you must have a lot of wonderful memories of her."

Janice remained quiet, staring at her husband's hand clutched in hers.

After wiping his eyes with his handkerchief, Eugene cleared his throat and replied, "Lauren was our only child. Janice and I had trouble having children. We even considered adoption. We had almost given up hope—Janice was thirty-three, I believe." He looked at his wife for confirmation, and she nodded. Eugene continued. "That was when we learned Janice was pregnant. It was one of the happiest days of our lives."

"How would you describe Lauren's childhood?" Darrin picked up the pen from the top of her legal pad.

"Lauren was a happy little girl, very athletic from an early age. Started playing soccer when she was five. She was a standout. And that continued through high school and college. You know she played at West Point?"

Darrin smiled approvingly. "I did not. That must have made the two of you very proud. But before we get to her college days, tell us more about what she was like growing up."

"What do you want to know?"

"Was she popular? Did she date anyone in particular? And, I think I know the answer to this, but did she ever get into any trouble?"

"Never any trouble. Never. Not even a speeding ticket. As far as dating, she was so busy with athletics—she played on the women's basketball team in high school in addition to varsity soccer—she didn't have much time for boys. As far as friends, she hung out with her teammates. They were like family."

"And how were her grades?" Jace asked.

Eugene turned his gaze away from Darrin to Jace. "Graduated at the top of her class. She wasn't valedictorian but pretty damn close. Several of the Ivies wanted her. I can't say I was that happy when she decided on West Point."

"Did she ever tell you why she made that decision?" Jace asked.

"We discussed it. She said she wanted to give back to her country. Plus, she thought women ought to have more of a role in our military. I didn't agree with her on that, but it was what she thought."

"How did she like West Point?"

"She didn't. Thought about transferring on several occasions."

"Why?"

"She told me it was still a 'good old boy' club. Lauren felt the male cadets only tolerated her. That's the way all women were treated, not just Lauren. But she made up her mind to stick with it. She was that way—very determined."

"Did she have any serious relationships while she was in college?"

Eugene seemed slightly irritated by Jace's question. "Like in high school, she was consumed with soccer and academics. And trying to learn how to be a good soldier—quite a transition."

"She obviously graduated," said Jace, quickly getting off the topic, trying to make sure the Hansons remained comfortable.

Eugene nodded. "Top ten percent of her class. After graduation, she was commissioned as a second lieutenant in the army and assigned to the 4th Battalion in Fort Campbell, Kentucky. Then she deployed to Kandahar, Afghanistan."

"Were you able to stay in contact with her after her deployment?"

"Not very often. Every month or so we were able to talk with her on Skype." Eugene smiled. "She looked good—and as happy as anyone could under the circumstances. She told us she really felt she was making a difference in our mission over there."

"How so?"

"Well, the cultural differences between the United States and the Afghans run deep; there's a lot of distrust. Lauren was selected as a member of an elite cultural support team to break down some of those barriers. She apparently bonded with some of the Afghan women and was making progress in achieving that goal until . . ." Eugene hesitated. He took a deep breath and continued. "Until she was killed by an IED on her way to the village where her team was working. Two other soldiers were wounded in the attack. Our daughter was the only one who didn't make it."

After several moments of silence, Eugene continued. "We had the funeral service in Hagstrom, just outside Fort Worth, where Lauren grew up and where Janice and I still live."

"Tell us about that day," Jace said.

"We decided to have a viewing at the church, St. Luke's Episcopal, and the funeral service in the sanctuary right afterwards. Her mother and I wanted to have an open casket. She was such a beautiful girl. Many of her friends hadn't seen her in quite a while, and we wanted to give them the opportunity to do so one last time."

Eugene refilled his glass with water and took a sip. "The funeral home did such a wonderful job. She looked angelic that morning, and so peaceful." Janice began to cry. Her husband squeezed her hand.

"What was the service like?"

"Very brief. I knew her mother and I were too broken up to handle a long one. I gave a short eulogy, and Father McCasland closed with a prayer."

"I know this is hard, but can you tell us what happened next?"

"Lauren's casket was placed in the hearse. Janice and I were directly behind the hearse in one of the funeral home's limousines. Others going to the graveside service followed. We were traveling along Main Street and headed for the cemetery where Lauren was going to be buried when our driver turned around and said something about there being a disturbance up ahead, that we should ignore it . . ."

"And what did you do?"

"Well, I couldn't believe it. I wanted to know what he was talking about. I leaned forward to see if I could make out anything."

"And?"

"That's when I saw them. There were these—these people, all dressed in white robes and dresses, marching around, holding up signs and chanting things."

"Could you make out what was on the signs?"

"Not all of them. One of them said something about women not having a place in the military. There was one about a woman's place being in the home and not on the battlefield."

"So what happened next?"

"I told the driver to stop the car, but he kept going. Said it wouldn't be a good idea. We were going pretty slowly, so I opened the door and jumped out. And then I saw this hateful-looking woman holding a sign that said God had killed Lauren because he hates"—the word momentarily stuck in his throat—"lesbians. That's when I lost it. I ran at her, tore the sign away from her, and stomped on it. I kept stomping until the police officer put his arms around me and pulled me back."

"Do you remember anything else?"

Eugene stood up and started to pace back and forth. "Yeah, I do. I remember that bitch—that coldhearted bitch—looking into my eyes, smirking and saying my daughter was in hell, where she belonged, because her mother and I hadn't raised her right. I don't remember much after that except for the officer pulling me back to the limo."

"And did you continue to the graveside service?"

"We did. But neither of us could stop the tears. I wish I could have I controlled myself better, but I had never been through anything like that."

Jace replied, "I don't think I would have done as well as you did. You don't have to apologize to anyone." He paused. "Now, let's talk about the judicial process and what we will need to prove to win. There's a church out of Kansas called the Westboro Baptist Church. They're not actually affiliated with the mainstream Baptist church, but they use the name anyway. The group that protested at Lauren's funeral, they call themselves the Brimstone Bible Church. They're a completely different bunch. As I recall, they have a compound out in West Texas, near Fort Stockton. Although these two groups are not affiliated with each other, they both share the belief that God is punishing America for condoning homosexuality by sending home dead soldiers."

Darrin and the Hansons shook their heads in disgust.

Jace continued. "The Westboro group protested at the funeral of a dead serviceman in Virginia or Maryland—somewhere up north—and the parents sued. The jury awarded them millions. But unfortunately, the story doesn't end well. The court of appeals took away the award, and the U.S. Supreme Court affirmed. They even charged the parents with court costs."

"That's ridiculous!" Eugene cried.

"I haven't read the entire opinion, but it was written by the Chief Justice. In the opinion, he reasoned that free speech about an issue of public importance is protected, regardless of whether or not it's offensive. Since the Westboro Baptist Church was voicing a belief on a hotly contested issue—homosexuality and the country's attitude toward it—they could not be sued successfully for damages."

"What is this country coming to when people can get away with something like that?"

"I seem to recall the court made some distinction between speech that is directed at a private person and speech that is addressing an issue of public importance," Jace said. "The first type is not protected, the second type is."

"Sounds like a distinction without a difference, a bunch of legal mumbo jumbo."

"I agree with you. It's like the court's rulings on what is and what isn't pornography," Jace grinned, trying to bring a little levity into the room. No one smiled. He continued. "What I am trying to say is that your case may be thrown out on summary judgment before it ever gets to trial unless we can find an important factual distinction between the Westboro case and yours. Finding that distinction may not be possible and, believe me, the trial prep will be expensive."

"I don't care about any of that. We owe it to our daughter, and to this country of ours, to go after those sick bastards. Now, I know we haven't talked about your fee, and from what I've heard, you don't come cheap. What is your rate, Jace?"

"I'm not going to charge you by the hour. You're right. That's usually the way I work, but it would be prohibitively expensive in this case. What if I take your case on a contingent fee basis—that is, we get paid a percentage of the recovery if we win, nothing if we lose. I'm thinking twenty percent. How does that sound?"

"I've either read, or heard, about some lawyers getting half. You sure you're okay with twenty percent?"

"Positive. Plus I'll front the pretrial expenses. Look, you and Janice are sacrificing plenty to see this through. It's the least I can do."

"We have a deal then. I am very grateful to you, Jace."

"We'll start working on drafting the complaint right away, and we'll be back in touch as soon as we have something for you to look at." Jace stood and extended his hand. "Mr. and Mrs. Hanson, again, I'm very sorry for your loss. I promise to do everything I can to win this lawsuit."

Eugene rose and gripped Jace's hand. "I know you will, Jace. I know you will."

The Hansons followed Jace and Darrin to the elevator. As the door slid open, Eugene turned around. "If there is anything I can do to help, anything—no matter how painful you may think it is—give me a call."

Jace nodded as the elevator door began to close.

J ace and Darrin were seated at the round conference table in Jace's office. Jace spoke. "This is going to be a tough case to win. You know that, don't you?"

"Why do you say that? If I were on a jury, I would give them big money."

"So would I. But the problem is getting this case to a jury. The First Amendment gets in the way."

"I know people in this country have the right to protest, but at the funeral of a fallen soldier? It's just unbelievable to me. What was the court thinking?"

"Well, I need an associate to do some research on this issue. How about Kirk? I know that Jarman case just settled. Maybe he's got some time. He should start with a careful review of the Westboro decision and go from there."

Darrin made a note on her legal pad. "I'll check with him. Knowing Kirk, I'm sure he'll make time."

Jace continued. "And work with him on drafting the complaint. I want to file this case in federal court here in Fort Worth as soon as possible. Also, I want you to draft some interrogatories and document requests to serve along with the complaint. I want to be aggressive from the get-go."

Darrin continued to scribble. "I agree."

"You will need to get medical authorizations from the Hansons so we can obtain their records for the last three years. Since we'll sue for mental anguish, whoever the BBC retains as a medical expert will be entitled to see those records to determine if they had any preexisting emotional problems."

"Got it."

"And I want you to find out everything you can about Lauren Hanson, from the time she was born until she died. Get her school records, her military records, talk with her friends. I want to know more about her than even her parents do."

"I think it's odd that Lauren never had any boyfriends."

Jace sighed. "Theoretically, whether Lauren was gay shouldn't impact our case one way or the other. Unfortunately, this is Texas, and as much as I love it, people down here aren't quite as accepting of that lifestyle as they should be. And if we get some jurors on the panel who are anti-gay, then we could be sunk."

"I'll see what I can find out about her."

"And Darrin, see if you can find out exactly what was written on those placards and what the protesters said at the funeral. Understandably, Eugene's memory may be a little hazy."

"I'll find out if someone recorded the protest and posted it on YouTube. And I'll be sure to include a document request that covers any signs or placards used at the demonstration."

"Good thinking." Jace got up from the table. "Let's get started."

Darrin remained seated. "Aren't you forgetting something?"

"What?"

"This so-called church and its members. We need to do our homework on them, don't we?"

"Absolutely, but your plate is way too full. I think we should hire a PI to do that."

"I'll call Boyce today and get him on it."

Jace shook his head. "This may be a little over Boyce's head."

"Really? So who do you have in mind?" Darrin asked.

"Jackie McLaughlin, the investigator down in Austin."

There was a long pause. "Jackie McLaughlin? Why?"

"She did a damn good job for us on our last case, don't you agree?"

Darrin was tight-lipped as she abruptly slid her chair out from underneath the table and stood. "Well, if that's all, I've got a lot to do."

"Wait. Do you have a problem with her?"

"No, Jace, of course not." Darrin quickly walked out the door and headed down the hall.

"Women," Jace muttered as he got up from the table. He pulled his cell phone from his pants pocket and dialed a number. A familiar voice answered. "Jackie, this is Jace. How are you?"

CHAPTER

3

Just blocks away Cal Connors took a bite of his chicken-fried steak and almost swallowed it whole, anxious to finish making his point. "Christine, I've never seen it this bad. That son of a bitch we have for a governor and all of his puppets in the statehouse have made it near impossible to get a plaintiff verdict in this state. Tort reform is killing us, just killing us."

Christine, his daughter and law partner, played with her salad, making sure she had given her dad ample time to vent before responding. She hadn't.

"And they are so damn sanctimonious." Cal shoveled down some mashed potatoes and followed it with a gulp of iced tea. "A doctor cuts out the good lung and leaves the cancer-eaten one in, and his poor patient can't get his full due from a jury of his peers. His award is capped without rhyme or reason. It's just a bunch of shit and you know it."

"Dad, you're preaching—"

Cal waved his daughter off with his fork. "And then there's the Texas Supreme Court. Well, they're 'supreme' at taking away verdicts awarded by ordinary working folk, but that's about it. They've turned the system on its head, all because of the sizable contributions made to their campaign by big bidness. Take that builder out of Dallas—he put up all of those shoddy homes, and when some poor son of a bitch finally got to trial and won, they took away the verdict on some trumped-up technicality. Just wore that guy and his poor ol' wife down to a frazzle. It's criminal, that's what it is."

There was a short lull before Christine spoke. "Dad, may I say something?"

Cal stopped his rant, gazed into the clear blue eyes of his only child, and then smiled. "I guess that's enough for today."

"Hey, I agree with everything you just said. The plaintiff bar—you and I included—got caught asleep at the switch and didn't put up enough money to get our people elected in the last go-round. It's that simple. That's why we're paying the price. We just need to learn from our mistakes and get ready for the next election cycle. The pollsters are predicting that it's just a matter of time before Texas goes blue, and when it does, we'll be right back in the saddle."

"It won't be soon enough for me."

"Well, at least we can still control the judicial races in certain counties. It's the statewide races that are the problem. We've got to get out the Latino and African American vote. Once we do that, we'll take back the state supreme court, the state legislature, and maybe even the governor's office. But it's going to be a gradual process."

"Well, what in the hell do we do in the meantime? Everything we have is leveraged to the hilt—our homes, our vacation homes, our plane, you name it. How are we going to make ends meet until things go back to the way they were?"

Christine took a last bite of salad and followed it with a sip of tea. "Funny you should ask. I got an interesting call from an insurance adjuster this morning."

Cal leaned forward across the table. "What is an insurance adjuster calling you for?"

"You remember those silica cases we filed several years ago, where we sued that sand company and respirator manufacturer for exposing our clients to all that dust? We paid some local docs to do pulmonary exams and they found lung obstructions in all of our clients. Is any of this ringing a bell?"

"I vaguely remember. You signed up the clients and filed the cases, right?"

"That's right. Well, this adjuster, Jamie Stein, has the insurance coverage for both defendants."

"What company?" Cal turned an ear toward his daughter.

"Empire Risk. They're headquartered in Hartford."

"Never heard of them."

"I hadn't either. But after I talked with Stein, I Googled them. The company's financially solid. They write only commercial lines—no homeowner or health care."

"So what did Stein want?" Cal stuck a toothpick in the corner of his mouth and began working it from side to side.

"He wanted to talk about settling all of our cases."

"How many cases do we have?"

"Two hundred and sixty-three, to be exact. I had Glenda run a report."

"Nice. So why did he contact you directly? Aren't the defendants represented by counsel?"

"Yeah, they are - by big firms out of Dallas and Houston. Stein says they're killing him on fees. A lot of make-work and phantom billable hours—you know the drill."

"Typical. But why doesn't he just move the files to other defense firms?"

"Stein felt they would be just as expensive. He wants to see if he can settle all of the cases now, lock, stock, and barrel."

The waitress came up to the table. "Mr. Connors, how about some homemade peach cobbler?"

Cal patted his stomach. "Nell, you know I would love some, but there's no room at the inn. Just bring me the check when you get a chance."

Nell slid it under his plate. "When you going to be in court again? I'd love to drop by on one of my days off and watch you in action."

"That's what Christine and I were just talking about. We're getting a big one ready. You'll be the first to know when we start picking a jury."

"Don't forget about me." Nell smiled warmly before heading to another table.

"Dad?" Christine shook her head disapprovingly as her father kept his eyes locked on Nell's wiggling posterior.

"Oh, c'mon. She's just a good friend, that's all." Cal sighed and quickly changed the topic. "So I assume you're going to meet with Stein?"

"I can't think of any reason not to, can you?"

"Hell, no. A hefty settlement just might be our ticket out of this financial mess. It could buy us enough time to rearrange the judicial playing field. Get us back to the good ol' days. How much is Stein offering?"

"We didn't talk numbers. He just wanted to feel me out, see if I had any interest."

"When are you gonna call him?"

"As soon as we get back to the office." Christine rose from the table. Cal gently took her arm and pulled her back down.

"By the way, anything new on that reporter? What was her name? Leah something?"

"Leah Rosen. I told you to quit worrying about her. That article will never see the light of day. You have my word."

"I just remember her coming up at the end of my last trial in the Valley with that look in her eye. She seemed so damned determined . . ."

"Forget it. We're not going to waste any more time talking about her. We've both got more important things to do."

Without looking at the check, Cal slid a crisp fifty-dollar bill under his plate, and the father-daughter team made their way to the door.

CHAPTER

Leah and Abe were seated in the kitchen at Abe's home in the Tarrytown neighborhood of Austin. A half-empty bottle of wine sat on the table between them.

"So what do you think I should I do, Abe? I can't stay here forever."

Abe slowly stroked his beard and, after a long pause, responded, "Well, you can stay here as long as you want. In the meantime, I would follow Officer Gomez's recommendation and schedule a meeting with that private investigator. What did you say her name was?"

"Jackie McLaughlin. Officer Gomez said she used to be with the Austin Police Department."

Abe poured some wine into Leah's glass and then emptied the rest into his.

"I don't know, Abe. This could be nothing. Maybe it was some kind of prank. If I get my apartment professionally cleaned and have the doorman walk me up when I get home from work, check it out with me, make sure no one is hiding in a closet, I think I'll be fine. I feel like I'm overreacting hiring an investigator. There are tons of people who live in my apartment building. It's not like I live in a secluded farmhouse in the middle of nowhere."

"Trust me. You should call in a professional. Just as a precaution."

"You may be right. I'll think about it. And Abe, you just don't know how much I appreciate your letting me stay here."

"My pleasure."

"I wonder if Christine Connors might have had something to do with this?"

"Why not Cal?"

"Well, when I met with Christine several months ago, I was trying to figure out if she worked on the cases involving Howell Crimm. I told her I had evidence of fraud in those cases, and she gave me a look that could kill. Maybe she's trying to scare me off the story."

"That may be. But I wouldn't push things right now. Be patient and let the dust settle. I assume you're going to wait a little while before scheduling an appointment in Topeka with Dr. Coleman?"

"Only until I get comfortable back in my apartment, which should be in a couple of days."

"Like I said, I wouldn't push it."

Leah glanced at the clock on the kitchen wall. "Abe, did you know it's almost one in the morning? I've got to be at work by nine. As you know, I have a very strict boss."

"He might make an exception since you found a dead fish on your pillow just hours ago," Abe winked. "You're in the bedroom just to the right after you go up the stairs. Do you need me to wake you in the morning? I am usually up at six regardless."

"I have my iPhone. I'll set the alarm." Leah picked up her overnight bag and headed toward the door. Abe remained seated at the table, finishing the last of his wine.

Leah stopped at the kitchen doorway. "Abe, you're the best. Thanks for being there for me."

Abe raised his glass. "I always will be, Leah."

CHAPTER

5

Jace handed the rental car keys to the valet and walked quickly toward the entrance to Malaga, a trendy tapas restaurant in downtown Austin. Traffic from the airport had been snarled, and he was twenty minutes late. He entered the restaurant and stopped at the reception desk. "I have a reservation for two at six-thirty. It's under Forman. I'm running a little late." As he spoke, Jace scanned the restaurant for his dinner companion.

"Yes, Mr. Forman. Your other party has already arrived. Please follow me."

Jace trailed a young woman not much older than his son as she weaved her way to a small table tucked cozily in one of the restaurant's corners.

"Here you are. Your waiter will be right with you." The hostess smiled politely and disappeared.

Jackie looked up as Jace pulled out the chair across from her and sat down. "Sorry I'm late, but rush hour traffic was a nightmare."

"No worries. I just got here ten minutes ago. I took the liberty of ordering a pitcher of sangria."

Jace poured a glass and took a sip. "Nice call. Haven't had sangria in years."

Jackie held up her glass. "I would like to propose a toast to your big win in the Stone case."

Jace followed suit and added, "Which, I might add, would never have happened without your assistance."

"That was such a weird case. In all of my years of police work, it was the first time I investigated a grave robbery. That poor girl's body, dug up and dragged off to that church. And her parents hiring Cal Connors to sue the cemetery. Anyway, Jace, I have to thank you. If you hadn't gotten me involved in that case, I would never have considered leaving the force and starting my own shop."

"Things have a way of working out for the best."

"Sometimes they do, sometimes they don't. I'll never forget that afternoon, though, when the chief summoned me to his office. No sooner had I walked in and taken a seat than he blurted out he was going to put a formal reprimand in my file, that the order came from on high, and he had no choice. I mean, I was only doing my job, and if the evidence happened to help you in your case, so much the better." Jackie took a sip of sangria and then chuckled. "I told him he could take that reprimand and stick it where the sun don't shine—I was quitting. You should have seen the look on his face."

"I'll bet. I can't prove it, but I'm pretty damn sure Cal was behind all of that. He had the assistant DA in his back pocket on that case. I mean, why else would he have focused on my son as a murder suspect in that poor girl's death?"

"Wouldn't surprise me one bit. That—" Jackie stopped in mid-sentence as the waiter positioned himself at their table, his hands clasped behind his back.

"Have you had a chance to look at the menu? I can come back if you need more time."

Jace looked up, "The last time I was here I had the assorted meat and cheese appetizer. The jamón serrano, chorizo, manchego . . ."

"A great choice for two."

"Jackie?"

"Perfect."

The waiter nodded and scurried toward the kitchen.

"Jace, I love the ambience of this place—the exposed brick walls and tile floors. I'm surprised I hadn't heard of it."

"I've been here once before with a client for lunch. I thought you might like it. The food's very different. People think that Spanish food is like Tex-Mex, but they couldn't be more wrong."

"Hey, I can't tell you how much I hated wimping out on our dinner in Fort Worth after your trial, but when I quit my job, I was kind of freaking out—trying to figure out how to start my private investigation business."

"Jackie, I feel I was partially responsible for your job—"

Jackie cut him off. "You shouldn't. Like I said, it was the best thing that ever happened to me. I'm my own boss now. Just starting to see the money roll in, but things take time."

"Well, this new case should help."

"I've already started looking into it, the Brimstone Bible Church. Ezekiel Shaw is its founder. He's got a whole flock of followers and a hundred-acre compound in a real isolated area out in West Texas, near Fort Stockton."

"Hey, I'm impressed."

"I try to please." Jackie grinned provocatively before taking another sip of sangria.

"I need you to find out everything you can about this Shaw guy and his cult. I'll be taking his deposition in the near future, and I want to take the son of a bitch apart."

"Understood."

The waiter reappeared with the appetizer and took their entrée orders.

Jace resumed the conversation. "I want to know how to get under this guy's skin, how to make the jury hate him."

Jackie lowered her voice to a whisper. "Anything in particular you have in mind?"

"I'd like to know how he treats women. The fact that his group is protesting the increasing prominence of women in the workforce tells me he may hold a grudge against women in general—maybe because of a bad experience as a child. I don't know."

"Interesting. That's certainly a possibility."

Jace kept their glasses full of sangria as they enjoyed their appetizer and discussed Jackie's assignments on the case.

"Before our entrées arrive, I think I'll visit the ladies' room." Jackie pushed her chair back from the table and stood as Jace politely did the same, their faces almost touching. "I'll only be a minute."

As she walked away from the table, Jace couldn't help but watch her. She was wearing a short brown knit dress, cinched in at the waist by a wide leather belt, brown suede knee-high boots completing the look. She faintly reminded Jace of a female investigator on a current television series. But the similarities stopped with the outfit, as he found Jackie much better looking, with softer features, including her wavy brown hair and big brown eyes.

While she was gone, the waiter cleared their appetizer dishes and delivered their entrées.

"You should have started without me."

"I didn't give it a thought."

Jackie took a bite of her grilled tenderloin and nodded approvingly. "So how's Ms. McKenzie? I do have her name right, don't I?"

"She goes by Darrin – you know that. And she's fine."

"I assume she will be working on this case as well."

"Of course."

"Jace, I don't mean to pry but I sense there may be something going on between the two of you. If I'm out of order here for asking, just tell me." Jackie took a heavy hit off her sangria as she waited for a reply.

Jace bit his lip and stared at the plate in front of him as he considered his response. He cleared his throat and said, "I don't know how to answer your question. Your instincts are right – there is something between us. It's just hard to say how serious it is."

"Is Ms. McKenzie – I'm sorry, is Darrin - a little more serious than you are?"

"I can't speak for Darrin. I do know that I'm not ready for any commitments right now."

"I can understand that. I mean, you just lost your wife in a car accident, what, two years ago?" Jackie's eyes begged for a response.

Jace sighed, "You should know the truth about that, Jackie." Jace paused momentarily before he continued. "My wife and I had been arguing when she raced out of the house and jumped into her car. She sped onto the freeway crashed into an eighteen-wheeler. I didn't know it at the time, but my son Matt was home and overheard the argument. It was bad enough to lose my wife, but Matt blames me for her death." Jace shook his head and took a deep breath.

"I'm so sorry, Jace. I had no idea." Jackie reached across the table and squeezed his hand gently. "How are things with your son now?"

39

"Better but still tough. I feel like I'm walking on egg shells whenever we're around each other. I just don't want to say the wrong thing, or do something that might set him off. It's a tricky situation. But that's enough about me." Jace switched gears, "How was your dinner?"

"I didn't like mine." Jackie grinned as she nodded at an empty plate.

"Glad you liked it."

"So, you got time for a nightcap before you head back? I know a really cool bar not far from my place that has this great jazz band."

"Maybe another time, Jackie. I've got meetings starting tomorrow morning at eight and going all day."

"I'm only talking about one little ol' drink. You'll be able to make the—" As she spoke, Jackie brushed the toe of her heel up and down Jace's leg.

"You know better than that. One drink would lead to another and...."

"So? That wouldn't be the end of the world, now would it? Southwest has an early-bird flight that would get you back in time to make your eight o'clock."

"Jackie, I don't think we should rush things." Jace glanced down at his watch and then motioned for the waiter to bring the check.

"So when are we going to reschedule that dinner at your place in Fort Worth?"

"As soon as I come up for air, I promise."

"I'm counting on it."

As the two walked out of Malaga, Jace saw a group of college kids walking toward them. One in particular caught his eye. "Matt?"

"Dad? What are you doing here?" Father and son awkwardly embraced. Jace turned and gestured toward Jackie.

"I would like to introduce you to Ms. McLaughlin. She used to be with the Austin Police Department but now has her own private investigation firm. I may have mentioned her name to you during the Stone case. She was a lifesaver, literally." Jace smiled in Jackie's direction. "I'm down here meeting with her on a new case we just filed."

"Nice to meet you, Ms. McLaughlin. I remember my dad talking about you."

"It's my pleasure, Matt. Jace has told me so much about you that I feel like I already know you."

Jace interrupted. "Matt, I would have called you, but this was a last-minute trip. I just came in for this dinner meeting and am catching the last flight back to Fort Worth. I'd love to buy you a beer, but I need to get a move on."

"Sure, Dad."

Jace hugged his son, then turned to Jackie. "Call me as soon as you learn anything." Jace handed his ticket to the valet. "I would wait for you, but if I don't hurry, I'll miss my flight."

"No problem. I'm a big girl."

"Don't worry, Dad. I'll wait around until Ms. McLaughlin gets her car."

As his dad drove off, Matt turned to Jackie. "So was this new case you were meeting on filed here in Austin?"

"No, Fort Worth."

"So why is he using an Austin investigator?"

"I guess he thinks I'm that good. And I am."

The valet pulled Jackie's car up to the curb. Before getting in, she smiled at Matt and said, "It's been a pleasure to finally meet you. I hope we'll see more of each other in the future." Without waiting for a response, Jackie slid in behind the wheel and drove away slowly, waving at Matt as her car merged into traffic.

CHAPTER

Darrin curled up on the sofa in her modest apartment and dialed a number on her cell. As she waited for an answer, she sipped a martini and nibbled on some cheese—dinner for the evening. Seconds later, a familiar voice came on the line.

"Sis, what's up?"

"Hi, Megan. Is this a good time?"

"As good as any. I just put the kids to bed—for the second time. Hopefully they'll stay down this time."

"Where's Mark?"

"At work, as usual. I hardly ever see him anymore. He's married to his practice—or fooling around with one of his nurses," Megan joked. "What have you been up to?"

"Same ol', same ol'. Just working."

"Anything as interesting as that weird grave robbery case?"

"Well, actually, there might be," Darrin said with a laugh. "We were just hired to sue a religious cult that stages protests at veterans' funerals. Their leader, Ezekiel Shaw, has been all over the news lately."

"I've seen that guy on television. He makes me sick. Hope you get millions and millions against those Bible-toting nuts."

"Yeah, me too."

"So how are things with Jace? Every time I ask, you politely change subjects. Don't you think it's time you filled me in. That's what sisters are for anyway."

"Honestly, I wish I had a good answer to that question. I really don't know how things are with Jace. He never tells me how he feels. And right now I've got this feeling he may have something going on with this PI we have been using down in Austin."

"What makes you think that?"

"I can't put my finger on it – just female intuition, I guess."

"Hmmm. So, I don't get it. Are y'all seeing each other or not?"

"I don't want to get into all that. Let's talk about something else."

"No, I'm serious, Sis. All I know is you have worked for him for years, and since his wife died, I can't figure out if y'all are seeing each other, just messing around, or what."

"Join the club. I mean, my feelings for him have changed over time. And since his wife died, things between us seem to be gradually changing."

"Yeah, but all you ever talk about now is how you and Jace worked through lunch, or you and Jace worked late and went out to dinner. I mean, it sounds to me like work is just an excuse for you guys to see each other."

"Well, we have been on a few real dates, Megan."

"So, are you guys sleeping together? Tell me the truth Darrin."

"Come on, Sis. Don't you think about anything but sex?"

"It's a pretty important signal as to what's going on inside a relationship."

Darrin hesitated before responding, "We've come pretty damn close."

Megan laughed. "You've got to be kidding me. So what's the hold-up?"

"I don't think I'm ready for that and Jace hasn't pushed it," Darrin replied, her tone defensive.

"And why don't you think you're ready? Because Jace hasn't put a ring on your finger, or told you he loved you? I hate to break your bubble but the days of knights in shining armor are long gone. Besides, before things go any further you need to find out whether you're good in bed together."

"I can't help it – I want to be sure before I sleep with him. I've got to get this right. It's complicated – having your personal life and work life all wrapped up together."

"I understand that but you'll never know for sure. Take Mark and me. We didn't sleep together before we got married – that Catholic guilt trip at work, I guess. Besides, I didn't think the physical part of a relationship was that important. The way I saw things you either loved someone or you didn't and, at the time, I just knew we were the perfect match. That was ten years ago and now look at us. We have two kids, our sex life is practically nonexistent, and he's never home. Not a pretty picture."

"Do you think he's seeing somebody?"

"I don't know. I joke about it, but what if he is? What would I do? Let's be honest, I haven't worked for over eight years—good luck finding a job. I'd be nuts to pull the plug on our marriage."

"But you're not happy, Megan."

"So. I live in a big house in a great neighborhood with two wonderful kids."

"Hmm. That's sort of a cop-out, don't you think? Have you talked with Mark about your feelings?"

"Tried to. He's always too busy—blows me off." Megan diverted. "Let's get back to your love life, Darrin, it's much more interesting. You're thirty-six, drop-dead gorgeous, smart, single, and have no children tying you down. If you're worried about mixing work and play, why don't you date around a little? Guys would line up for the chance to go out with you. All you need to do is put out the word. I know several doctors . . ."

"Very funny. I really don't want that right now. I wish I did, but I just can't get my mind off Jace."

"Does he know about your first marriage?"

"I think it came up briefly in one of our dinner conversations, but he left it alone—didn't pry."

"Well, you certainly don't want a repeat of that fiasco."

"Come on, Megan. I was so young. I didn't have a clue as to what marriage was about. It didn't even last a year."

"That's what I'm talking about. What was that guy's name – Clifton?"

Darrin tried unsuccessfully to stifle her laugh.

"I thought he was a little full of himself at the time – it was all about Clifton. I think I may have told you that but you wouldn't listen. No, you were too much in love, or so you thought. And, if I recall correctly, you didn't have sex prior to tying the knot. You were saving yourself, as the saying goes."

"Okay, okay. But I'm not exactly rushing into this thing with Jace. We've been working together for years. I love being around the guy—I can't help it. I actually look forward to going to work."

"What if you found out he really does have something going on with that girl down in Austin? How would that make you feel?"

"Like one stupid bitch. There would be no going back if that happened. I'd quit and move back to Houston."

"That's what you say now."

"No, I'm serious. I wouldn't be able to trust him—ever."

"Oh, come on, Darrin. From what you've told me, Jace hasn't made any commitments to you. You've had some dates and you enjoy being together but that's as far as it's gone. If I were you, I wouldn't pull the line too tight, or you might lose him. I know you don't want him to play the field. I wouldn't either if I were in your shoes. But the alternative might be a lot worse – think about it. Look, I've got to go. I just heard the front door open. Dr. McDreamy must be home."

"Tell him 'hi' for me. And please don't mention any of this to him, or anybody, for that matter."

"Don't worry, Sis. Your little secret is safe with me."

"Night, Megan. I'll talk to you soon."

Darrin felt a sense of relief after chatting with her sister. Megan was a good shrink – one Darrin could completely trust, someone who called it like she saw it. She made another martini, curled back up on the couch, turned on a *Seinfeld* rerun, and laughed out loud as Kramer, sporting a tux and top hat, took George's in-laws for a romantic ride through Central Park on a carriage drawn by a gassy horse.

CHAPTER

7

Christine walked briskly out of the W Hotel in Union Square in the direction of the Blue Water Grill. Dressed conservatively in a beige business suit and matching pumps, she exuded confidence as she made her way through throngs of people engaged in various diversions in the square. Arriving at the restaurant promptly at noon, she smiled at the maître d' and announced, "I'm here for lunch with Mr. Jamie Stein."

"Please follow me."

Soon she was seated across from a ruggedly handsome man who appeared to be in his late thirties. His black hair was combed straight back, his eyes a deep brown. He wore a fashionably slender pink silk tie with a dark-blue suit, a matching handkerchief barely showing from his jacket pocket.

"Ms. Connors, thanks for making the trip. I know New York City is a long way from Fort Worth."

"My pleasure. I love coming here."

"So when did you get in?"

"Yesterday afternoon. Spent some time just strolling around the West Village. I usually stay in Midtown or on the Park, so this is quite a change for me."

"How do you like it?"

"A lot, actually. It has more of a neighborhood feel. Not so many tall buildings. Nice choice, Mr. Stein."

"Jamie. Mind if I call you Christine?"

"Be my guest."

The waiter appeared and took their drink orders—Jamie a vodka tonic and Christine a bloody mary.

"You know this restaurant used to be a bank? Still has the vault. Kind of appropriate that we are meeting here."

Christine laughed politely. "I guess you could say that. I'm staying at the W, and the concierge said the food here is fantastic."

"The concierge is right. The food is great and the ambience is pretty damn nice as well."

The waiter delivered their drinks, which they both slowly stirred as he disappeared.

"The other thing I like about this place is they don't rush you. So many restaurants make you feel like you're imposing when you take the time to enjoy your meal."

"You seem to know your way around Manhattan. Did you grow up in the City?"

"Brooklyn. The accent's a dead giveaway, wouldn't you say?" Jamie smiled, fidgeted with his fork, and then continued. "So as you folks say down in Texas, you ready to talk a little bidness, or would you prefer to wait until after we eat?"

"Your call. Either is fine with me."

"Well, why don't we go ahead and order, get that out of the way."

Christine nodded, and Jamie lifted his hand to signal the waiter. They placed their orders, then Jamie said, "I assume you're still interested in settling all of those silica cases your firm has against my insureds?"

"At the right price, that's correct," Christine replied, her expression giving away nothing.

"And what might that be?" Jamie drained the last of his drink and motioned for another. He rested his arms on the table and leaned forward, his eyes searching Christine's for clues.

"Well, I've had one of our paralegals put together a chart from our database that details the name of the plaintiff, the diagnosing doctor, the date of the diagnosis, the plaintiff's age, his lost earnings—that type of info."

"I assume you have a copy for me?"

"Of course." Christine retrieved the soft leather satchel from beside her chair and opened it. After taking out two copies of a multi-page document, one for Jamie and one for herself, she returned the satchel to the side of her chair. "I'll give you a minute to look it over."

She watched his reaction as his eyes scoured the document. After he finished, he folded it up and placed it in the inside pocket of his jacket.

"Very thorough, Christine. Kudos to your paralegal. The only thing that's missing is a number. Let's cut to the chase. What will it take to settle all of these cases?"

Without hesitation, Christine responded, "Seventy million."

Jamie laughed mockingly and rolled his eyes. "I thought you said you wanted to settle these cases. You are wasting my time."

"We have confirmed diagnoses of silicosis for every one of—"

"From doctors who would swear to anything for a buck. You know that and I know that. The only reason I'm interested in settling your crappy cases is because these defense lawyers are killing me on fees, and there's no end in sight."

"So what number did you have in mind? And don't insult me or I'm getting up and walking out of here."

"Half of that."

Christine didn't stand, but her stare signaled disappointment, skillfully camouflaging her elation. "You know I can't do that. I couldn't recommend it, and my clients wouldn't take it even if I did." She finished her bloody mary before continuing. "If we take these cases to trial, how much do you think Empire Risk will spend on lawyer fees? My bet is you'd spend at least what you're offering me to settle, and you'd still have the possibility of getting hammered at trial."

Jamie didn't respond.

"Okay, I'll tell you what. I might be able—I say 'might be able'—to get my clients to take sixty. But it'd be a stretch."

Jamie sighed. "Look, I'm going to give you my bottom line. No more negotiating, no more posturing. I will settle all of your cases for fifty million under one condition."

"And what might that be?"

"Ten of that comes back to me."

Christine gasped. "You know I can't do that. You're talking about a bribe."

"I wouldn't use that word. It has such a bad connotation." Jamie smiled and then took another sip of his vodka tonic.

"Well, if that's a deal breaker then—"

"It is. Why else would I be interested in cutting out the defense lawyers? There has to be something in it for me."

Christine rose from the table. "I'm sorry, Mr. Stein, but we have nothing else to talk about."

As she turned to walk toward the exit, Jamie called out, "You know how to reach me. Think about it. It's a lot of money. Talk to your dad and law partner about it. He's been in this business a long time, and I'm sure he's done worse—a lot worse—than what we've been discussing. Have a safe flight back to Cowtown."

Without responding, Christine walked swiftly to the door. Seconds later, the waiter arrived at the table with their orders and glanced nervously at Christine exiting the restaurant. "Sir, I apologize if …"

"No need. Your service has been perfect. Just leave both of the entrées with me. And another vodka tonic to wash it all down."

"Right away, sir!"

Jamie took a bite and smiled. He would know her answer in a day or so, and he was pretty sure what it would be.

Christine rested her head on the back of her airplane seat and closed her eyes. A bribe! Stein was proposing an illegal kickback! It couldn't be characterized any other way. But fifty million was a shitload of money, especially for those "dog" cases that should have never been filed in the first place and certainly couldn't be won at trial. And the law firm's cut of 40 percent would be a godsend, considering she had been scrambling to pay the firm's overhead the past several months. Christine needed to run it by her dad and get his thoughts. But there was little doubt in her mind as to what he was going to say.

The flight attendant interrupted her trance. "Can I get you something to drink?"

Christine opened her eyes and smiled. "Yes, please. Jack Daniel's and a glass of ice." She would have three more before her plane landed at DFW several hours later, plunging her into an alcohol-induced respite from the crazy life she had chosen.

CHAPTER

Jace was up early. While shaving, he occasionally glanced at the small flat-screen television in the upper corner of his bathroom, which was tuned to the local news. He heard the female reporter say the name "Hanson" and quickly picked up the remote and increased the volume. With shaving cream still covering half his face, he watched the screen and listened intently as the reporter continued with her story.

"Although not yet confirmed, Janice Hanson, whose daughter was tragically killed in Afghanistan just a few months ago, died of an apparent overdose of sleeping pills. The authorities are not yet saying whether that overdose was accidental or intentional. Her husband, Eugene Hanson, has been taken to John Peter Smith Hospital for observation."

Jace hit the off button and quickly finished shaving. He threw on a sports jacket and a pair of slacks. On his way out the door, he grabbed a cup of coffee before getting in his Range Rover and heading to the hospital.

"I'm sorry, Mr. Forman, but visiting hours don't begin until eight. You'll need to wait in the reception area or come back in thirty minutes. Please help yourself to a complimentary cup of coffee. Or, if you're hungry, there's a cafeteria just down the hall."

Jace nodded at the soft-spoken elderly lady manning the information desk. "Thank you, ma'am. I didn't make time for breakfast this morning. I think I'll head down to the cafeteria."

"Try their pancakes. They're my favorite."

Thirty minutes later, Jace was standing in front of the same receptionist. "What room did you say Mr. Hanson was in?"

"Room 313. Take the elevator down the hall behind me to the third floor. The desk nurse will direct you to Mr. Hanson's room."

"Thank you so much."

Standing in front of room 313, Jace slowly pushed the door open to reveal a motionless Eugene Hanson, lying in bed, his eyes tightly closed. Jace tiptoed into the room and whispered, "Eugene, can you hear me?"

No response.

Jace repeated the words, this time a little louder.

The patient turned his head and slowly opened his eyes.

"Eugene, it's me. Jace Forman. How are you feeling?"

Eugene shook his head.

A nurse walked in and picked up the chart hanging at the edge of the bed.

Jace read the nurse's name tag. "Cheryl, how is Mr. Hanson doing?"

"He was very upset when he arrived at the hospital. We administered a sedative through an IV drip, which has calmed him down considerably. He's probably still a little groggy."

"Has anyone been here to see him?"

"You're the first." Nurse Cheryl checked her patient's vitals, took his temperature, and recorded the results on his chart. She glanced at the IV drip, then said, "Everything looks fine. The doctor should be in later this morning during rounds." The nurse left, and Jace turned his attention back to his client, whose eyes were now wide open.

"Jace?"

"Yes, Eugene, it's me. I am so sorry to hear about Janice." Jace took his client's hand. Eugene squeezed it, his eyes tearing up.

"He killed her. You know that, don't you?"

"He?" asked Jake. "Who's he?"

"Ezekiel Shaw. What he and his people did out there at the funeral to my Janice was nothing less than murder." Eugene looked straight into Jace's eyes. "She was all I had left."

"I know, Eugene. We'll make him pay."

"Could you help me adjust my bed? I'm a little out of it."

Jace pushed a button, slowly raising the back of the bed. "How's that?"

"Better, much better." Eugene swallowed. "Damn right we're going to make him pay. I'm going to kill that bastard."

"Whoa—wait a minute! You're not going to kill anybody." Jace laughed nervously. "The last thing we need is for you to end up in jail. Hell, I wouldn't have a client."

"No, Jace, I mean it. I'm going to kill that bastard Shaw. This is all his fault. Janice was never the same after that son of a bitch and his cult picketed Lauren's funeral."

"And that's what lawsuits are for. I promise you—we'll shut Shaw and his church down. He won't be able to do this to anyone else ever again."

"I'd like to believe that. But you said yourself our chances aren't good. And how many times have we seen our criminal justice system turn rapists and murderers back on the street only to see them commit the same crimes again?"

"Your case is a civil suit and—"

"I know, but doesn't that put us in an even tougher position? Say we get a money judgment. You know he's going to appeal, and that will tie us up in court for years and years. Meanwhile, he and his followers will just keep right on protesting. It'll be business as usual."

Jace was silent. His client was right, and getting more lucid by the minute.

"Jace, my life might as well be over. With Lauren gone and now Janice, I have nothing."

"Come on, now," Jace said. He squeezed Eugene's hand, needing to stall. "I'll make a deal with you. Just give me a little time. Let me take Shaw's deposition. You can be there. Let's see how the lawsuit goes."

"I don't know, Jace."

"I've promised you that I'd put this guy out of business. Just give me the chance to prove it."

Eugene forced a smile. "I guess I owe you that."

"Good. I'll be back to check on you later today."

"I hope to be out of here soon. I need to make arrangements for Janice . . ."

"Eugene, I'll speak with the funeral home and let them know you are going to need a little time."

"Thank you, Jace. I appreciate it."

"Call me if you need anything—anything at all." Jace noticed his client was already nodding off as he quietly exited the room.

CHAPTER

9

Dressed in worn blue jeans, a wrinkled T-shirt, and sandals, Jackie grabbed the laptop off her desk and plopped down in the overstuffed chair in the corner of the bedroom she had recently converted into an office. She kicked off the sandals and rested her bare feet on the ottoman in front of her, balancing the MacBook Air on her lap. She typed "brimstonebiblechurch.com" and hit the enter key. A professional-looking website appeared.

She scrolled to the "Photos" tab and clicked. There were four photographs available for viewing. She chose the first. An image of a man's face filled the screen. He had shoulder-length brown hair, a shadowy beard, and alluring brown eyes. He was staring directly into the camera, a faint smile on his lips. Underneath the image was the simple description: "Savior Ezekiel Shaw, founder and leader of the Brimstone Bible Church. Prophet to Mankind."

She clicked on the next photo. Shaw, dressed in a flowing white robe, stood behind a wooden pulpit, his outstretched arms reaching toward heaven, his eyes gazing upward. There was no caption.

Jackie went to the third photo. The setting was pastoral. Shaw stood among a group of men, women, and children who were seated at his feet, their gaze fixed upon him. Again, he was dressed simply in a white robe, leather sandals on his feet.

The last photo depicted Shaw seated on the ground with his legs crossed, in the middle of a group of young children, a baby cradled in his arms, a narrow river flowing in the background. His head was bowed.

Jackie returned to the first photo and stared at it. There was something about those eyes. They drew you in and didn't let go. She shook her head and entered the "About Us" section, which she slowly read to herself.

The Doctrine of the Brimstone Bible Church

1) The Bible is the Word of God and is to be read and enforced literally. Everything in It is inerrant and not to be challenged or changed.

2) Ezekiel Shaw is God's only living prophet. He receives revelations directly from God, which are not to be challenged or questioned. Anyone who questions his teachings or disobeys his commands will suffer eternal damnation.

3) The only true religion is that of the Brimstone Bible Church. All other religions are heretical and blasphemous. They lead not to Heaven but to eternal damnation.

4) Brothers and Sisters of the Brimstone Bible Church must give all their worldly possessions to the Church. The rich have no place in Heaven, as they have chosen to worship the idol of money rather than God.

5) Women are to be wholly subservient to men.

6) Men, women, and children shall be wholly subservient to the only living prophet and diviner of God's will, Savior

Ezekiel Shaw. Savior Shaw shall be subservient only to God. Failure to strictly adhere to this tenet of faith will lead to eternal damnation.

7) Homosexuality is a cardinal sin and will lead to eternal damnation.

8) The Brimstone Bible Church has the obligation to bring God's True Word to the world and to educate sinners as to their evil ways.

9) Strict adherence to this Doctrine will lead to an afterlife in Heaven filled with happiness and devoid of sorrow.

In disbelief, Jackie finished reading and clicked on "FAQs." It was more of the same. Gays don't make it to heaven. A woman's place is in the home. Women should be seen, not heard. The USA has turned its back on these guiding principles and is being punished. The Pope is a fraud. Even Billy Graham is a liar. Anyone who does not become a practicing member of the BBC is destined for hell and eternal damnation.

Jackie needed a break. She closed her laptop and headed to the kitchen for a sandwich. She threw together a ham and cheese on rye and chased it with a Shiner Bock.

After finishing her lunch, she settled back into her chair and placed the half-empty Shiner on the table next to her. She closed the BBC website and typed in "cult leader characteristics." A number of sites came up. She clicked on one and began reading. According to the article, cult leaders were charismatic, emotionally manipulative, narcissistic, deeply insecure, and paranoid. They were pathological liars, indifferent to the hurt they inflicted upon others, intolerant of dissent, and prone to fits of rage.

Several names flashed to the forefront of Jackie's mind: Hitler, Mussolini, Idi Amin. But weren't they dictators, not leaders of a religious cult? She wondered whether the psychological profiles of dictators and cult leaders were significantly different. Weren't both types driven by power? Weren't Jim Jones, the crazed cult leader who orchestrated a mass suicide of his followers on a compound in Guyana, and Adolph Hitler, who, in messianic fashion, drove his country down the path of ruin while systematically murdering six million Jews, cut from the same cloth? Wasn't Nazism, with its credo of unquestioning loyalty and obedience, remarkably similar to the teachings of the Peoples Temple, whose leader required its members to take the ultimate test of loyalty and obedience by drinking cyanide-laced Kool-Aid?

Jackie minimized the site and did Internet searches for Warren Jeffs, of the Fundamentalist Church of Jesus Christ of Latter-Day Saints; David Koresh, of the Branch Davidians; L. Ron Hubbard, the science fiction writer who founded Scientology; and Jim and Tammy Faye Bakker, of *PTL Club* fame. What she found was surprisingly similar: they were charismatic, sociological scam artists who made their followers totally dependent upon and subservient to them. Ezekiel fit the mold perfectly.

Jackie placed her laptop on the ottoman and reached for a manila folder she had placed on the table. It was labeled "Ezekiel Shaw" and contained the results of her investigation so far. She glanced over the report she had prepared for Jace.

Jimmy Wayne Watkins was born on November 18, 1978, in DeSoto, Texas, to a fourteen-year old single mother named Pearl Watkins. Raised by his grandmother, he ran away at sixteen, roaming from town to town before finally settling in Austin, where he began attending services at the Fundamentalist Family Church, presided over by the Reverend Josiah James. Enthralled by Reverend James's lively sermons, Jimmy Wayne was "born again" at nineteen and changed his name to Ezekiel Shaw. He began preaching at the Fundamentalist Family Church when Reverend James was away or ill, eventually developing a following of his own.

After a dispute with Reverend James over the interpretation of Scripture's role for women, Ezekiel and his followers left Fundamentalist Family to form their own house of worship, naming it the Brimstone Bible Church.

After several years of holding services at a rented warehouse, one of the members inherited several million dollars, which she promptly bequeathed to the church. The funds were used to purchase a hundred-acre compound near Fort Stockton, which had formerly been used as a hunting lodge. Subsequently, the BBC members improved the compound's buildings and erected a temple where they could hold their services. It is believed that between seventy-five and one hundred people currently live on the compound.

There have been rumors that the men in the congregation, known as Brothers, practice bigamy and that girls as young as fourteen have been forced to have sexual relations with men many years older. No charges have been filed as of this writing.

Jackie took the last sip of her Shiner and closed the file. She picked up her cell phone, dialed a number from memory, and waited for an answer.

"This is Gomez."

"Jorge, how's my ol' partner doing?"

"We're missing you, Jackie. The department just ain't the same."

"You're too kind."

"No, I'm serious as a heart attack. That was a stupid move the chief made. I know he feels bad about it, but the folks over in the DA's office forced his hand."

"Well, sometimes things work out for the best."

"How is it having your own business? By the way, I referred a client to you the other day."

"Yeah, what's his name?"

"It's a she. Leah something—starts with an *R*, I think. Did she call you?"

"Not yet. What would she need me for?"

"Somebody put a dead fish in her bed. It's not clear why. She's a reporter for *Texas Matters*. Just a guess, but someone may be trying to scare her off a story."

"What type of story?"

"It's all guesswork at this point, but she's working on an exposé about a lawyer—Cal somebody. I'm not good with last names."

Jackie's interest was piqued. "Was it Cal Connors?"

"Yeah, that's it. Do you know him?"

"I know of him. He's a showboat lawyer out of Fort Worth. Thanks for the referral. I'll let you know if she calls." Jackie transitioned. "Jorge, I need a couple of favors."

"Anything for you. What can I help you with?"

"I'm working on a case and I need as much information as I can get on an Ezekiel Shaw. Born Jimmy Wayne Watkins—changed his name when he found religion."

Jorge made a note. "Got it. What are you looking for?"

"Anything you can find. He was in Austin for a while. Maybe he had some run-ins with the law while he was here. And, Jorge, don't limit your search to Austin—make it statewide."

"No problem. I'll run those names through our database and see what pops up."

"Would you also check with your buddies over in Fort Stockton? Shaw is head of a religious sect known as the Brimstone Bible Church—"

Jorge interrupted, "Nice."

"Yeah, I know. The BBC owns a hundred-acre compound about forty miles from Fort Stockton. I assume they have to go into town for supplies from time to time. Find out if the cult members have had any run-ins with the law."

"Anything else?"

"That's it for now. And Jorge, thanks for all your help."

"My pleasure. I'll be in touch."

CHAPTER

10

Cal leaned back in the chair and rested his custom-made boots on the desk. "I thought you'd call me after you met with Stein. I've been on the edge of my seat."

"I would have but I wanted to tell you in person, for a number of reasons."

His interest piqued, Cal cocked his head. "I'm all ears."

"Well, we met at the Blue Water Grill, in Union Square."

"I have no idea where that is. You know how I hate New York—too many damn people."

"I know, I know. I'm just trying to set the stage."

"I'm not interested in the damn stage—I'm only interested in the money. I would hope you got around to talking numbers."

"We did."

"And?"

"He's willing to settle all of our cases for fifty mil."

"Holy shit!" Cal jerked his boots off the desk and, smiling broadly, walked over to Christine, who was seated in the chair in front of his desk, and gave her a kiss on the forehead. "So why aren't you smiling, my dear? This could save our firm—get us back to the good ol' days."

"There's a catch."

"Damn! I knew it was too good to be true."

"Stein wants ten million of that amount to come back to him personally."

"He what?"

"You heard me."

"Why, that stupid son of a bitch. We could all go to jail."

"That's why I ended the meeting."

There was a prolonged silence in the room before Cal spoke. "So how did Mr. Stein propose we pay him the damn money? Does he want it wired to some secret account?"

"We didn't get that far. I was so shocked I got up and left the restaurant."

"And how did he react?"

"Cool, calm, and collected. As I was rushing out of the restaurant, he hollered something like 'That's a lot of money, Christine—think about it.'"

"So let's do think about it." Cal was back in his chair, his boots up on the desk again, his gaze fixed on the ceiling.

"There's nothing to think about. Your initial instincts were right on. What Stein's proposing is an illegal kickback, any way you take it. He's offering to commit his employer to settle a bunch of shitty cases for a boatload of money—not because he thinks it's a good settlement but because his palms are getting greased. I mean, he knows these cases are dogs. He came right out and said so during our meeting."

"Well, he's right about one thing—it is a lot of money. Our cut of the forty million would go a long way to getting this firm back on its feet financially. Besides, I wouldn't give you a rat's ass for a single one of those cases. Hell, our clients will be jumping for joy to get anything. And just think about the alternative. If we don't do this deal, everything you and I have worked for will all go up in smoke—poof!" Cal abruptly extended the fingers of both hands for effect. "The banks will foreclose on our plane, our homes, our island—you name it." He hesitated before sliding his boots off the top of his desk and leaning forward, his eyes locked on his daughter's. "Life as we know it will be gone—up a bear's ass."

Christine got up from her chair and walked toward the window. "Dad, we're talking about jail time here. Don't forget that."

"I don't think so. Look at all those Wall Street big shots. They stole billions, literally billions, of taxpayer dollars. How many of them do you see doing jail time? Not a damn one. And you and I both know that any prosecutor, state or federal, would think twice before taking us on. We have a squeaky clean record, and they know we would fight them tooth and nail. And the fact that we've been big contributors to local charities, judges, and politicians don't hurt a damn bit." Cal smiled for the first time since learning of Stein's proposal.

"I don't know. I'm the one out front on this. If this scheme unraveled, I might not do jail time, but I'd likely lose my law license."

"'If.' You said it—'if.'"

"So what are you proposing?"

"We don't have enough facts to make a well-reasoned decision. Get more details from Stein as to how his share would be paid, the safeguards that would be put in place to make sure the money can't be traced—that sort of thing."

"I guess another conversation couldn't hurt—nothing criminal about that."

"Don't call him at work. Call him on his cell."

Christine shook her head. "Dad, I'm not an idiot. Give me a little credit." She finally smiled.

"When are you gonna call him?"

"There's no sense in delaying. Let's find out the details and make a decision. I don't like uncertainty." Christine paused in the doorway. "I'm not making any promises as to how I'll come down on this—none whatsoever."

"I know, I know. Just make the call and we'll talk."

After Christine left, Cal did a quick calculation in his head. The firm would net roughly twenty million out of this deal, enough to keep things afloat at Connors & Connors for the foreseeable future. Yes, this deal needed to happen, and the Lone Wolf would make sure it did. His daughter just needed a little fatherly influence and reassurance. It now seemed they had weathered the storm, and it was just a matter of time before the clouds would start to clear.

CHAPTER

11

Eugene Hanson unsteadily poured himself another drink from the half-empty bottle of Jack Daniel's, which he then plunked down on the desk in front of him. He held the glass up and made a silent toast to no one before downing its contents. He adjusted his reading glasses and stared at the image of Ezekiel Shaw on his laptop screen.

Slurring, he muttered, "Savior Shaw, is it? You're the one who's gonna need a savior, because I'm gonna blow your fucking brains out." Eugene used his right hand to make an imaginary pistol, took aim at the image in front of him, and then whispered, "Pow. And just like that, there'll be no more Ezekiel Shaw and no more Brimstone Bible Church." Eugene began to laugh, slowly at first and then hysterically.

After several seconds the laughter subsided, and he turned his attention to the computer keyboard. He typed in "assault rifles," and several links appeared. He selected one and, after quickly reviewing the contents, printed the pages from the site and put them in a manila folder on the desk.

Next, he typed in the words "photographs Brimstone Bible Church compound Fort Stockton" and pressed the "enter" key. Again, a number of sites came up. He scrolled down to the sixth one and clicked on it. A sinister smile crossed his face. There were numerous aerial photos of the compound, with each of its structures numbered in red; there was a legend underneath linking a description of the structure to its corresponding number. Again, Eugene printed the site's contents and inserted the pages in the manila folder.

He looked up from the laptop, his bloodshot eyes settling on the fifth of Jack, which was now almost empty. He grabbed the bottle by the neck and guzzled the remaining contents, wiping his mouth with his shirtsleeve and then tossing the bottle in the trash can in the corner of his study. Then he typed "how to make a videotaped will." His laptop screen filled with sites. He chose one and, after scanning it, scrolled to the print icon at the top of the screen. He waited as the pages printed, then retrieved them and slid them into the manila folder. He crossed his arms over the file, laid his head down, and passed out.

PART TWO

CHAPTER

12

Leah settled into the first empty aisle seat on her return flight from Kansas City to Austin. It had been a hectic day. She had caught the red-eye that morning, rented a car at the Kansas City airport, and then driven to Topeka for her 2:00 appointment with Dr. Seth Coleman. Arriving several hours early, she had elected to grab a sandwich and latte at a nearby Starbucks, where she had checked emails and returned phone calls. The doctor had been tied up in several "emergencies," so she hadn't been able to see him until almost 4:30, making her chances of catching the 7:00 flight back to Austin dicey. She sighed with relief as she boarded the plane and found a seat. She fished her cell phone out of her purse and tapped on Abe's name. "Hi Abe! My flight is about to leave so I don't have long to talk. Bottom line, the meeting went much better than I expected. I think he just might talk."

"Leah, that's great!"

"Yes, the good doctor seemed shocked when I showed him the expert report Crimm had sworn to in the Zilantin case. It took him all of thirty seconds to realize that Crimm was making everything up—or, at the least, had ignored all of Coleman's research."

"Did he say anything?"

"No, but his body language was very telling. His face turned beet red—almost as red as the color of his hair."

"I assume he said something."

"He read the report several times and then asked if he could keep it. I told him he could, that I had several copies. I asked him if he agreed with Crimm's conclusions."

"And . . ."

"He avoided my question. But he did say it looked like there had been some mistake. I asked him to be more specific, but he declined. Unfortunately, his cell phone rang, and he rushed out saying he had another emergency—obviously a stall tactic."

"So what did you do?"

"There was nothing more I could do. He had the report and was obviously troubled by its conclusions. So I left right after he did so I could catch the seven o'clock back to Austin."

The flight attendant announced that they had been cleared for takeoff and asked the passengers to turn off all electronic devices. She began to walk down the aisle in search of offenders.

"Abe, I've got to go. We're getting ready to take off. I'll be in the office early tomorrow. We can talk then."

"Be safe, Leah."

"I will."

As the 737 climbed toward its cruising altitude, Leah smiled. This could be her big break. If Coleman cracked, then the accusations about Crimm would be corroborated, *Texas Matters* would run the story, and Cal Connors would be in a world of hurt.

Leah pulled into the parking garage underneath her apartment building and took the elevator to the lobby. She wanted to ask the security guard on duty to escort her up to her apartment and do a quick walk-through, but he was engaged in an animated discussion about sports with one of the other tenants. She was exhausted and didn't feel like waiting.

Leah walked straight to the tower elevators and pressed the button. Minutes later, she was in her kitchen pouring a glass of wine. She opened the freezer and pulled out a frozen dinner. The only one left was Salisbury steak with a side of macaroni and cheese; she rolled her eyes in disgust as she popped the container into the microwave. Wineglass in hand, she walked to her bedroom to make sure she didn't have any unwanted company. She looked in the closet bedroom and then the bath. Mission completed, she returned, took out the plastic tray, and forced down a few bites, chasing them with healthy sips of wine.

Her hunger semi-satisfied, she headed back to her bedroom to take a shower. She felt grimy from her long travel day and decided she would sleep better after letting the pulsating streams of hot water massage her aching muscles. She pulled off her heels, threw them in the bottom of her bedroom closet, and walked barefoot into her bathroom. She turned on the shower and stared at herself in the mirror over the sink. The bags under her bloodshot eyes told the story—she had been pushing herself a little too hard. She needed to slow down.

She opened the glass shower door and tested the water temperature—perfect! She took off her blouse and bra and tossed them into the clothes hamper. After unzipping her khaki skirt, she wiggled out of it and her panties, picking up both from the tile floor and dropping them into the hamper. As Leah stepped into the shower, she closed her eyes as rivulets of water streamed down her face.

Leah arrived at the office a little before eight the next morning. She had slept hard, and she felt rested for the first time in several days. She grabbed a bagel and coffee on the way to work— not her normal routine but she had wanted to get there early. She had so much to do before Abe arrived. She could hardly wait to strategize with him about the next step she should take to get her story in print.

Uncharacteristically, she hadn't taken time to read her emails before she left for work. She opened her laptop and clicked on the mail icon. She started scrolling through her emails until her eyes came to an unusual sender address: newsworthy@gmail. com. It referenced a story she was working on for one of the senior editors. She opened the email. She cringed as she read the text: "Stop, or this goes viral."

There was an attachment. Should she open it? She had to. After that cryptic message she had little choice. She winced and then double clicked. It appeared to be some type of video. She hit the arrow and the video started to roll. She gasped in horror. She was watching herself from the night before—in her bathroom, brushing her teeth, peering at herself in the mirror, taking off her blouse, her bra, her skirt, and then her panties.

Leah paused the video. She could feel her heart pounding. But she had to know what else was on it. She hit play, and the video resumed, revealing close-ups of her as she washed every inch of her body. The video ended abruptly after she wrapped a towel around herself and stepped out of the shower.

Leah rose from her chair and began to pace frantically around the office, her mind racing. She rifled through her purse and speed-dialed the only person in the world she felt she could trust. Abe answered. "Leah, are you okay? Where are you?"

Her tone frantic, Leah pleaded, "At the office. I'm at the office. I need you, Abe. I need you to get here as soon as you can. Something terrible has happened."

"What? What's happened? What are you talking about?" Abe hurriedly threw on a pair of wrinkled khakis and a sports jacket as he talked. "Leah, are you there?"

"Yes, I'm here."

"Leah, you need to listen to me. Calm down and tell me what's going on. Slowly."

Leah took a deep breath. "I got—I got this email this morning and . . ."

Abe could hear a muffled sob in the background. He sat down on the side of the bed and started pulling on his socks, his cell phone cradled between his ear and shoulder. "And what was in the email?"

Leah's voice quivered as she replied, "There was a video attachment of me in my bathroom undressing . . ."

"Who received the email?"

"I was so upset I didn't look." Leah scrolled to the list of addressees. "Thank God! It looks like it was just sent to me."

"Okay, listen to me. I'm going to call our tech guy and have him immediately run a trace to figure out who sent it, or at least the computer or server it was sent from. And call that private investigator. Call her right now."

Leah clicked off and rummaged through her purse, found the business card Officer Gomez had given her, and dialed the number written on the back. "Ms. McLaughlin, this is Leah Rosen. Officer Gomez gave me your name. I need to schedule an appointment right away."

CHAPTER

13

It was seven in the morning, and Maurice Morgan sat hunched over his desk scanning the latest edition of the *Fort Worth Daily Record*. As was his routine, he had been the first to arrive at Hadley and Morgan—the law firm he had started thirty-seven years before—and he was on the prowl for new business. The *Record* listed every new lawsuit that had been filed in Tarrant County the day before. It had been his practice for years to read the *Record* carefully first thing in the morning and, if he recognized the name of one of the parties sued, call and advise that person or company that there had been a lawsuit filed against them—as a matter of professional courtesy, of course. If luck went his way, the call resulted in Hadley and Morgan being hired to represent the unfortunate party.

He took a sip of black coffee and readjusted the gold-rimmed glasses on the bridge of his hawk-like nose. He squinted as he turned to the next page and slicked back a few errant strands of thinning gray hair that had fallen in his line of vision. As he read down the list of lawsuits, he sat up in his chair when he saw "Hanson v. *The Brimstone Bible Church and Ezekiel Shaw*." He had read an article or two about some of the church's protests, but that wasn't what caught his attention. What did was the name of the lawyer who had filed the suit: his former law partner Jace Forman.

Maurice circled the lawsuit with a red pen and pursed his thin lips. His memory took him back to the day when, years ago, Jace had come into his office, demanding an increase in pay. Forman had compiled a list of all the lawsuits he had won, all the clients he had brought in, all the other contributions he had made to the firm that, in his view, clearly justified a generous bump in salary. Maurice had listened without interrupting, his reasonable reply being "Your time will come. Continue to pay your dues and you will be rewarded." That was the way it had always been done at Hadley and Morgan and the way it would continue to be done—discussion over.

But his explanation hadn't satisfied his former law partner. Eighteen months later, Forman—along with several other Hadley and Morgan lawyers, paralegals, and support staff—had defected to form a new firm. Some of Hadley and Morgan's most lucrative clients had gone with him, the lost revenue almost bankrupting the firm that Maurice had, through untold sacrifice and hard work, built over many years. He had been biding his time, waiting for an opportunity to even the score. Now smiling, Maurice whispered, "It's payback time." He buzzed his secretary, who appeared in his doorway.

"Yes, Mr. Morgan."

"Have Prater come to my office."

Cromwell Prater IV had joined Hadley and Morgan the same year as Jace. They had been friends at first, but over time competition had taken its toll, and their camaraderie had evolved into distrust. When Jace formed his new firm, Prater was not asked to join. What had previously been distrust morphed into hate, and as Jace's impressive victories in the courtroom mounted and his firm's reputation grew, Prater became consumed with jealousy.

As he strutted rapidly down the hall toward the office of his mentor and the managing partner of Hadley and Morgan, he wondered what their hastily called meeting might entail. He entered Maurice's office and stood erect, as if at attention. "You wanted to see me?"

"Yes, Crom. Have a seat, please." Maurice motioned to one of the two chairs in front of his desk. "As I always do, I was looking through the *Record* this morning, and guess whose name I came across."

Crom furrowed his brow. "I have no idea."

"Our old friend Jace Forman."

Crom's lips stretched into a tight line, his green eyes narrowed.

Maurice continued. "Mr. Forman has sued the Brimstone Bible Church. You've heard of them, haven't you?"

"Isn't that the group that recently protested at a soldier's funeral over in Hagstrom?"

"That's the one. I assume that protest is the reason for Forman's lawsuit."

"That would be my bet."

"You interested in doing a little *pro bono* work?"

Crom tilted his head. "What did you have in mind?"

"I'm sure the Brimstone Bible Church will need representation, and they probably can't afford our rates."

"I see where you're going." Crom smiled.

"Do you have time to take this on?"

"I'll make time. It'd be my pleasure to go up against our old friend in a case that's sure to garner lots of publicity."

"I thought you'd see it that way."

"What's our next step?"

"I'll give their leader a call. He's been individually sued in the lawsuit. His name is Ezekiel Shaw. I'll tell him about the lawsuit and see what he says. I have little doubt that he'll ask me if we can represent him as well as that church of his." Maurice smiled and sighed. "Crom, I've been waiting for this opportunity for a long time—ever since that cocky bastard walked out the door."

"So have I, Maurice. So have I." Crom rose from his seat and walked determinedly out of the office.

CHAPTER

14

Leah and Jackie were seated in a booth at 24 Diner, on Sixth and Lamar, a few blocks from Leah's condo. Since Jackie worked out of her home and really had no need for a formal office, she thought it best to meet her clients at a location of their choosing.

Having gotten the introductions and pleasantries out of the way, Jackie dove in. "So let's start from the beginning. Just tell me what happened, and don't leave anything out. What might not seem important to you might to me."

Leah related the events of the past few weeks, including her observations, feelings, and every detail she could recall. Jackie listened intently, scribbling notes on a small spiral notepad.

"So is there a way you can trace who sent that email? I talked to our IT guy at Texas Matters and he had never run across anything like this." Leah shuddered. "This all seems like such a bad dream, like it can't be happening. I mean, I just can't believe there is a video of me like that out there." Leah sighed and looked down at the table.

Before responding, Jackie reached over and squeezed Leah's hand. "I can only imagine what you're going through. Now, to answer your question, with a little luck we will probably be able to determine where the email originated. Figuring out who sent it gets trickier, but it has been done."

"Well, I was hoping for better, but at least there's a chance."

"And you can rest assured I'll make sure everything is done to figure out who did this. Trust me on that. Now, let's switch gears a moment, Leah. Tell me about your job. What do you do at *Texas Matters*?"

"Well, my duties and job description have changed a lot over time. Right now I'm researching several different stories for other reporters more senior to me. And I'm working on compiling the information I need to write my first solo piece."

"What's it about?"

"The title is 'Texas Justice Gone Wrong'—at least, that's what I'm calling it right now."

"Catchy title."

"I thought so. Anyway, I covered this case down in the Valley. One of the lawyers in the case was a Fort Worth attorney. His name is Cal Connors—some call him the Lone Wolf. Ever heard of him?"

Jackie nodded. "As a matter of fact, I have. Connors represented the plaintiffs in a grave-robbery case in Fort Worth. It was a civil suit against the cemetery, but there was a criminal investigation going on at the same time. There was a question as to whether the young girl whose body was stolen had been murdered. I was involved in the criminal investigation."

"And Jace Forman represented the cemetery, right?" Leah asked.

"How did you know?"

"Small world! I interviewed him not too long ago in connection with the article. I tracked down as many lawyers as I could who had tried cases against Connors. I wanted to know what they thought of him."

"Well, what did you learn from Jace?"

"Honestly, not much. He played it pretty close to the vest—said Connors was a worthy opponent and that was about it. He wouldn't elaborate no matter how creative I got in my questioning."

Jackie smiled knowingly. "Typical response from a lawyer."

"I totally agree." Leah laughed. "But seriously, the more I learned about Connors and his form of justice, the more I became convinced he was part of one big fraud."

"Wow, that's a pretty serious allegation. How'd you come to that conclusion?"

"It was pretty simple. He never lost! He tried all these cases against Big Pharma and used the same expert in every case, a well-credentialed doctor named Howell Crimm. Interestingly, the reports in every case were worded exactly the same. The drugs were different, but the conclusions Crimm reached were always identical. He swore in every one of the cases I investigated that the pharmaceutical company had manipulated the data to get FDA approval. That made me suspicious."

"So what'd you do?"

"I found out who Dr. Crimm's research assistants were when he wrote the reports. Both had been in medical school when they did the research."

"Names?"

"Sanjay Patel and Seth Coleman. Dr. Patel is in Nashville at Vanderbilt doing his residency. Dr. Coleman is in private practice in Topeka, Kansas."

"So did they talk to you?"

"One did, Dr. Patel. During our initial phone conversation, he had nothing but good things to say about Crimm. A few days after that, the jury in the case I was covering down in the Valley awarded Connors's client this humongous verdict against the pharmaceutical company. It drew national press coverage. Dr. Patel read about the verdict in the *New York Times* and called me. He couldn't believe it—all the research he had done for Crimm on the drug that was the subject of the case had indicated it was safe. I told Patel that the sworn statement Crimm had filed in the case painted a different story. He wanted to help but was worried about getting involved. Ultimately, he supplied me with some incriminating documentation that, in my opinion, proved Crimm had falsified his findings."

"So you had enough to get your story published?"

"I thought so, but Connors called Steve Blumenthal, the owner of *Texas Matters,* and threatened him with a lawsuit if he published a story that was the least bit critical of him or his firm."

"And Blumenthal backed off . . ."

"Unless and until I could get some corroborating proof. That's what I am working on now."

"The pieces are beginning to fit together."

"You think that email has something to do with my story, don't you?" Leah asked.

"That would be my guess."

"You think Connors is behind this?"

"Knowing Connors, it's likely, but I can't be sure—not just yet." Jackie paused. "I'll need to do a little investigation. First, I want to see if I can determine the source of the email. I have a tech guy I used while I was on the force. If anyone can trace it, he can."

Leah nodded.

"Next, I am personally going to conduct a thorough sweep of your apartment from one end to the other and destroy all hidden cameras, taps, and whatever surveillance equipment I find. By the time I get through, I guarantee your apartment will be clean."

Leah sighed. "That makes me feel a lot better."

"Then I think we should do a little surveillance of our own. I'm going to mount a small, undetectable camera above the door to your apartment. It's triggered by motion. We'll get a good look at any uninvited guest who might try to get in." Jackie paused. "And we'll have your locks changed and a dead bolt installed on the inside. How does all that sound?"

"Great."

"And there's one other thing. I want you to carry a concealed handgun and a can of Mace with you wherever you go."

Leah frowned. "I'm okay with the Mace, but I don't know about a handgun. I'm a big proponent of gun control."

"Do you think whoever filmed you in your bathroom is?"

Leah stared down at her hands and then looked up at Jackie. "I've never even shot a gun. I think I'd be so nervous I'd probably shoot myself!"

"That's easy enough to fix. There's a shooting range just outside the city limits. It's called 'Aimless.'"

"Seriously!" Leah laughed.

"I know, the name is pretty funny. It was started by a bunch of libertarians back in the Sixties. They didn't believe the government should regulate anything—abortion, pot, guns. I have a friend there, Chip Holt. A few lessons from him, and not only will you be able to shoot a gun, but you'll be damn good at it."

"I'm a little skeptical, but I'll take your word for it. When will you be able to get my apartment cleared?"

"I'll start on it as soon as we finish here. Don't worry. We're going to get the son of a bitch who did this to you—and anybody and everybody who may be involved."

CHAPTER

15

Clad only in a bra and panties, Christine reached for a Neiman Marcus hanging bag containing her outfit for the evening: a lambskin suede jacket, a low-cut scoop neck top, and a pencil skirt, all in midnight blue. She unzipped the bag and pulled on the top, eyeing herself in the full-wall mirror in her luxurious bathroom. She nodded approvingly—just the right amount of cleavage.

She wiggled into the pencil skirt, tucked in her top, and guided the zipper up the side, straightening the skirt with her hands in the process. Perfect—tight-fitting and sexy, showing off her curvy hips and exposing just enough of her shapely legs.

She slid her slender feet into dark blue suede, pointy-toed pumps—no stiletto heels tonight but high enough to grab attention. Looking at her reflection, she smiled admiringly.

She had saved the best for last, a buttery soft lambskin jacket with notched lapels and a yoked back. She slipped on the jacket, adjusting the lapels and the back to her taste. She cinched in the belt to outline her wasp-like waist, modeled one last time in front of the mirror, and strutted back into her bedroom. She looked at the rolled joint resting on her bedside table. Very tempting but risky—she had a business deal to close tonight. Besides, it would be waiting for her when she got home. In her experience, there was no better way to ensure a good night's sleep than burning one down right before getting under the covers.

She grabbed her matching Gucci evening bag and walked out the door.

Christine arrived at the Ritz-Carlton in Dallas twenty minutes late. She gave her car key to the valet and walked confidently through the hotel lobby toward the award-winning restaurant of Chef Dean Fearing. After introducing herself to the maître d', she was led to a table for two in the back.

Jamie Stein rose as the two approached. "Christine, so good to see you again."

"Likewise. Sorry I'm late, but the traffic . . ." She seated herself in the chair pulled out by the maître d', who then disappeared.

"No worries. I'm in no hurry. I've got all night." Jamie smiled at his date for the evening. "You look amazing. I love that jacket."

"Thank you. It's a little warm in here, though." She began to pull the jacket off her shoulders.

"Let me help you with that." Jamie rose and hustled around to Christine's side of the table. As she slid out of the jacket, he intentionally brushed her shoulders with his hands. She pretended not to notice. He draped the jacket over the back of her chair and returned to his seat. "That any better?"

"Yes, that's great." Christine pushed her hair back as Jamie's eyes were drawn to her plunging neckline, now clearly visible.

"So, how have you been?"

"Good. And you?"

"Same. I was wondering how long it was going to take you to call."

Christine grinned. "How could you be so sure I would?"

"Oh, I don't know. Just instinct."

The waiter appeared and took their drink orders. Jamie ordered his second scotch on the rocks and Christine a glass of pinot grigio.

"Your proposal still on the table?"

Jamie chuckled. "And why wouldn't it be?"

Christine picked up the napkin folded in front of her and placed it in her lap. "Oh, I don't know. You seem like the fickle sort."

"Not me. Reliable as they come."

"I do have some concerns."

"I figured you would. Try me."

Christine hesitated, searching for the right words. Conveniently, the waiter delivered their drinks and left. "Your compensation—how would that be handled?"

"I assume you use outside investigators at your law firm from time to time?"

"We do."

"Well, a close friend of mine owns a private investigation company called Security Plus, with offices throughout the country—New York City, Atlanta, Vegas, New Orleans, L.A., Chicago, and, conveniently, Dallas."

"I'm impressed. What does Security Plus do?"

"Investigation stuff."

"I see." Christine took a sip of wine. "And I assume you have no traceable affiliation with this company?"

"You assume correctly. None whatsoever."

The waiter appeared and, after reciting the evening's menu, left the couple to decide.

Christine leaned forward across the table and whispered, "If we do this deal, how do we get your money to you?"

"You will wire ninety-five thousand a month to three separate Security Plus bank accounts. I know you have cases in Texas, and I suspect you are considering filing some in California and Louisiana."

"And why would you suspect that?"

"Good venue for plaintiffs—no tort reform. Am I right?"

"You could be. Go on."

"All of the accounts are with small, locally-owned banks whose presidents are all friends with my buddy at Security Plus. These are, shall we say, mutually beneficial relationships, and these bankers – well, they know not to ask any questions. Follow me so far?"

Christine nodded.

"You will receive invoices from the Security Plus offices in these cities every month with the notation 'monthly retainer' on them. Make sure you wire the money to the accounts within five days of the invoice date."

"At that rate you won't get your money for a couple of years."

"That's correct. Makes for a nice little annuity."

"I assume the payments are under six figures, so no bank regulator's curiosity is aroused."

"Yes."

"And you have no affiliation with this company, so it would be difficult, if not impossible, to trace the money back to you."

"You're a quick study."

The waiter appeared again, took their order, and rushed off to another table.

"I'm impressed, Jamie. Seems you have thought of everything." Christine smiled.

"I have thought of everything," Jamie said confidently.

"One more question," Christine said coolly. "What makes you think we'll pay you one penny after we receive the settlement proceeds from Empire? Why wouldn't we simply cut you out?"

"Let's just say my good friend at Security Plus has been snooping around and has run across some information that I don't think you, or your dad, would want getting out."

Christine scoffed. "I have no idea what you are talking about."

"Oh, I think you do. Does the name Howell Crimm ring a bell? Just to refresh your recollection, your dad used him as an expert in your firm's lawsuits against Big Pharma. The conclusions Crimm swore to in all of those cases were remarkably similar—in fact, almost verbatim. Doesn't it strike you as a bit odd that an expert could reach identical opinions regarding distinctly different drugs?" Jamie smiled.

"I don't know what you have or what you think you have, but I don't appreciate the threat."

"Well, you asked. No offense intended."

"Okay. None taken. This is business. So when do I get the wiring instructions and the other details?"

"I have a packet for you—in my room." Jamie's eyes met Christine's and lingered tellingly.

Before Christine could respond, their entrées were served. Jamie sliced into his blood-red buffalo tenderloin. "Have you ever had buffalo? It's delicious. You should try a bite."

Christine waved him off. "I'm fine with the scallops, but thanks anyway."

"So, Christine, how's the firm doing?"

"As you probably know, we've seen better days. But our business is like that. It's either feast or famine, as the old saying goes. And how are things at Empire Risk?"

"I hate the fucking insurance business. I get paid like shit, but the company gives me the authority to make million-dollar deals. Go figure."

"So why stay in it?"

"Let's say there are perks that keep me around, like cutting deals that have something in it for me. I mean, there are so many cases being handled in my department that I can fly under the radar pretty easily—nobody looking over my shoulder." Jamie cut another bite of tenderloin and stuffed it into his mouth, continuing the conversation while he chewed. "So enough about business. You seeing anyone?"

"Don't have time—too much going on. And you?"

"Divorced for the second time. Can't seem to get it right. I think I'll stay single for a while."

"Kids?"

"No, thank goodness. You ever been married?"

"No, and I don't know that I ever want to be. I'm just too selfish. I don't like to share and I'm not ashamed to admit it." Christine finished her wine.

As the waiter cleared away their plates, Christine smiled at her dinner companion. His rugged appeal and don't-give-a-shit attitude had grown on her. She was drawn to men willing to take risks. After all, that's what had made her father so successful. She wondered how Jamie would be in bed, and she intended to find out.

Jamie drained the last of his third scotch. "Dessert?"

"How about a bottle of champagne in your room? I think a little celebration is in order." Christine leaned forward, exposing just the right amount of cleavage.

"I couldn't agree more." Jamie raised his hand and motioned for the check.

CHAPTER

16

"Any indication who will be representing Shaw and the BBC?" Jace took the last bite of his sandwich, crumpled up the wrapper, and launched it toward the trash can in the conference room corner. It ricocheted off the side of the can, landing on the floor. "Shit. I used to be able to hit that shot."

Kirk laughed. "At least you hit the can. And no, I'm not surprised we haven't heard anything on our lawsuit. The answer date isn't until day after tomorrow." Fresh out of law school, Kirk had made the ballsy decision to leave Hadley and Morgan with Jace and the other defectors when the Forman Firm was formed. Jace never forgot Kirk's loyalty and awarded him by giving him one plum assignment after another. Kirk always delivered in spades, whether he was asked to take a key deposition, draft a critical brief, or research a pivotal legal issue. He had become Jace's go-to associate and now was in line to make partner. Although swamped with other cases and assignments, Kirk had shown little hesitation when Darrin asked him if he wanted to be on the team in the Hanson case.

"So where are you on your research?"

"Well, I've read the Westboro case several times, looking for nuances in the majority opinion—"

Jace interrupted. "Have you found any?"

"The court goes out of its way to draw distinctions between speech directed to issues of public importance, like homosexuality and abortion, and speech of a personal nature, like insults and lies. Speech on public issues is protected by the First Amendment but insults and lies—not so much. Interestingly, the court declined to consider a post on the Westboro Baptist Church website, reasoning in a footnote that it was outside the appellate record."

"Do you agree with the court's refusal to consider that evidence?"

"No, I don't. It seemed to me that the justices wanted to reach the result they did and ignored anything that got in the way, including the website post."

"Tell me about the post."

"One of the picketers put it up several days after the protest. I don't remember the exact words, but it was very personal— talked about the deceased soldier, how the parents had raised him for the devil, that he was an adulterer. That was the gist of it."

"How in the world could the court ignore that?"

"Like I said, it made it easier for them to reach the result they wanted to reach."

"What else caught your attention?"

"Chief Justice Roberts wrote the majority opinion. He made it clear that this was a 'narrow' decision, which is another way of saying it was a very close call. If we can present some evidence showing distinctions between what the BBC did and what the Westboro Baptist Church did, the ruling just might go the other way."

The conference room door opened and Darrin stepped in. "Sorry I'm late, but I got caught up in a conference call on another case." She quickly slid into one of the chairs directly across the table from Jace.

"No problem. Kirk was just filling me in on his research." Jace smiled at Darrin and then turned back to Kirk. "Anything else?"

"That's all I have right now."

Jace turned his attention to Darrin. "What have you found out so far?"

"I've ordered the Hansons' medical records. Lauren's West Point and military records are being assembled and should be in my hands in a few days. As Kirk has probably told you, no answer has been filed so . . .

"We don't know who will be representing these dirtbags."

Darrin nodded.

"What have you learned about the protest? Did the BBC dot all the i's and cross all the t's?"

"I checked with the police department in Hagstrom. The BBC applied for, and received, all the required permits."

"Figures, but it was worth a try." Jace sighed. "Well, let me know when the answer comes in. It'll be interesting to see who we're going to be up against—probably the ACLU, but who knows."

Kirk gathered his files from the table and left the conference room. Darrin lingered.

"Jace, do you have a moment?"

"Always."

Darrin hesitated before continuing. "I don't know how to put this."

Jace remained silent, his eyes focused on Darrin's.

"I'm so confused."

"About what?"

"Us?"

"What do you mean, Darrin? I love being with you. You know that."

Darrin nodded. "I get that feeling but I have no idea where our relationship is headed. At times, I think there is something there and, at other times, I just don't have a clue."

Jace sighed. "To be completely honest, I'm confused as well. What happened to my wife really took its toll. And you know things aren't great with Matt. Yeah, they seem to be getting better but I sense there's still a lot of pent-up anger there. Bottom line, I don't want to tell you something just because I know that's what you want to hear. I just can't do that. It wouldn't be fair to you or to me." Jace slowly moved toward Darrin, put his hands on her shoulders, leaned over and kissed her gently on the lips. He then pulled back and stared deeply into her eyes. "I can't make any promises but I do know there is something between us. Let's give it some time and see what happens."

Darrin glanced down at the floor before looking back at Jace. She nodded and then put her arms around his neck, pulling him to her. Their lips met and melted together, their bodies pressed against each other. Darrin gently pulled back, looked up at Jace, and whispered, "You have no idea how hard it was for me to turn down your invitation to go to St. Croix with you after the Stone case."

"You're wrong about that because I wanted to hear a 'yes' worse than you'll ever know. But I didn't want to push you."

Darrin laughed softly. "I wish you had." She dropped her arms from around his neck and turned to walk toward the window. "It's hard on me – working with you and then feeling the way I do. Which is why I am thinking maybe I should get a job somewhere else. There are plenty of good paralegals out there. You'd find someone to take my place in no time."

"That's bullshit, and you know it. No one could fill your shoes."

"Jackie McLaughlin would love to try."

Jace walked up behind Darrin as she gazed out the window and put his arms around her waist. "So that's what this is all about. Do I sense a little jealously here?"

Darrin slid out of Jace's embrace and turned to face him. "I'm not kidding about this. Is there something going on between you and Jackie?"

In a calm voice, Jace responded, "I like Jackie. She's a helluva good investigator. But I'm not seeing her, if that's what you're asking me."

"Well, the other day you sure seemed determined to use her on this case—"

Jace interrupted. "That's because your plate was full, and I wanted to make sure everyone's responsibilities were clear."

"You are one smooth talker, Jace Forman. A born trial lawyer. I'll give things some time but, if I find out you've been lying to me about her, then I'm out of here. I mean it, Jace."

Jace gave Darrin his million-dollar smile.

Darrin shook her head and tried unsuccessfully to suppress a grin. "I'm not kidding Jace," and walked out of the conference room, closing the door behind her.

Alone, Jace ran his fingers through his thick brown hair and sighed. Darrin was right—he did have feelings for Jackie. He just didn't know how deeply they ran. He had been married for years and he wasn't ready to do that again, not even close to ready. But he couldn't afford to take a chance on losing Darrin, personally or professionally. He would have to walk a fine line—a very fine line. He grabbed his case file off the conference room table and headed back down the long corridor to his office.

CHAPTER

17

Leah's cell phone vibrated. She picked it up from the corner of her desk and glanced at the caller id: Jackie McLaughlin. She quickly answered. "Jackie, I've been on pins and needles. What have you learned?"

"Well, we're dealing with a professional. There were small video cams throughout your apartment. Whoever placed them there could literally record everything you did while you were in your apartment."

"I can't believe I didn't notice them."

"I can. Whoever did this replaced the smoke detectors in every room with clones that contained concealed cameras. No reason for you, or anyone else, to notice."

"Oh my gosh. That's unbelievable!"

"Not in today's world. And the hanger in your bathroom on the back of the door, the one you hang your robe on—it had a tiny camera in it as well."

"Who makes these things? Aren't they illegal?"

"There are a number of companies in the market. They advertise them as home security devices—you know, so people can check on their maids, nannies, or their home when they are out of town. And they're cheap—a few hundred dollars."

"I had no idea. That's so disturbing."

Jackie sighed. "I'm sorry, Leah."

"Anything else I should know?"

"The good news is we installed a video cam in the hallway just above the door to your apartment and a dead bolt on the inside."

"Are you sure you found all the cameras?"

"One hundred percent sure. You have nothing to worry about in that regard."

"So it's safe to stay in my apartment?"

"Safer than it's ever been." Jackie paused. "I had my tech guy look at that email on your laptop. He thinks he may—I say 'may'—be able to trace it back to the IP address it was sent from. But that's a complicated and time-consuming process. I'll let you know if he turns up anything."

"So what about this pervert's threat to post the video on YouTube? What can we do to stop him?"

"Nothing at this point."

"Nothing? What am I supposed to do while your guy tries to determine who sent this?"

"I would lay off that story you're working on. At least for now."

"But we don't know for sure that Connors is behind this, do we?"

"No, not for sure, but that's my guess at this point."

"So you're saying I don't have a choice?"

"Not in my opinion." Jackie changed course. "Have you scheduled anything at the firing range?"

"I have my first lesson tomorrow."

"Good. Have you purchased a gun yet?"

"No. I thought it would be better to wait and see what Chip recommends for me."

"I agree. My bet is he'll tell you to buy a Glock 19. They're small, lightweight, and hold fifteen rounds. Perfect for carrying in your purse."

"I'll let you know what he says."

"And you have my number if you need me. Don't think twice about calling—anytime, day or night."

"I won't. Thanks, Jackie."

"You're welcome. I'll call you when I have something."

CHAPTER
18

Cromwell Prater IV slid behind the wheel of his red Porsche 911 Carrera, placed his portable coffee cup in the holder next to him, and turned the ignition key. The turbo engine purred. He smiled at the sound and eased the stick shift into reverse. As he backed out of the driveway, he glanced at the jewel-studded Rolex on his wrist—7:00 a.m. At an average of eighty-five miles per hour, the four hundred mile drive to the BBC compound would take him no more than five hours, his ETA a little before noon, just in time for lunch with his new client, Ezekiel Shaw.

Ten minutes later he steered the Carrera onto the entrance ramp at I-20 and slid an audiobook into the CD player—Glenn Beck's *Agenda 21*. In Crom's opinion, Beck was a true patriot, a man unafraid to speak out against big government and the liberal agenda that had infected the country. He had read all of Beck's previous books, his favorite being *Common Sense*. Who could really argue with someone who wanted the country to return to the road map laid out by Thomas Paine? He adjusted his leather seat and set the cruise control on eighty-five, his attention momentarily focused on a futuristic society with little hope and limited purpose.

After fifteen minutes, he ejected the CD. He was too distracted, his thoughts consumed by memories of a previous time. He grimaced as he recalled Maurice coming into his office to tell him that Jace Forman and several other Hadley and Morgan lawyers had decided to leave and form their own practice. And Jace hadn't asked him to join the new enterprise, hadn't even mentioned it. Crom had considered Jace a close friend—what a fool he had been!

Through the years he'd watched as the Forman Firm grew, and his old partner, and so-called friend, amassed an impressive record of courthouse victories. Sure, Crom had done well at Hadley and Morgan, serving on numerous committees and ultimately being asked to chair the firm's litigation section. But the sting of being overlooked by Jace still lingered. The way Jace got praised in the news media stung even more. Crom knew he was just as good a lawyer as Jace Forman—and now the time for payback had finally arrived. He and Jace would face off in a federal courtroom in Fort Worth, Texas—like gladiators in an arena—and only one would walk away victorious. As Crom's Carrera sped down the highway, a wry smile crossed his lips. He would do anything to win that contest—anything.

T
he members of the Brimstone Bible Church had all taken their assigned seats in the pews of the rustic log chapel where morning devotionals were held each day. The men were dressed in their typical work uniforms: khaki shirts, bib overalls, and Red Wing steel-toed boots. The women wore white cotton

dresses buttoned at the neck and extending to the tops of their black granny boots, their heads covered by white bonnets tied securely under their chins. All heads were bowed, all eyes closed, all hands clasped in prayer.

Once everyone had assembled, Ezekiel entered the simple sanctuary from a side door and slowly made his way up the winding stairway that led to a pulpit six feet above the rough-hewn planked floor. Upon reaching the top, he gazed out at the congregants, a satisfied smile forming on his lips. He addressed his followers in a deep, comforting voice. "Brothers and Sisters, welcome. I am so glad to see your smiling faces on this beautiful morning. Now, before we begin our morning service, I would like to make a short announcement. I am expecting a visitor today."

Several of the male members gave him a questioning look. Some grumbled their displeasure. Ezekiel just smiled.

"Although he is not one of us, he comes to help us—to help us fight that wickedness that has been filed by the nonbelievers. I will be with him at all times. He will not be speaking with any of you, so you need not worry. Just tend to your chores and flash him a warm smile if he looks your way. Now let us proceed with our morning devotional. Please bow your heads in prayer." Ezekiel lowered his head reverently and clasped his hands on the lectern in front of him. Before speaking, he cracked one eye to make sure all in the congregation had obediently followed his lead. They had. He then began the service.

Just before noon Crom pulled up in front of a wrought-iron gate graced by an eyebrow arch inscribed with the words "Brimstone Bible Church." A rudimentary cross was prominently displayed at the arch's apex. Crom lowered his window and punched the speaker button on the keypad to his left. A familiar voice answered.

"Mr. Prater, welcome to A World Apart. The gate should be opening as I speak. Please follow the signs to my house. I look forward to meeting you."

Crom eased through the entrance as the gate slowly opened and followed the signs to a two-story log cabin. A lanky, long-haired man simply clad in a white robe and leather sandals waited at the front door. He waved as Crom's Carrera approached and then walked toward the car as it came to a stop in the gravel driveway.

"Mr. Prater, so glad you made it here safely. I'm Ezekiel Shaw." Ezekiel extended his hand, which Crom eagerly took.

"Savior Shaw, it's—"

"Ezekiel is fine. One of the congregants started calling me Savior years ago and the title stuck. If that's what they want to call me, fine. But you—please call me by my first name. It's much less formal."

"Ezekiel it is."

Ezekiel walked back toward the log cabin, his attorney in tow. Their conversation continued.

"How long have you and your congregation been here?"

"Several years. We are a self-sufficient community. We do our own construction, farming, teaching—you name it. Don't have to rely on anyone outside the faith to do anything for us." Ezekiel grinned. "Well, that's not entirely true. We don't have any lawyers in our community. That's why we need you."

Ezekiel stopped at the front door and motioned Crom inside. "We're going to meet in my study. It's just down the hall, first door on the left. My assistant made some sandwiches. I hope you don't mind this being a working lunch. I have some activities I must lead starting at two this afternoon."

Once they entered the study, Ezekiel motioned to an oval rough-hewn oak table in the corner of the room, a tray of sandwiches, paper plates, and two glasses of water on top. "This all right? Hope you like ham. We raise hogs here at the commune."

"Perfect." Crom took a seat at the table and Ezekiel followed.

"So, it's okay if I call you Crom, isn't it?"

"Of course. I would be insulted if you didn't."

Ezekiel grinned, took a bite of his sandwich, and continued. "I don't understand this lawsuit. Our church has never been sued before. We always follow the local laws and regulations regarding peaceful protests. And that's exactly what we did here. Isn't this just a nuisance suit?"

"That's what we'll argue. And the Supreme Court has recently handed down a decision—"

Ezekiel interrupted. "The Westboro case. I've read it. Although I'm no lawyer, it seems to provide an absolute defense. I apologize for hitting you with a barrage of questions while you're trying to eat."

"Don't worry. I can eat and talk at the same time." Crom nibbled at the sandwich, unsure as to its safety, and then sipped some water. "I tend to agree, but we do need to take their case seriously. To start with, I need a little background. Tell me about the Brimstone Bible Church and what you believe."

"Well, first and foremost, we believe the Bible is the inerrant word of God to be literally interpreted and followed."

"That's not surprising. I believe many Christian denominations share that conviction."

Ezekiel stood and walked over to the built-in bookcase. He pulled out a leather Bible, its cover worn and frayed at the corners. "This book—written ages ago—contains the road map to a life of grace and goodness, as well as the key to eternal salvation." He returned to the table, slid back into his chair, and leaned across the table toward Crom. "Do you believe that?"

Crom's eyes widened. "I was raised a Methodist, if that's what you mean."

"That means nothing—absolutely nothing. You have to find God yourself. You have to read his word. You have to study his word. You have to pray about understanding his word." Ezekiel paused and leaned back, resting his head on the back of the chair and gazing up at the bead-board ceiling. "Have you ever read the Bible? Now, I don't mean a verse or two when you go to church. I mean starting with the first chapter of Genesis and ending with the last chapter of Revelation. Have you done that, Crom?"

Crom shifted uncomfortably in his chair. "No, I'm embarrassed to say I haven't. I've been meaning to but, with my heavy caseload and all, I just haven't gotten around to it."

"Didn't think so. The vast majority of people who call themselves Christians haven't either, so you have plenty of company. And that's the problem—they don't know God's will because they haven't taken the time to even read his word."

"So let's get back to what you and your followers believe. You've told me you believe the Bible is the inerrant word of God. What else?"

"From that fundamental truth flows the rest of our doctrine. Obviously, the Ten Commandments should be followed to the letter. To me it's blasphemous that this country won't even permit those divine proclamations to be posted in public places. Crom, they are God's law, as he gave it to Moses. Why shouldn't they be this country's as well? Why shouldn't they be prominently displayed in every courthouse, school, and government building?"

"Because of the First Amendment, the establishment—"

"I know the argument, but it's hogwash. Jews came up with that tortured interpretation."

Crom shifted uncomfortably in his chair.

"Homosexuality is an unpardonable sin. Women should be submissive to men. They should never, ever be in positions of authority. That is a contravention of the clear teachings of the Bible."

"Where do you find that in the Bible?"

"There are many references: Genesis 3:16, Isaiah 3:12, 1 Corinthians 11:3, 1 Corinthians 14:34–36. Need I go on?"

"Please." Crom scribbled on his legal pad.

"Ephesians 5:22–24, Colossians 3:18, 1 Timothy 2:11–15. Just wait until you read those verses. They make it clear as a bell what a woman's role should be."

"Any more references?"

"Let's see." Ezekiel scratched his stubbly beard as he searched his memory. "Well, there's Titus 2:4–5 and 1 Peter 3:1." He paused and peered again at the ceiling. "There are probably more verses that speak to this issue, but those are the ones that come to mind."

"So how do you treat women here?"

Ezekiel cleared his throat and responded, "We treat our women well, very well. They know their place in the world God created, and they're comfortable with that."

"So is that the reason you protested at Lauren Hanson's funeral?"

"Absolutely. We need to wake up this country, get it to return to the teachings of the Bible. You think the founders would have ever permitted women to serve in the military? I mean, do you think George Washington would have ever allowed a woman to command any of his troops? I can answer those questions. Absolutely not. And that's why God is sending soldiers like Second Lieutenant Lauren Hanson home in a body bag—to punish us, to get us to change our ways."

"But why put her parents through that? Why not protest somewhere else?"

"The answer is simple. We are trying to get as many people as possible to focus on our message. In the book of Ezekiel, God orders us to show others the evil of their ways. Otherwise, we are committing a sin by our own inaction. And that is what we are doing when we stage these protests: trying to show the multitudes the error of their ways."

"I think I understand your position."

"I would hope so. It's not rocket science."

Crom ignored the insult. "Do you have the signs that were used at the protest?"

"They've all been destroyed."

"Why?"

"Why would we keep a bunch of cardboard placards that have already served their purpose?"

"Were there any videos taken of the protest?"

"Not that I'm aware of."

"Did you hear any of your followers direct any personal insults at Mr. or Mrs. Hanson?"

"That would never happen. All of the Brothers and Sisters know to stick to the script, and it's a simple one. Crom, a woman's place is in the home—not in the armed services, not in corporate boardrooms, not in law firms. Speaking of, I saw on your website that your firm employs female lawyers, is that true?"

"Yes, we do."

"You should rethink your hiring practices."

"There is a law—"

"I knew you were going to say that. And therein lies the problem. That law needs to be repealed, taken off the books."

Crom opened his leather briefcase and inserted his legal pad and pen. "I'd like to take a quick tour of the compound, if that's possible."

"It would be my pleasure to personally escort you around, but I would prefer you use the word 'commune' to describe our community. 'Compound' sounds like a military installation, and this certainly is no military installation."

"'Commune' it is, then."

"Crom, we are very proud of what we have built here with God's blessing and support. It's been an answered prayer, and I mean that literally with every fiber of my being. We have been blessed with acres of ruggedly beautiful land that, as of yet, has escaped the tarnish of man's materialism. And we intend to keep it that way. Although our buildings aren't ornate or showy, they adequately serve our purposes. We believe God wants us to live simple lives and shun material indulgences."

Crom thought of his $150,000 sports car parked in Ezekiel's driveway and winced. He quickly pulled his jacket sleeve over the diamond-studded Rolex on his wrist and changed topics. "At some point, I will need to interview all of the people who participated in the protest."

"And you will have free rein to do so," Ezekiel lied. "Just let me know when you want to schedule the interviews. I can tell you there are no documents that fit within the categories the other lawyer has outlined—not a one. And I suspect those you interview will have recollections similar to mine. But I know you have to go through the motions."

Ezekiel rose from his chair and headed toward the door. His guest followed. An hour later, Crom was speeding back across Texas on I-20, straight to Fort Worth, his mind racing as fast as his Porsche's turbo-charged engine.

CHAPTER

19

"Guess who's representing the BBC and Shaw?" Darrin walked into Jace's office a little before 7:00 p.m. holding a thick bundle of papers in her hand.

"No idea."

"Cromwell Prater IV."

"You've got to be kidding!"

"Nope. I checked the fax machine just as I was leaving and found their answer, a motion for summary judgment to dismiss our case on First Amendment grounds and a stack of discovery requests."

Darrin handed a twelve-inch stack of papers to Jace, who immediately started flipping through the pages. "This is going to be an all-out war! I know Prater has been waiting for a chance to kick my ass. I bet he's as happy as a pig in shit—not to mention that asshole Maurice Morgan." Before he could say any more his phone rang. Jace glanced at the number and quickly grabbed the receiver. "Matt, what a pleasant surprise!"

Assuming Jace would want a little privacy, Darrin smiled at him and left his office, closing the door behind her.

"Hey, Dad. Do you have a minute?" Matt's tone was foreboding.

"Always, Son. What's going on?"

"Well, I've got some big news." He hesitated a moment to work up his nerve.

"Don't keep me guessing. What's your big news? You're not getting married or anything crazy like that, are you?"

"I've enlisted in the Navy! I'm going to be a Navy SEAL!"

Jace was speechless.

"Dad? Are you there?"

Jace cleared his throat before responding. "I'm here, all right. Just a little shocked, that's all. I would be lying if I didn't say this news caught me by surprise. How long have you been—"

Matt interrupted. "For a few months. I just think I need to give something back to my country and—"

"I understand that, but what about your college degree? You are a junior and will graduate next year. Why not wait?"

"I'm just not into school right now. My classes are boring as hell. I'm sick of all the fraternity crap. I want to do something that has some meaning."

"Well, I am a little disappointed you didn't talk with me about this before you pulled the trigger. I mean, it's a huge decision. And training to be a SEAL—I don't know all the details, but I do know it's damn tough. Not to mention the fact that you might be sent on some high-risk mission to Afghanistan, Iraq, or who knows where."

"I've considered all that." Matt's voice turned defensive and a bit defiant.

"Is there something more to this than serving your country? You seemed a little miffed the other night when you bumped into me and my business associate outside of Malaga."

"Business associate? Is that what you are calling them these days?"

"That's not fair, Matt. Ms. McLaughlin is a PI who is helping me on a new case, that's all."

"You have to go all the way to Austin to get a PI? That's a stretch, Dad. I'm not an idiot."

Jace bit his lip. "So did your feelings about me factor into your decision?"

"Not in the least. Like I said, I'm doing this to give back to my country."

Jake sensed Matt was lying. But he also didn't see any point in starting an argument. "So what's the timeline?" he asked.

"I head to Chicago for SEAL prep school in a few weeks. The training is supposed to be pretty intense, so I don't know if I'll even make the cut."

"How long is this prep school?"

"Eight weeks."

Jace sighed. "When can I see you, Matt? Are you sure we can't have one long sit-down talk before you leave? This is not going to be easy for either one of us."

"Well, I'm pretty swamped right now. I've got to withdraw from my classes, turn in my books, pack up my apartment. Let me get through all of that crap, and I'll give you a call. I'll definitely make it back to Fort Worth before I start training."

"You know you could wait until after you graduate from college to join," Jace said.

"Dad, I can get a degree later. My mind is made up."

"All right then, I'll see you in a few weeks. I love you, Son."

"You too, Dad."

Jace stared at the receiver in disbelief before returning it to the cradle. Instinctively, he hurried down the hall to Darrin's office.

She glanced up at her boss from the pile of papers on her desk. "You look like you've just seen a ghost. What's wrong?"

Jace sat down in the chair across from her. "I can't believe this. It's like something out of a bad dream."

"What is?"

"I just got off the phone with Matt. He's enlisted in the Navy. He wants to be a SEAL."

Darrin leaned forward. "He what?"

"You heard it right. He's going to SEAL prep school in a few weeks."

"Why?"

"I have no idea." Jace hedged. "Maybe he's still pissed at me over his mother's accident. Hell, I don't know. I thought things were getting a lot better, but I guess I was wrong."

"Anything happen that might have set him off?"

Jace hesitated, then shook his head. "I don't know. He's hard to read."

"What about school?"

"Says he'll get his degree after he gets out. I wish there were something I could do to stop this, but it's out of my control."

"Why don't we get some dinner and a bottle of wine? We can talk about it then." Darrin smiled empathetically. "How does that sound?"

"Let me grab my jacket and briefcase. I'll meet you at the elevator in five minutes."

CHAPTER

20

Maurice Morgan slouched in his leather office chair. He looked over his reading glasses and across the desk at Crom. "How's our lawsuit against Forman going? Any developments?"

"It's early in the case, so not a lot to report. I filed an answer and a motion for summary judgment earlier this week."

"Who's the judge?"

"The Honorable Barbara Zimmerman."

Maurice shook his head. "Oh, well. She wouldn't have been my first choice, but we'll have to play the cards we've been dealt, so to speak."

"I haven't had any cases before her, have you?" Crom asked.

"Fortunately, I haven't. You know, she was appointed by that liberal bastard Clinton. I guess Slick Willy figured he could fill his minority quota by appointing a Jew and a woman at the same time—kill two birds with one stone."

Maurice chuckled. Crom, who didn't exactly share his boss's political leanings, winced undetectably.

"What kind of reputation does she have?" Crom asked.

"What you'd expect. She's liberal as hell, just like that son of a bitch who appointed her. Always rules for the 'little man.' Oh, excuse me, the 'little person.' Got to be politically correct these days."

"Any idea whether Forman has tried any cases in her court?"

"No, but you should get that paralegal of yours to do a search. Forman has tried a lot of cases. I'd be surprised if one of those didn't end up in Zimmerman's court. Let me know what you find out."

"I will."

"So tell me about your meeting with our new client Ezekiel Shaw. What was he like?"

"His appearance is odd, to say the least. He wears a long robe and sandals."

"You can clean him up before trial—that is, if Forman gets past summary judgment."

"I don't know about that. Shaw seems pretty stubborn about having the final say on everything, which I assume includes the way he dresses."

"A lot of clients seem stubborn until their asses are on the line. Then they become a little more practical. Wouldn't you agree?"

"Typically that's the case. But Shaw believes in the Bible—in a very literal sense. To him, it is black and white and should be followed exactly as it was written centuries ago."

"Good for him. That's what I believe."

"Have you read the Bible from cover to cover, Maurice?"

Maurice shifted in his chair. "That's a strange question. Why would you ask me something like that?"

"That's what Shaw asked me. When I told him I attended church and had studied passages from the Bible, he scoffed at me—told me that's what all the fake Christians do."

"I don't agree with him there. It doesn't hurt to have a minister more knowledgeable than you take you through the most meaningful parts."

"Not the way he sees it. He thinks that is an abomination. Shaw doesn't believe anyone should be able to cherry-pick Scripture. To him, anyone who calls himself a Christian has the solemn obligation to read every single verse in the Bible, New and Old Testament, and abide by each and every one—literally."

Maurice coughed. "So what does our client believe the Bible says?"

"There are a number of things, like the BBC has the only true faith, homosexuality is an unpardonable sin, the Ten Commandments were literally handed down from God to Moses—those types of things. But the most important from the standpoint of our lawsuit against Forman is the BBC's take on women's rights."

"And that is?"

"They shouldn't have any. Men should run the show."

"I'm growing to like this guy. He got any more room at that commune of his?" Maurice laughed.

"Well, actually, there is plenty of support in the Bible for his position. I can't tell you how many passages he quoted when I challenged him on this issue. He started with Genesis and Eve's sinful influence on Adam and then moved all the way through the New Testament. He spit verse after verse out from memory. His biblical knowledge was pretty damn impressive. After he finished, he asked me if we had any female attorneys. When I answered yes, he told me we should fire them all, that we were engaging in sinful conduct."

"Hell, I wish we could," Maurice said, as Crom bit his tongue. "I'm so tired of having to work around pregnancy leave, flex time, watching what I say around them. I wish we could go back to the days when I first started practicing. This profession was a club of good ol' boys, pure and simple." Maurice smiled as he reminisced. "Anyway, bottom line Crom, what kind of witness is this guy going to make? If the case goes to trial, the outcome will likely turn on how well he holds up under Forman's cross-examination."

"Maurice, the guy is mesmerizing—something about the way his eyes lock on yours and don't leave. And he seems deeply certain of his beliefs and unshakable in his recollection that his followers did not direct any personal insults at the Hansons or their daughter. My initial impression is that he'll make a great witness. And he does have a point—that they protested an issue, not the dead girl specifically."

"You sure about that? And are you sure there are no untidy loose ends? No one who might turn on him?"

Crom wanted to say that Shaw's views on women could hurt him with the judge and jury, but decided against it. "I haven't seen anything yet that might damage the case," Crom said. "So far, so good."

"Good to hear." Maurice smiled. "Keep me posted."

"Of course." Crom took the cue, stood, and left the office.

CHAPTER

21

Darrin walked up the sidewalk to the modest ranch-style home of Eugene Hanson. She rang the doorbell and looked around the neighborhood as she waited.

The door opened. Eugene stared at her, his eyes unblinking. For a moment Darrin wondered if he was on medication.

"Ms. McKenzie. Please, please come in."

Darrin crossed the threshold. "Thank you, Mr. Hanson."

"Eugene, please. Would you care for a cup of coffee? I just made a fresh pot."

"I'd love one."

"Let's meet in the study." Eugene gestured toward a door just down the hall. "Why don't you make yourself at home while I get the coffee. Do you take cream or sugar?"

"Just black."

Darrin headed toward the study. She took a quick survey of the room and noticed a lone file resting on top of the desk. She looked over her shoulder to make sure she was alone and then picked up the file. The tab had the initials "BBC" written on it.

She opened the file, and her eyes widened at a series of aerial photographs, labeled "A World Apart—The BBC Commune." There were a number of buildings depicted in the photographs, with descriptions underneath each.

Why, she wondered, would Eugene have photos of the specific buildings in Shaw's compound? She quickly flipped through the rest of the documents in the file. There were various photographs of Shaw and some of his followers. There were a couple of news articles about Shaw going to West Texas. Then Darrin took a breath. In the back of the folder were several printed pages from a website advertising automatic weapons and ammunition.

She heard footsteps, quickly closed the file, returned it to the desk, and dashed over to a bookshelf lined with old paperbacks. Trying to regain her composure, she pulled one from the shelf and began to leaf through the pages. Seconds later, Eugene entered the room, a cup of coffee in each hand. Darrin returned the paperback to its slot and turned to face her host. He handed Darrin her coffee and then sat in the swivel chair behind the desk, motioning for Darrin to take the seat in front of him.

Darrin eased into the chair, cradling the coffee cup with both hands, and said, "Before we get started, Eugene, I just want to tell you how sorry I am about your wife. I know this must be a tough time for you, considering how many years the two of you were married. And the funeral, it was so moving. I don't think there was a dry eye in the church."

"There was no one like Janice. She was the only woman I ever really loved. I'm just glad those bastards—forgive my language, but there is no other word to describe them—didn't show up and turn her service into some kind of circus. I don't think I could have taken that."

Darrin noticed Eugene's eyes were starting to water. He swiped his shirtsleeve across his face. "So what's this motion that their lawyer has filed? As I told you, I have never been involved in a lawsuit and don't get all the legal mumbo jumbo."

"The BBC and Mr. Shaw have filed a motion for summary judgment to have our case dismissed on First Amendment grounds."

"Excuse me, but what in the world does that mean?" Eugene tilted his head, furrowing his brow in the process.

"I'll try to make this as simple as I can. Basically, they are asking the court to throw the case out without having a jury trial."

Eugene snorted derisively. "The judge can't do that, can he? I mean, everyone's entitled to a jury trial. That's one of those fundamental rights that's in the Constitution, isn't it?"

"Well, as a general rule, you're right, but there is an exception. If the judge finds that there are no fact issues for a jury to resolve, then he or, in this instance she, can decide the case based strictly upon the law."

"I am not sure I follow that. And I certainly don't agree that that's the way it should be. But if you say it's so, then I'll take your word for it. Is there any chance of the judge granting the motion?"

"As Mr. Forman already indicated to you, a recent case out of the Supreme Court does present some problems for us. Their motion is based on that decision." Darrin took a sip of coffee, which had turned lukewarm.

"So what do you need from me?"

"We need an affidavit from you swearing to what you heard and saw at the protest."

"And how will that help?"

"If the judge believes there's evidence that the BBC's statements were personal insults against you, your wife, or your daughter, then she'll likely deny the motion for summary judgment. We'll be able to go to trial."

Eugene slammed his fist down on the desk. "Damn right they were personal. Those people were out to get us. And they are going to pay."

Thinking about what she had seen in the folder on his desk, Darrin tensed. "We've put together an affidavit that mirrors what you told us you heard and saw when we first met with you in our offices." Darrin took out a three-page document and handed it to Eugene.

After reading it slowly, he looked up across the desk at Darrin. "That is exactly what I heard and saw. Do I just sign here at the bottom? Who's going to notarize this? I see there's a place for a notary's signature."

"I will. I have my license."

Eugene reached across the desk to retrieve a pen that lay in the corner. He scribbled his signature on the last page and pushed the document back to Darrin.

"Thank you, Eugene. I'll notarize it when I get back to the office."

"Anything else?" Eugene asked abruptly.

"I'm also leaving with you a copy of some interrogatories and document requests the opposing lawyer has served on us. I'm in the process of preparing some draft responses, but in the meantime, I wanted you to have a copy. I'd like for you to review them carefully and give me a call in the next day or so."

Eugene shook his head as he leafed through the lengthy documents. His unblinking stare was back. "All of this legalese is just a bunch of shit, isn't it?"

"What do you mean?"

"It's just a waste of time. A way to avoid the truth."

Darrin tried to smile politely. "I promise you, we are going to do everything we can to see that you get your day in court."

Eugene just shook his head.

Darrin rose from her chair. "I hate to run, but I have to get back to the office. Call me if you have any questions."

They said their goodbyes, then Darrin almost ran to her car. Once inside, she fumbled through her purse until she found her cell phone. She dialed a number. "Jace, we've got a problem—a big problem."

D arrin paced in front of Jace's desk. "I'm worried about our client. I can't tell you how freaky our meeting was, from the time he opened the door until I left. He seemed so agitated, like he was ready to explode at any minute."

"I know you're upset, but let's go over it again—this time with a little less emotion," Jace said, leaning back in his chair. "It might help if you sat down."

Darrin shot a reprimanding look at her boss. "You're not taking me seriously. I'm telling you—"

"I'm taking you very seriously, I swear. I just want to make sure I understand exactly what happened before making any decisions. Does that make sense?"

"I'm sorry, Jace. I'm more than a little shook up right now. Just bear with me." She took a sip of water and then sat on the edge of the chair in front of Jace's desk. After taking a couple of deep breaths, she detailed her morning with Mr. Hanson. "Jace, what are we going to do? I know, deep down, that our client is planning to kill Ezekiel Shaw and maybe all of his followers. We've got to go to the police."

Jace rose from his chair and walked toward his office window. He gazed out as he spoke. "Our client—and you can't forget that—hasn't done anything illegal. Nothing you have described to me—"

Darrin jumped up from her chair and walked hurriedly toward Jace. She squeezed his arm. "Jace, you're not hearing me. Our client is crazy! I saw that look in his eyes. He's going to kill someone if we don't stop him."

"Eugene Hanson has done nothing illegal. Everything you found in his file is easily accessible on the Internet. Even if we went to the police, they wouldn't have any basis to arrest him. And aren't you forgetting about the attorney-client privilege? Your entire meeting today is covered by it."

Darrin loosened her grip on Jace's arm and walked back to her chair. She sat down and sighed. "You're right. I was so flustered I didn't even think about that. But we've got to do something. I really am afraid he is going to try to kill Shaw."

"He threatened to do just that when I visited him in the hospital, but I talked him out of it. I asked him to give me the opportunity to shut Shaw and the BBC down through the legal system. He gave me his word he would give me that chance."

"And you believed him?"

"I did then, and I do now. I admit that Eugene's a little unstable right now. But homicidal? I don't think so. If we contacted the police, we'd lose any control we currently have over Eugene. He would feel betrayed and likely fire us for divulging attorney-client secrets. And I wouldn't blame him. No, we can't go to the police with what you learned today—way too risky."

Darrin shook her head again. "I guess you're right. But I'm still concerned that he might do something horrible."

"We just need to keep a close eye on him. We don't really have any other alternative. I'll give him a call later today and check his temperature. If I sense anything alarming, I'll figure out something. I promise."

CHAPTER

22

Leah pulled off a county road fifteen miles outside the Austin city limits and parked her car in front of a nondescript prefab building with the words "AIMLESS" painted in large burnt-orange letters on either side of the entrance. She stared at the building as she sat in her car, in disbelief that she was there.

Minutes later, she was standing at the counter inside, guns of every size and shape positioned on the wall behind. There were several salespeople helping customers. One of them nodded in her direction, signaling he would be with her shortly. Leah nodded back and smiled. As she waited, she pulled her cell phone from her purse and began returning text messages before being interrupted by a burly man with a full black beard dressed in camo. "Can I help you, ma'am?"

Leah looked up, startled by his deep voice. "Yes, I'm here for a lesson with Chip Holt."

Without taking his eyes off Leah, the bearded salesman hollered, "Chip, there's a young lady here to see you." In a lowered voice, he added, "He'll be right with you," and then moved down the counter to assist another customer. Leah looked around, nervously wondering what her instructor would be like. She didn't have to wait long. The curtain behind the sales area opened and a thirty-something man of medium build, sunbleached hair, and a natural tan appeared. He held his hand out across the counter.

"Ms. Rosen, I'm Chip Holt."

Leah's eyes widened as she smiled at her new acquaintance. She shook his hand and replied, "Mr. Holt—"

"Chip."

"Chip. I've heard so much about you from Jackie McLaughlin."

"You can't believe all you hear."

"It was all good."

Chip leaned over the counter, his blue eyes a pleasing contrast to his brown skin and sandy hair. "I'm crazy about Jackie. I still don't get why she left the department—best investigator they had."

"Well, I'm glad she did. I couldn't get any help from the police. They're so busy solving the big stuff, you know. But I am very thankful Officer Gomez referred me to Jackie."

Chip led Leah to the gun display. "So, what do you know about guns?"

"That I don't like them. I've supported practically every candidate who has advocated for gun control."

Chip grinned sheepishly. "I take it you'd rather be almost any place other than here?"

What Leah wanted to say was "I did until I met you," but she replied, "I apologize for being so blunt, but I can't help it. And the answer to your question is yes."

"So tell me—why are you here?"

"My apartment was broken into and Jackie suggested I carry a gun for protection."

"Good advice. Any idea as to the type of firearm you want? They come in all shapes and sizes."

"What would you recommend?"

Chip responded without hesitation. "Glock 19."

Leah grinned. "I can't believe it. That's exactly what Jackie said you'd say."

"That's because it's the perfect gun for someone like you—light, compact, and easy to use. Let's look at one." Chip slid open the glass door to the display case, pulled out a gun, and placed it on the counter in front of Leah. "This little baby here is a nine-millimeter, comes with a magazine that holds fifteen rounds." He offered the gun to Leah. "Go ahead, pick it up. It won't bite." Chip smiled.

"It's not loaded, is it?"

"No. Don't worry. Just check out the weight—get a feel for it."

Leah tentatively picked the gun up off the counter. "Wow! I didn't expect it to be so light. I could carry it in my purse."

"That's the idea. Do you want to shoot it?"

"Today? I thought you might want me to review some instructional material or something first."

"The best way to learn how to shoot a gun is by doing it. And I'll be there with you—to make sure you don't blow your foot off."

Leah's eyes lingered on Chip's a little too long before she responded. "Well, let's do it. Do you have an indoor shooting range? You know, like the ones I've seen on TV?"

"Nope. We're going to jump in one of the mules I keep out back and drive to our outdoor range. You're going to learn how to shoot a gun while looking out on some of the most beautiful countryside in the whole world. You mind leaving your purse in our safe? You won't need it where we're going."

Without hesitation, Leah handed him her purse, which he locked in a safe under the counter. "What's a mule anyway? I've never heard that term."

Chip smiled. "Sorry about that. Just think all-terrain golf cart."

"Got it." Leah returned the smile.

"I'll drive around and meet you out front."

"Sounds good." As Leah walked toward the entrance, she couldn't help but look over her shoulder. Chip grinned knowingly as he caught her glance.

Chip coasted to a stop in a hilly, uninhabited expanse of land dotted by scrub oak and cedar.

"We purchased this land—over a hundred acres—years ago for practically nothing. With Austin growing like it is, we've been offered three times what we paid. But none of us—my partners and me, that is—are interested in selling. We love it too damn much." Chip extended his hand to Leah as she stepped down from the four-wheeler and handed her some electronic earmuffs and a pair of safety glasses. "You ready to get started?"

"Ready as I'll ever be."

After going over the safety precautions and demonstrating how to insert the magazine, Chip stepped away from Leah to demonstrate how to shoot. He pointed the Glock at some metal pots hanging from wooden frames and began his instruction.

"Those are our targets. The closest ones are fifteen to twenty yards away and the farthest are around seventy-five. All right, put on your ear protection and safety glasses. I'm going to do a little shootin'."

Chip smiled at his student, who could feel a little blush coming on. He turned toward the targets, aimed the Glock with both hands, and fired off fifteen rounds in succession. Leah could see the pans swing as the bullets hit their mark. After he finished, Chip slid the earmuffs down until they rested around his neck, turned, and walked back toward Leah.

"Wow, that was impressive." Her ear protection still firmly in place, Leah was yelling.

Chip reached over and pulled the muffs off her ears. "You don't need to wear these when no one's shooting. You might hear a little better without them."

"Sorry about that." Leah laughed.

"So you ready to give it a try?"

"Absolutely."

Chip handed Leah the Glock and a fully loaded magazine. Without difficulty, she inserted the magazine into the slot in the gun handle and pulled the slide. The distinct sound of the first round entering the chamber broke the silence.

"Nicely done. You're a quick study."

"So how should I stand when I shoot?" Leah walked toward the spot where Chip had fired his rounds and then turned around.

"There is no right answer to that question. Everyone has their own style. I like to position my legs shoulder-width apart with my right one a little in front of my left."

Leah followed Chip's advice.

"Now, take the safety off, aim the gun with both hands, and let her rip. But first put your hearing protection back on."

"Got it." Leah fired fifteen rounds in succession. None of the targets moved. She stood there staring at the motionless pans and turned around to look at Chip. "What did I do wrong?"

Chip motioned for her to remove the ear guards.

"I liked your stance, but you didn't take time to aim through the sight, and you let the pistol move around too much. But I was damn impressed. Much better than most of the beginners I teach. Want to go again?"

Leah nodded. On her third mag, Leah hit some targets. After finishing the round, she walked hurriedly toward Chip. This time she pulled down the ear protection instinctively. "I hit one!"

"You hit several. Nice shooting."

Leah smiled and looked at her watch. "Sheesh, I've got to get back to work. I have a meeting at two. When can we do this again?"

"You're the client."

"I actually am enjoying this—go figure. How about tomorrow, same time?"

"I think I can make that work." Chip motioned toward the Kawasaki. "Shall we?"

As they rode back to the store, Leah could feel Chip's leg pushing gently against hers. She turned and smiled at her new instructor. She couldn't wait until her next lesson.

CHAPTER

23

"Christine?"

Christine looked at the caller id on her office phone – unknown number. "I'm sorry, who's this?"

"I thought you might have recognized my voice. It's Michael Randazzo."

"Yes, Mr. Randazzo, what can I do for you?"

"It's Mike. Remember, we're old friends."

No response.

"Well, I'm calling to give you a status report."

"I thought we weren't going to talk."

"Something has come up. I need your direction."

"And what might that be?"

"Our friend has hired a PI. She used to be with the Austin PD. Her name's McLaughlin, Jackie McLaughlin. According to my source, she was one of the best on the force. Got caught up in some internal politics and left."

"So why are you telling me all this?"

"McLaughlin did a sweep of that little bitch's condo. All of my devices have been removed, every damn one of them."

"I see. That's unfortunate."

"No shit. Bottom line, I don't know who our friend is talking to, or what about. And I'm not following her because I'm afraid her PI might be tailing me. Understand our problem here?"

"Yes, I do." Christine fidgeted with a paperweight of the scales of justice, a permanent fixture on her desk. "So what would you recommend? We certainly don't want that story to run."

"I get that. My last little trick might have scared her off. The only problem is, I don't know for sure. And I'd prefer not to follow up on that threat I made. I'm pretty sure if I did, it would scare her enough to drop the story. But it also might get the attention of the FBI, and that's the last thing we want."

"Right." Christine glanced at the ceiling in her office and hesitated briefly before continuing. "You said earlier that we don't know who she is talking to, is that correct?"

"We did but not anymore."

"Is there another way to get that info?"

"Like hacking into her cell?"

"You said it, I didn't."

Randazzo chuckled. "Call old Rupert Murdoch—he can tell you."

Christine's tone was firm. "This is no time for joking, Michael."

"Just trying to lighten the mood. My apologies."

"Can you make arrangements to, uh, listen in on her cell phone conversations, check her voice mails, that type of thing?"

"That's one of the services we offer."

"Well, we have no choice. Like I said, we can't take a chance on that article running."

"There's one more thing."

"And what's that?"

"Well, your initial retainer was generous—"

"But it's about gone."

"Correction—it is gone."

"How much more do you need?"

"Another twenty."

"This is getting expensive."

"You're asking me to take a lot of risk, and risk is expensive."

"Okay, okay. How do I get you the money?"

"I'm still in Austin."

"I'll meet you in the lobby of the Stephen F. Austin tomorrow afternoon at three."

"I'll be there." Pause. "Christine, always a pleasure to do business with you."

Christine grimaced as she hung up the phone. She looked at her watch—it was a little before five. She rose from her chair and walked slowly down the hallway, wondering what she should tell the Lone Wolf and, more importantly, what she shouldn't.

Cal leaned back in his chair as the door opened and his daughter walked in. A big smile creased his lips. "Well, what a perfect way to end the day. How's my little girl doing?"

Christine grimaced. She hated it when he called her that but had quit telling him so. Her complaints hadn't done any good up to this point, so why bother? "I've had better days."

"Anything I can help you with? Those chicken-shit defense lawyers making life difficult for you?"

"Dad, it's not that." Christine slumped down in the chair in front of her dad's desk. "Haven't you had days when you just wanted to chuck it all—do something else other than practice law? This rat race of a life we have chosen gets old after a while."

139

Cal got up, walked around the desk, and took the seat next to his daughter's. Before responding, he draped his arm over the back of her chair. "Hell, I've felt the way you're feeling more times than I can count. Matter of fact, I felt that way after the Stone trial. Just wanted to hang it up for good. But you and I both know we couldn't get along without it. We'd miss the game too much. The losses are hard to take, but the wins—well, you can't beat that feeling."

Christine turned toward her dad and smiled. "I guess you're right. Thanks for the pep talk."

"Let's focus on something positive. You closed on that deal with Stein yet?"

"Money's in the bank—every penny of it."

"How about the settlement docs? I never asked you—how was Stein able to get his defense lawyers to sign off on this deal? I bet they were madder'n hell when he went around them."

"He wasn't worried about those stuffed shirts doing anything. Told me he threatened to have their legal bills audited if they didn't behave. That did the trick."

Cal smiled. "So all of the cases have been dismissed?"

"The dismissal orders have been signed by me and defense counsel. We are just waiting on the judge."

"And you don't anticipate a problem there, do you?"

"No. My guess is we'll have them this time next week."

"Good, good. And tell me the logistics of how our friend in Hartford is going to be compensated for his hard work?" Cal chuckled.

"No need to get into the details—the less you know, the better. Suffice it to say, Mr. Stein is one happy man."

Cal nodded. "You're probably right—no need to confuse me with minutiae." He hesitated. "So any news on that reporter gal down in Austin?"

"Again, Dad, the less you know, the better. Like I told you before, I've got all of our bases covered."

"You'd tell me if anything changed?"

"Have I ever let you down?"

"Never."

"So why would I start now?"

Christine shot her dad a devilish look as she stood and exited his office.

CHAPTER

24

Eugene walked into his study, sat down at his desk, and, at the top of a blank legal-size piece of paper, wrote "The Last Will and Testament of Eugene Hanson." He glanced at the instructions on how to make a holographic will, which he had printed off the Internet. He had committed the instructions to memory but wanted to have them next to him—just in case.

It was two o'clock in the afternoon, and he uncharacteristically hadn't consumed a drop of alcohol. He needed to be of sound mind. For the first time since losing his daughter and then his wife, he felt a sense of control, a strange yet comforting peace that things were about to change for the better, that good would ultimately triumph over evil. He put his pen down and walked over to the stereo system in the cabinet under the bookcase. His fingers instinctively found one of his favorite CDs, *Peer Gynt,* by Edvard Grieg. He smiled peacefully as he pushed the CD into the player and turned on the receiver. The melodic "Morning Mood" broke the silence. He hummed along as he triumphantly walked back to his desk and took his seat like a concert pianist at a sold-out venue. He continued writing.

"*I, Eugene Hanson, of sound mind and body hereby, in my own handwriting, make my last will and testament. I am making this will of my own volition and am not being coerced or influenced by any other person. I hereby appoint my personal attorney, Jace Forman, to be executor of my will to serve without bond. My executor is directed to pay all of my debts and taxes before he makes any other distributions. He may dispose of any of my property, real or personal, to do so.*"

Eugene reread the words—so far, so good. He took a sip of black coffee and continued.

"*After paying all of my taxes and debts, my executor is directed to establish the Lauren M. Hanson Trust (the "Trust"). All of the assets I have, including my $1,000,000 life insurance policy with the Travelers Insurance Company, the net proceeds from the sale of my house and the contents thereof, my 2007 Ford Taurus, my wedding ring and watch, and all other personal property or realty I may own at the time of my death, shall, after payment of all lawful commissions and expenses incurred in selling these assets, be transferred to the Trust. Additionally, any damages of whatever nature that may be awarded in the case I have filed against the Brimstone Bible Church and Ezekiel Shaw, less attorney fees and expenses, shall be transferred into the Trust. Jace Forman is appointed trustee of the Trust and shall have full discretion to invest and distribute the proceeds consistent with my intent that the income from the Trust be distributed on an annual basis in pro rata*" *fashion to the families of those who have lost loved ones in the armed services of the United States of America and who have suffered the mental pain and anguish of having the Brimstone Bible Church protest their loved ones' funerals."*

Eugene carefully proofed the last paragraph and smiled in satisfaction. He completed the document by writing,

"This is my last will and testament, which I have written entirely in my own hand as evidenced by my signature below and the date inscribed next to it."

He executed the document with his distinctive signature and inked in the date. He sighed in relief. But his job was not over.

He drank the last of the coffee, rose from his chair, and opened the closet door. He removed a box containing a brand-new, top-of-the-line Samsung video recorder and, with a letter opener retrieved from the desk drawer, began to open the box and remove the contents. He carefully assembled the camera and mounted it on the tripod. He directed the lens toward the swivel chair positioned behind his desk and peered through it, making some minor adjustments. He punched the record button and walked back to his desk.

After taking his seat, he faced the camera and cleared his throat. He picked up the will he had just written and, in a strong voice, stated, "I am making this video recording of my last will and testament, which I shall read verbatim." He then calmly and deliberately read each and every word. Upon finishing, he turned off the recorder, poured himself a full glass of Jack, downed the contents, and then poured another. As Grieg's "Hall of the Mountain King" played in the background at a frenetic pace, Eugene used his pen as a conductor's wand. His movements were wildly exaggerated, yet his tempo was perfect.

CHAPTER

25

"Leah, there is a Ms. McLaughlin here to see you. She said you would know what it was about."

"I'll be right out to get her." Leah rose from her chair and scurried down the hall to the reception area.

Jackie was seated on a corner sofa talking on her cell. Upon seeing Leah, she smiled and held up one finger. "Okay, gotta go. I'll call you later this afternoon." She stuffed the iPhone into her purse and stood. "Leah, I was in the area and decided to drop by."

"I'm glad you did. Come on back." Leah led the way to her office. "Can I get you any coffee?"

"No, thanks. I'm coffee'd out."

"I hear you. I drink too much of it myself." Leah motioned to the chair across from her desk. "Have a seat."

"So how are you?"

"Great. I wondered how it would be, sleeping in my apartment again. I'm not going to lie. It was pretty nerve-racking the first night or two, but once I got through those, no problem."

"That's good to hear. Any more incidents?"

"Nope. Not unless you know something I don't."

"Well, that's one of the reasons I wanted to meet with you."

Leah's face paled. "You've got to be—"

Jackie cut her off. "No, it's nothing for you to be concerned about. In fact, this could be good news. We may be getting closer to catching that son of a bitch."

Leah's eyes widened as she leaned forward on her desk. "That's not just good news—that's great news. Fill me in on the details."

"Well, you remember I told you I had this tech guru who might be able to trace the email you received back to its source?"

"Vaguely. I was such a mess back then."

"Well, he was able to determine the sender's IP address."

"I'm somewhat tech savvy, but I'm not sure what you're telling me."

"He was able to determine that the email was sent from a computer in the Newport Beach area of California."

"That doesn't narrow it down much."

"That's where I picked up the trail. I made the assumption that whoever wants you off the story would hire a PI firm to follow you, learn your habits, and then do what it takes to scare you enough to drop the story. I have access to a database that lists all the private investigators across the country. I limited my search to the Newport Beach area, and a number of names came up."

"And?"

"I made a guess—and that's all it is at this point—that, if Connors were behind this, he would hire the best in the business. And there is one guy who fits that description."

"What's his name?"

"Michael Randazzo. He's pretty high profile. Gets the dirt on celebrities for other celebrities when they have business disputes, custody battles, you name it." Jackie paused dramatically before continuing. "And get this. An L.A. reporter has filed a lawsuit alleging that he tried to scare her off a story."

"That is awesome, Jackie. Can you have him arrested?"

"Unfortunately, at this point we don't have any hard evidence that he did anything to you. Plus, I have no idea where he is."

"Do you think he could be in Austin?"

"That's definitely a possibility. I don't mean to alarm you, but have you been to see Chip?"

Leah leaned over, pulled a Glock 19 from her purse, and held it up for Jackie to see. "I've had two lessons. I'm a pretty good shot—at least that's what Chip says. I really like him, by the way."

"I knew you would."

"So what do you suggest I do now that we suspect Randazzo might be camping out in Austin?"

"Do what you've been doing. Never go out without the Glock in your purse and be aware of your surroundings."

Leah nodded.

"You have my cell number. Don't hesitate to call it if you feel unsafe or notice something suspicious."

"Don't worry. But before you go, I have one last question. And, please, don't take it the wrong way. How much is all of this costing? You are doing so much, and I don't have a lot of money."

"When I got permission from Abe to have my guy examine your computer, he told me *Texas Matters* would be responsible for my fee and asked me to send my bills to his attention."

Leah smiled. "Which probably means he is going to pay the bills personally."

"I can't answer that, but I will say you are very lucky to have such a great boss."

"You're right about that. And thanks so much for dropping by today. It makes me feel a little better to know you are all over this."

"My pleasure."

"Can I walk you to the elevators?

"No need. I can find my way. Be safe." Jackie rose from her chair and disappeared out the door.

CHAPTER

26

"Mr. Prater, it's good to see you again. Brothers and Sisters, as you may recall, Mr. Prater is defending us in that blasphemous lawsuit." Ezekiel Shaw spoke from the head of a rough-hewn rectangular table, his tone formal. On one side of the table were four men and on the other four women. They nodded but said nothing. "Mr. Prater, please tell us how we can help."

"If possible, I'd like to speak with each person separately about their individual recollections of the Hanson protest. In my many years of experience with trial work, that approach has proven much more effective in getting an accurate portrayal of what actually happened that led up to the lawsuit."

Ezekiel Shaw chuckled. "That may be your experience with nonbelievers, but we are God's people. We speak with one voice. We have no secrets from one another. Your secular rules ceased to apply once you entered the gates to our spiritual home."

"But—"

Shaw interrupted. "I'm sorry, Mr. Prater, but the issue is decided. Please ask your questions. My people have chores to tend to."

Flustered, Crom fished around in his briefcase and pulled out a legal pad and pen. Seated at the opposite end of the table from Ezekiel, he turned his gaze toward the gray-haired woman on his left and asked, "Could you please tell me your name?" He followed his question with a polite smile.

The response came from Shaw. "Her name is Sister Rebekah." The woman nodded in agreement.

Realizing the hopelessness of his cause, Crom capitulated. "I assume then that I should direct all my questions to you?"

"Your assumption is correct. The meeting will go much more quickly that way."

"So be it. Do any of your followers have any documents, and by that term I mean emails, notes, sketches, scribblings, letters— anything of a written nature—that might relate to the protest held at Lauren Hanson's funeral?"

"They do not." All assembled nodded in agreement.

"And just let me make sure, were all of you present at that protest?"

"They were." Again, more nods.

"And are all the people who attended that protest on behalf of the BBC here today?"

"I don't understand your question, Mr. Prater."

"I'm sorry, Ezekiel, but—"

"Savior Shaw."

Crom's face reddened. "I stand corrected, Savior Shaw. I merely want to make sure that all of the people from the BBC who attended the protest are here in this room today."

"I would prefer that you use the full name of our congregation and not an acronym. I don't want us to be confused with that ungodly news-reporting agency." Shaw paused. "And the answer to your question is yes."

"Understood," Crom said. "I have one last question. Do any of you remember hearing anyone in your membership say anything personally insulting to the Hanson family?"

"They do not. Isn't that right, Brothers and Sisters?"

A chorus of "amens" followed.

Crom stuffed his pad and pen into his briefcase and stood. "Thank you all for your time. I hate to say it, but each of you may have to testify in this case as to your individual recollection of the facts surrounding the protest. That's something I can't prevent, nor could any lawyer, no matter how skilled."

"But that's not going to be necessary since Judge Zimmerman is going to grant your motion for summary judgment before we get into all of that. Isn't that what you told me, Mr. Prater?"

"I said we had a good chance of winning, but there are no guarantees in my business."

"Very well then." Shaw stood. "Thank you for making the trip. And thank you for your efforts on behalf of my people. Brother Isaiah will show you out."

Brother Isaiah stood and led the way to the door. A deeply frustrated and confused Crom followed.

"You are all excused except Sister Rebekah."

After the other members left, Shaw turned to Sister Rebekah. "I didn't lie when I told our attorney every member of our church that attended the protest was present in the room. But we all know that someone else attended that protest that was not in the room—that sinning, trouble-making daughter of yours."

Rebekah looked down at her folded hands and nodded sheepishly.

"Where is she? Where is your daughter Maddy? She is no longer worthy of the spiritual name 'Sister Mary.' She has chosen the world of non-believers over God's kingdom here on earth. She will face eternal damnation, you know that, don't you?"

Tears began to form in Sister Rebekah's eyes as she replied, "I know, Savior Shaw. I know."

"I sensed when we were at that little motel just before the protest that she was not worthy. I knew when she couldn't answer any of my questions."

Sister Rebekah nodded her head. "I am so ashamed. But I don't know where Sister Mary—Maddy—is. I had no idea she was even thinking about leaving, and I haven't spoken to her since she left. You know our rules—we are forbidden to speak with anyone who has deserted us."

"Deserted God, you mean. And you were right not to contact her." Ezekiel stroked his chin. "But there are exceptions to all rules. She could endanger the future of our people, and our way of life. You must find her. Surely, as the one who raised her, you would have the best instincts as to where she might have gone."

"I will try my best. May I have permission to leave the commune?"

"You may, but keep me informed of your whereabouts at all times. I will provide you with a car and a cell phone."

"Thank you, Savior Shaw."

"You're dismissed."

CHAPTER
27

"So how did your prep session with Eugene go?" Darrin looked across her desk at a visibly distraught Jace. The dark circles under his eyes told a troubling tale of heavy stress and little sleep.

"Not good. I'm really worried about how he's going to hold up tomorrow at his deposition."

"No surprise there. What happened?"

"You really want to know all the details?"

"Maybe I can help."

Jace seemed to relax a bit. He sat back in the chair and took a deep breath. "Well, things started off okay. He hadn't been drinking, which was a definite plus. He looked all right—clean-shaven, dressed in a white shirt and khakis."

"That's a big improvement from what I encountered."

"We covered all the things you and I discussed with him and his wife in our first meeting. His memory hadn't faded. He stuck to his story pretty damn well."

"That's good."

Jace sighed. "And then the shit hit the proverbial fan. I told him Prater would likely question him about his wife's psychiatric problems."

"That's a given, isn't it? Prater wouldn't be doing his job if he didn't."

"That's what I told Eugene, but it didn't sit well with him. He started pacing around the conference room, muttering that this lawsuit was a waste of time, that he should have already taken care of things. The same kinds of things he said to you."

"Were you able to calm him down?" Darrin asked.

"Well, I did it by lying. I told him that Judge Zimmerman probably wouldn't admit any evidence of his wife's psychiatric diagnoses at trial."

Darrin smiled. "That's a lie, but one that needed telling. And it worked?"

"Well, he let me continue with the prep session."

"Did you show him the medical records Prater will probably use at the deposition? The ones showing Janice's multiple admissions to Timberlake for clinical depression?"

"No. I sensed that would set him off."

"But you know Prater's going to use them."

"No doubt about it. That's one of the issues I'm really concerned about. Then I had to bring up Lauren's lack of boyfriends and what Prater might infer from that."

"Ouch. Glad I wasn't in the room when you broached that topic. What did he do?"

"For a moment I thought he might hit me."

"So were you able to work your magic a second time?"

"I guess you could say that. I told him I saw this type of crap in every case I handled, shysters—that's what I called Prater—trying every trick in the book to rattle the other side."

"And he bought it?"

"Well, he quit yelling at me and promised not to hit me." Jace grinned at his contrived attempt at humor.

"Any chance he won't show tomorrow?"

"There's always a chance, but I think the odds are against it."

"Why do you say that?"

"I told him that if he failed to show, Judge Zimmerman would throw his case out."

"And she might."

"But probably wouldn't—she'd likely just enter an order compelling Eugene's appearance. Nevertheless, I wanted to scare the hell out of him so he wouldn't even think about not showing."

"Nice. So do you need anything else from me before the deposition?"

"Just make sure Harriett gets the conference room set up by nine."

"Don't worry. I'll take care of it myself."

"Well, I guess I'll head home and stare at the ceiling for the rest of the night."

"Is there anything else bothering you?"

Jace hesitated and then muttered, "I don't want to get into it."

"It's Matt, isn't it? I can always tell. What happened?"

"I talked with him last night from the SEAL training camp, prep school, whatever you call it. Our conversation was a train wreck."

"How so?"

"I asked him again why in the world he had made such a rash decision to quit UT and enlist in the SEAL training program."

"And?"

"Truth came out. He yelled at me. Called me a cheater and a liar. Accused me of causing his mother's death. Said he would never forgive me for that. Said he just wanted to get away."

"Oh, Jace. I'm so sorry. Do you have any idea what brought this on?"

"Obviously he feels strongly about it."

"But the two of you were on pretty good terms a month or so ago, weren't you?"

"It was getting better. But I ran into Matt and a friend of his after I had dinner with Jackie in Austin."

"You had dinner with Jackie?"

Jace realized his blunder and started backpedaling. "You knew I had to meet with her on the Hanson case. I had to go over what I wanted her to do—"

"And that could have been handled over the phone, Jace."

"I do better in—"

"I'm not buying it. You wanted to see her, plain and simple."

"It was totally innocent. It was just a business dinner—that's it. I flew home right after."

Darrin shook her head. There was no use arguing with a man who wins arguments for a living. "Look, I'm sorry about what's going on between you and Matt. I know you're deeply hurt and going through a lot. Plus, you've got an unstable client on your hands and a tough case to try. But that doesn't excuse you for sneaking down to Austin for a dinner with Jackie."

"That's not what happened."

"I'm not going to desert you at a time like this, but if you continue whatever thing you've got going with Jackie, I'm out of here—no advance notice, no nothing."

"Darrin, I really don't need this right now. You are being totally unreasonable. Jackie is a hired investigator. We have a working relationship, and that's the extent of it. She is in the middle of an ongoing investigation in this case, and you know as well as I do that I'll need to talk with her from time to time."

"I understand that part, Jace. But it's got to be all business with her. I'm not going to be part of some love triangle. And as far as her findings are concerned, that's what phones are for—no candlelit dinner meetings." Darrin grabbed her purse and rose from her chair. "I'm exhausted—physically, mentally, and emotionally. I'm going home. I'll see you in the morning."

Darrin walked out of her office. As she hurried down the hall, she wondered if she had made the right decision. Maybe she should have quit right then and there. Jace needed a wakeup call. That was painfully apparent. Hopefully she had gotten his attention. She stopped in front of the elevator and wiped a tear from her cheek before punching the down arrow.

CHAPTER

28

"Mr. Hanson, you are aware that you are suing my clients, alleging they caused your wife to take her own life. That's a true statement, is it not?" Crom leaned forward on the conference table, his eyes boring into those of his prey.

Eugene continued to stare at his interrogator without responding.

"Was there something confusing about my question? Would you like for me to repeat it?"

"Yeah, I would like you to repeat it."

Jace cringed at the tone of his client's voice and hoped a total meltdown wasn't just around the corner.

"I'm going to ask the court reporter to please read back my last question."

The court reporter complied.

Without hesitation, Eugene responded, "Yes, Mr. Prater, it is."

"At the time of her death, how long had you and Mrs. Hanson been married?"

"We were coming up on our fortieth wedding anniversary."

"And I assume that you and Mrs. Hanson were very open with one another, that you didn't keep secrets?" Crom smiled insincerely after finishing the question.

"That's a fair assumption."

Jace fidgeted in his chair, sensing a setup.

"Before the incident that is the subject matter of this lawsuit, did your wife ever tell you she was unhappy?"

"Aren't we all from time to time?"

"So the answer to my question would be yes?"

"I suppose so."

"Did she ever tell you she was so unhappy that she felt she needed medical treatment?"

Eugene nodded.

"You'll need to answer out loud. The court reporter can't record gestures."

"Yes."

Crom pulled out two copies of a document from a manila file folder on the table to his right. He handed one to the court reporter and one to Jace. "Please mark this as an exhibit."

The court reporter applied a sticker to the exhibit and handed it back to Crom. Jace tried to maintain a poker face as he scanned the document.

"Mr. Hanson, I am going to hand you what the court reporter has marked as Exhibit 4 to your deposition and ask you if you can identify that document."

Eugene took the document from his interrogator and briefly reviewed it. "No, I cannot."

"Does it appear to be a medical record of the Timberlake Psychiatric Hospital?"

"That's what it appears to be, but I've never worked there, so I couldn't say for sure."

Faking sympathy, Crom continued. "I understand. Let me put it another way. Do you remember taking your wife to that facility in November 2011?"

"I can't be sure about the date."

"But you do remember taking her there somewhere around that time?"

Eugene nodded.

"I hate to do this again, but I'll have to ask you to speak out loud so the court reporter can take down your response.

"Yes."

"And this wasn't her first stay at that facility, now was it, Mr. Hanson?"

"No, it wasn't." To Jace's surprise, Eugene's demeanor was remarkably calm and composed. It was as if he knew exactly what he was doing when he nodded instead of directly answering Crom's questions, just to get under his skin. Maybe Jace had prepped the witness better than he thought.

"Now, I would like you to read into the record the sentences I have taken the liberty of highlighting on page two of the exhibit."

Eugene turned back to page two and read the highlighted portion to himself. "Your question again, Counselor?"

"Please read the highlighted portion into the record."

"The document says what it says. You can read, can't you?"

"But I would like for you to read it into the record."

"I would prefer not to." Eugene started to rise from his seat. Jace stretched his arm across his client's chest, creating a barrier between him and opposing counsel.

"I agree with my client. He doesn't need to read any portion of that document into the record. It says what it says. You are harassing Mr. Hanson."

Eugene leaned back in his chair, comforted by his lawyer's support.

"Should we call Judge Zimmerman?" Crom asked.

"Be my guest. The phone is on the credenza. I doubt the judge will be very happy to be interrupted about such a petty matter."

Crom glared at Jace and said, "I'll read it into the record then." Eugene handed it back to him. "It says, 'Ms. Hanson reports frequent thoughts of suicide.' Did I read that correctly?"

Eugene answered, "You did."

"So it's true, is it not, that your wife had thought about taking her own life years before the incident in question?"

"That's true. But it's also true that she never did—not until your clients pushed her over the edge."

Jace fought to conceal his smile. Crom's face reddened.

"This is a good place to take a short break. I'm moving to another topic."

"Fine with us. How long?"

"Fifteen minutes."

"We'll be back at eleven-fifteen. Eugene, let's give Mr. Prater some privacy." Jace rose and walked out the conference room door, his client close behind.

Eugene followed Jace into his office and closed the door behind them.

"Eugene, you were incredible in there. Incredible."

Eugene grinned at the compliment. "It wasn't easy. There were times I wanted to beat the crap out of that pompous little shit."

"I know, I know. So did I. But I'm so glad you didn't."

"How much longer do you think this will go?"

"I don't know." Jace looked at his watch. "Probably another couple of hours or so. You need anything to drink?"

"No, but I'll need to take a pit stop on the way back to the conference room. That coffee's doing a number on me."

"You and me both."

"So what's the bastard going to cover next?"

"My guess would be your recollection of the protest or how you came up with the amount of damages you want the jury to award."

Eugene nodded.

"And he'll likely try to get you to admit your daughter was—"

Eugene cut Jace off. "Why don't you object or something? What in the hell has that got to do with anything?"

"Unfortunately, it's fair game. We are going to say that the protest sign calling your daughter a lesbian was libelous. Truth would be a defense to that claim."

"You're not—"

"No, no. I don't believe it for a minute, but I can't object to Prater's trying to prove it. Just don't let it get to you."

"I'll try not to, but I can't make any promises. Think about what you would do under similar circumstances."

"Understood. We need to get back in there. The sooner we get this over with, the better."

"Mr. Hanson, we are back on the record. You understand you're still under oath?"

"I do."

"I want to ask you some questions about your daughter's social life. Let's start with high school. Did Lauren have any boyfriends?"

Eugene stared at Crom for an uncomfortably long period of time before responding, "I'm sure there were some, but I can't give you any names. It's been a long time, a lot of water's gone under the bridge."

"Can you describe any of her boyfriends? I'm sure they came to pick her up at your house before going on dates."

"Is that a question?"

"It was. Can you describe any of her boyfriends back in high school?"

"Like I said, that was a long time ago."

"I take that as a no."

"You can take it any way you want."

"Okay, Mr. Hanson, let's turn our attention to your daughter's West Point days. Did she ever mention any boyfriends to you?"

"I seem to recall her saying she was seeing someone."

"Did she ever say who that someone was?"

"Not that I recall."

"Did she ever bring anyone home with her for you and Ms. Hanson to meet?"

"She was busy—academics, athletics. She was involved in everything. She didn't have a lot of spare time on her hands."

"Let me summarize your testimony, if I might. You cannot testify as to the name of any boy your daughter ever dated, isn't that true?"

"I just can't remember their names. That doesn't mean she didn't have any."

"But you can't give me one name, can you?"

"What's this got to do with the fact that your clients dragged Lauren, her mother, and me through the mud? My daughter was a courageous young lady who was defending the freedoms you, and your clients, currently enjoy—something I bet you never did, did you?"

"I'm asking the questions here."

"Not anymore. I'm done with this."

"I have more questions."

"Not for me you don't. This deposition is over." Eugene rose from his seat and marched out the door, Jace in quick pursuit.

"Eugene, you can't—"

"I just did."

"Can I speak with you briefly in my office?"

Eugene did an about-face and stopped Jace in his tracks. "Look, if you're worried about me doing something stupid, you can rest easy. I just couldn't continue sitting there while that little chickenshit took pot shots at my daughter. Look, Jace, I don't know if Lauren liked guys, girls or both. The truth of the matter is her mother and I would have loved her regardless. And what that asshole is trying to do in there is disgusting and I'm not going along with it, end of story. My bet is if he takes this up with the judge, she will see it my way. I know she will if she has children—no doubt about that." "I don't know what Judge Zimmerman will do."

"Well, I'm going home. Give my regards to Ms. McKenzie." Eugene turned around and walked determinedly toward the elevator.

Darrin stuck her head into Jace's office. "You aren't finished yet, are you? I thought the deposition would go at least another hour or so."

"Come on in and I'll bring you up to speed."

Darrin stepped into the office and closed the door behind her. She slid into the seat across from Jace's desk.

"Our client just ended the deposition." Jace smiled and shook his head. "Pretty ballsy move."

"I don't get it."

"He was doing great. He got through all the difficult questions about his wife's psychiatric problems like a champ. Nothing rattled him."

"I wouldn't have predicted that in a lifetime."

"I wouldn't have either. I think it threw Prater for a loop. It was a beautiful thing to behold." Jace paused, and then continued. "Then Prater started asking about Lauren's social life, implying she was a lesbian. That's when the wheels came off."

"So did Eugene go nuts?"

"Not really. He calmly said something to the effect of 'this deposition is over.' It was actually kind of fun watching Prater's reaction. He didn't know whether to brush his teeth or wind his watch. He started sputtering about how he had more questions. Eugene just ignored him and walked out the door."

"You gotta love him for it."

"I don't think I would have had the guts to do something like that."

"Are you worried about him, Jace? Do you think—"

"He'll do something crazy? No, I don't. I talked with him on his way to the elevator and he assured me he was fine, just tired of sitting there while Prater took shots at his daughter."

"What do you think Prater will do?"

"File a motion with the court for sanctions, try to get Judge Zimmerman to dismiss our case."

"You don't think there's any chance of that happening, do you?"

"Not really. The judge might order Eugene to finish the deposition, but I think that's the worst that could happen. And considering the kinds of questions Prater was asking, she might not even do that."

"By the way, we got some good news in the mail this morning. It's there on your desk."

Jace began to shuffle through the pile in front of him. "What is it?"

"Keep going. I don't want to spoil the surprise."

Jace pulled a two-page document from the file and began to eagerly scan its contents. As he neared the end, his eyes brightened and a big smile creased his lips. He then kissed the document before uttering, "Thank you, Judge Zimmerman. She denied Prater's motion for summary judgment. I would love to see Prater's face when he reads this."

"It's not all good news, Jace. Check the footnote at the bottom of the last page of the judge's opinion."

Jace's gaze returned to the document. "Hmm. Looks like the court wants more evidence than just testimony from Eugene. Otherwise, she's going to throw out the case."

"Jace, I've scoured YouTube for videos of the protest and only came up with one. The quality was so poor you couldn't really hear what the protesters were saying or make out what was written on the signs."

"Keep looking. I know you'll find something. Let's just savor this victory for the moment."

Darrin walked toward the door and lingered before opening it. "And about last night—"

"I had it coming. Poor judgment on my part. Won't happen again."

"I was a little too hard on you. I believe you about the dinner being just business. I can't help it, Jace - I'm the jealous type. But don't let anything I said keep you from doing what you need to do to win this case. If you need to meet with her, go ahead. Just keep—"

"I get the picture." Jace grinned. "I wish we weren't in the office right now. I would—"

"There will be plenty of time for that once we win this case." Darrin smiled as she backed out of the office and quietly shut the door.

Eugene pulled into the garage of his home. He opened the door adjoining the kitchen, stepped inside, and hurried into his bedroom. He pulled out an overnight bag from the top of his closet and threw it on his bed. After hastily packing, he zipped up the bag and carried it down the hall to the study.

His expression grim, he opened the closet door and removed the AK-47 he had purchased several days before. He gently leaned the rifle against his desk and returned to the closet to retrieve two extra magazines. He threw the magazines into a backpack, hoisted it over his shoulder, grabbed the rifle and the overnight bag, and headed toward the kitchen.

He hurried out the door to the garage, popped open the trunk of his car, and threw in the gun and his bags. After sliding behind the steering wheel, he closed his eyes and breathed a sigh of relief. He would finally get the chance he had been waiting for. The BBC had posted on their website that Shaw and his followers would be staging a protest at the funeral of Private First Class Andrea Dalton in Norman, Oklahoma the following morning. And Eugene would be there to make sure it was their last.

He stared at the dashboard and took a deep breath before turning the ignition key and backing out of the garage. He would stop by the post office on the way to I-35 to mail his last will and testament, and a DVD of himself reading its contents, to his lawyer and soon-to-be executor of his estate. He had patiently waited for this moment. The time to savor the sweet taste of revenge had finally arrived.

PART THREE

CHAPTER

29

The crowd had turned unruly. Shaw and his followers were surrounded by several hundred people. Some were waving American flags and gesturing wildly at the besieged group, some were singing the national anthem loudly and off-key, and some were hoisting patriotic placards into the air with a vengeance that bordered on hysteria. The crowd spewed insults at Shaw and his disciples in rapid-fire succession—"You go straight to hell!" "Jesus preached love, not hate!" "Death is too good for you!" "Your mothers must have slept with the devil!"

As the pandemonium continued to build, the local police, who had positioned themselves in a circle around the perimeter of the First Samaritan Christian Church, looked around in all directions, scanning the area for any sign of trouble.

Shaw's eyes darted back and forth in search of an escape hatch. Finding none, he motioned for his disciples to put down their signs and gather around him. All immediately complied. He began to calmly repeat in mantra-like fashion, "Forgive them, Father, for they know not what they do." The others joined in.

Several blocks away, Eugene stopped his Ford Taurus at the entrance to a three-story public parking garage. He lowered his window and pressed the entry button, took a ticket from the dispenser, and began to drive through the gate as the automatic arm slowly ascended. There were plenty of vacant spaces on the first, second, and third levels, but he continued up the ramp to the roof. As the ramp opened to daylight, he conducted a quick recon and smiled. The roof was completely deserted, just as he had expected.

Eugene parked the car, got out, and walked hurriedly to the trunk. He popped it open, took out the AK-47, and slung the backpack containing the extra magazines over his shoulder. He made his way to the northwest corner of the parking garage roof, crouching down just before he reached the four-foot wall that ran along the roof's perimeter. He slowly raised his head and peered over the wall at the scene unfolding just blocks away. Eugene shook his head and sneered as his eyes settled on a tall bearded man dressed in a long white robe. Eugene muttered, "I've got you now, you no-good son of a bitch."

Without looking away, he reached down for the AK-47, brought it slowly to his right shoulder, and rested the barrel on the concrete barrier in front. He gazed through the sight, moving the barrel slowly until Shaw came into view. Eugene took a deep breath, which would be his last. Before he could squeeze the trigger a shot rang out from below. Eugene Hanson, forlorn father and would-be assassin, collapsed on the pavement in a pool of blood.

"Bruce, I am standing across the street from a public parking garage just blocks away from the First Samaritan

Christian Church here in Norman, where the Brimstone Bible Church was holding a protest today. As you can see, there are police cars behind me. Details are sketchy at this point, but what we do know is that someone on the roof of this parking garage was shot minutes ago by one of the police officers assigned to maintain order at the protest."

"What can you tell us about his condition?"

"I have been told by one of the officers that the individual suffered a head wound and died instantly."

"What do we know about the deceased at this time?"

"He was a white male, heavily armed and driving a Ford Taurus with Texas plates. There is speculation – and that's all it is at this point - that he came to the protest with the intent to kill some, or all of the protesters."

"And what about the group that staged this demonstration?" The anchor glanced down at a notepad in front of him. "The Brimstone Bible Church—were any of its members injured?"

"No. Immediately after the incident, all of the protesters, including their leader Ezekiel Shaw, were whisked away from the scene by local police. I am told they are currently under heavy guard at an undisclosed location."

"Haylie, thanks for your excellent reporting." The anchor turned back to the camera. "If you are joining us late, there has been a shooting at the protest staged by the Brimstone Bible Church at the funeral of Private First Class Andrea Dalton. The victim's identity has not been disclosed pending notification of relatives. We do know that none of the members of the Brimstone Bible Church were injured in the incident. As more details become available, they will be accessible on our website, www.sinnews. com."

Darrin stopped the video, closed her laptop, and collapsed into the chair across from Jace's desk. "This is so sad. That poor man!"

"You were right. I should have done something, Darrin. If I had, Eugene might be alive today." Jace looked up at the ceiling and ran his hands through his hair.

"You can't beat yourself up over this, Jace. There was nothing you, or anyone for that matter, could have done to prevent this tragedy. Our client was a man on a mission."

Jace sighed. "Well, maybe so. There's nothing I can do now, anyway. Hey, when you were working on the discovery responses with him, did you find out if Eugene had any relatives—any siblings, uncles, cousins?"

Darrin shook her head. "He didn't mention anyone."

"Well, the news will be all over the paper tomorrow. Let's see what happens. In the meantime, I'll make a call to the Norman Police Department. From the description that reporter gave there's no question it was Eugene, but I'll see if I can get some of the details. Also, someone needs to make funeral arrangements if Eugene didn't have any relatives."

Darrin rose from her chair, walked over to Jace, leaned down, and put her arms around his neck. "You okay?"

Jace looked up into her eyes and forced a smile. "I will be. It may take a little time."

"I'll be right down the hall if you need me."

"That's good to know."

Darrin walked slowly toward the door, pausing at the threshold. "And Jace, we'll get through this. I promise."

CHAPTER

30

Jamie Stein eased his fire engine–red Ferrari 458 Italia convertible into the storage facility he had rented in Bloomfield, Connecticut. He turned off the ignition and smiled as he breathed deeply, taking in the intoxicating aroma of its black leather interior. He pressed the clutch gently to the floor, shifting from first to neutral and then back again before opening the door and walking around his recent acquisition, his eyes admiring its sleek lines. This wasn't just a car—it was a piece of art worth every penny of the $245,000 price tag. And it was Jamie's ticket out of obscurity—his escape, albeit temporary, from a life of boredom and monotony to one of excitement and glamour, a life he had always coveted but found out of reach.

He walked out of the garage, pulled down the door, and turned the lock with the shiny brass key the attendant had given him several days before when he rented the space. He walked briskly to the Honda Civic in the storage facility's parking lot, looking around to make sure he wasn't being watched. Relieved, he opened the Civic's door, slid behind the steering wheel, and turned the ignition key. Thirty minutes later he was in his modest one-bedroom apartment in downtown Hartford. He poured himself a glass of Jameson Irish Whiskey and settled into a chair facing an old flat-screen TV sitting on top of a chest against the wall. He took a sip of the whiskey and licked a lingering drop from his upper lip. He looked around the apartment—what a shithole! He had to get out of this place. And he would. It was just a matter of time. Lady Luck had begun to smile on him.

So far, Christine had made good on her end of the bargain. The payments had been wired to the accounts he had designated. He had decided to use half of the money to finance a lifestyle he had never been able to afford: expensive wines, high-end restaurants, gorgeous women, and a badass car. He smiled at the mental image of his new Ferrari. The wine and women were just around the corner. He would continue to work at Empire Risk, at least temporarily; any sudden change would no doubt draw suspicion. On the weekends he would morph into a different person, the person he had always dreamed of being. He would trade his Honda Civic for the Ferrari; jump on I-95 to Manhattan; stay at the Plaza, the Palace, or one of the many high-end hotels the city had to offer; dine at her finest restaurants; and, with a little luck, pick up some young out-of-towner looking for a good time away from home. If he struck out, he had the number of the best escort service in town. It wasn't beneath him to pay for an evening of sexual fantasy with a gorgeous professional who knew the right buttons to push. After all, Eliot Spitzer had done it. So why not Jamie Stein?

The remainder of the monthly payments would be transferred to an untraceable offshore bank account known only to him. Heaven forbid, but he just might need a rainy day fund in the event that his plan to live the high life hit a snag. Jamie was a resourceful man. He always had a plan B - always.

CHAPTER

31

"Thanks for meeting me on such short notice." Jackie took a sip of her Shiner Bock as she exchanged smiles with Leah.

"I was packing up my briefcase to leave work for the day when you called. It's good to see you, Jackie." Leah tasted her vodka tonic and nodded approvingly.

"Things going okay?" Jackie asked.

"Yeah, but I get a little scared whenever I get ready for bed. It creeps me out to be in that bathroom, especially late at night. I guess I'm kind of a wimp."

"Not at all. Those feelings are totally normal. I mean, I would have been shocked if you hadn't felt a little antsy." Jackie paused before getting to the purpose of the visit. After taking another sip of Shiner, she continued. "I've been thinking about how to catch this guy, and I've come up with a plan. Like we discussed last time, my bet is it's that Randazzo guy from L.A. But I don't have a trace of evidence to back that up. It's just a hunch, and that's it. In any event, I think we might be able to flush out the person who's been doing this shit to you."

Leah leaned forward across the table, her eyes wide with anticipation. "That's great! So what's your plan?"

"Well, don't freak out, but I'm pretty sure your cell has been hacked."

Leah gasped. "What makes you think that?"

"Just a hunch of mine, and with all the years I've been in this business, my hunches are usually right on."

"So should I trade in the phone?"

Jackie shook her head. "No, I have a better idea. Let's use it to slip this jerk some bad info—bait him."

Leah furrowed her brow. "I don't know that I follow you."

"Okay. You've been working on this story about Connors, right?"

Leah nodded.

"And as I recall, you need some corroboration before your editor will go to print with it."

"That's right."

"So what type of corroboration does your editor want?"

"Another source. Right now, we only have one, and he's been a bit shaky."

"Understood. So let's assume that this person who is trying to scare you off the story is working for Connors."

"Okay."

"And let's further assume he learns you've gotten what you need to go to print. What do you think this asshole would do?"

"Probably go ballistic and do whatever he thinks it would take to stop me."

"That's my thinking too."

"So what's the plan?" Leah sipped her vodka tonic.

"You call your boss . . ." Jackie hesitated, searching her memory for his name.

"Abe. Abe Levine."

"Right. And you'll have to talk with Abe first. He's got to be in on this from the outset."

"No problem there."

"Tell Abe you've got the corroborating information you need to run the story. Give him whatever details you want. Make it sound authentic. Then tell him you want to rent a secluded getaway on Lake Travis where you can hole up for several days and finish the article without any distractions."

"You have a place in mind?"

"Yeah, it's about thirty miles from Austin, on the opposite side of the lake. It'll take you about an hour to get there by car." Jackie handed Leah an envelope. "The address, directions, key to the house—everything you need is in here."

"So I would be the bait?" Leah questioned apprehensively.

"That's one way to put it. But believe it or not, you'll be safer there than you are here in Austin."

"How can you be so sure?"

"Because Officer Gomez and I are going to be watching the place the whole time you are there. If that asshole shows up, we'll nab him," Jackie responded reassuringly.

"But you told me he's dangerous and one of the best in the business, isn't that right?"

"That's what I told you and that's what I believe. But like I said, Gomez and I are going to be watching the place for several hours before you even get there. Remember, we've both done this type of work for a number of years."

"I'm not doubting you, Jackie. I'm just a little scared, that's all."

"That's understandable." Jackie hesitated for a second. "I don't want to scare you, but there's one other thing I'd like to do, just to give us a little insurance."

"I'm afraid to ask what that might be. But go ahead. Tell me."

"Leah, I want to install a software program on your laptop."

"What type of program?"

"Goes by the acronym RAT, which stands for 'remote administration tools.'"

"What does this software do?"

"It will allow me to access your laptop from mine."

"And why would you want to do that?" Leah asked.

"You have a MacBook Pro, right?"

Leah nodded.

"Which has a built-in webcam, correct?"

"Correct. So?"

"If you put the laptop in your bedroom, this program will allow me to see and hear what's going on in there at all times."

"Are you kidding me? There's software that will allow you to do that?"

"Yes, there is. Unfortunately, hackers use it to watch unsuspecting young women undress. Like this guy out in California—he was able to get some nude pictures of Miss Teen USA, which he then tried to use to blackmail her. Fortunately, they caught the sleaze bucket."

Leah shook her head in disgust. "Geez, I had no idea. I guess there is no such thing anymore as the privacy of one's home."

"Not like there used to be. Accessing your laptop may be overkill, but it would make me feel better to know what's going on inside the house as well as outside. Even if I can't see everything, I should be able to hear what's going on."

"I think that's a good idea. I'd feel safer knowing you're watching."

"It's settled then."

"So how do you install this RAT software?" Leah asked.

"Remotely. You won't even notice."

Leah folded and unfolded her drink napkin as she spoke. "Jackie, you've hit me with a lot of stuff today. I need some time to think about it."

"Can I be honest with you, Leah? I really don't think you have a choice. I just don't know how long I can keep you safe here in Austin. We've got to catch this guy. And to do that, we've got to take some calculated risks."

Leah studied Jackie's face before responding, "All right. Well, let me sleep on it and I'll be back in touch."

Jackie reached in her purse and pulled out a disposable cell phone, which she slid across the table to Leah.

Leah looked confused.

"From now on, call me on this. It's not hacked."

"You think of everything." Leah dropped the cell in her briefcase. "I'll let you know tomorrow."

"I'll be waiting for your call."

CHAPTER

32

J amie pulled his red Ferrari up to the valet stand in front of the W Hotel in Union Square. He grabbed his leather overnight bag out of the backseat, exchanged his ignition key for a ticket from the valet, and strutted through the hotel entrance to the reception desk. An attractive blonde in her twenties smiled at him. "Good afternoon! How may I help you?"

While fishing for the wallet in his back pocket, Jamie returned the smile and responded, "I have a reservation for two nights. The name is Stein, Jamie Stein."

The blond attendant typed in his name on her computer and then slid a document across the counter. "Yes, Mr. Stein. I have you down for tonight and tomorrow night, departing on Sunday morning. You have our weekend luxury package. If you could please initial next to the X confirming your agreement to the rate."

Jamie looked at the rate—$1,200 a night—initialed next to the X, and signed at the bottom.

"And what card would you like to use, Mr. Stein?"

"American Express." He handed her the card, which she imprinted and returned to him, along with two card keys to the room and a metal key to the in-room bar.

"You're on the sixth floor. The elevators are directly behind me and to the right. Enjoy your stay."

Jamie picked up his bag and headed to the elevator. He got off on the sixth floor and found his room. Looking around, he grinned with pleasure. He had big plans for the weekend. First, he would check out the bar scene downstairs. With a little luck, he might find a twenty-something looking for a good time. Assuming he scored, there were plenty of good restaurants in the area, and the club scene in Greenwich Village was inferior to none. A nightcap in the room would naturally follow and then several hours of playful sex.

The drive from Bloomfield had taken almost two hours, and he wanted to freshen up. He hopped in the shower and, afterward, put on the Armani sports jacket and slacks he had purchased several days before, along with a pair of Cole Haan tasseled loafers. He pocketed his billfold and room key and then glanced at himself in the full-length mirror before confidently heading out the door.

It was happy hour in the bar, and the place was rocking—wall-to-wall people. Scanning the room, he caught the eye of a willowy brunette seated with several of her girlfriends at a corner table. She smiled, which Jamie acknowledged with a nod. Seconds later, he was talking with one of the most beautiful women he had ever seen.

"Thanks," he said. "I don't think I would ever have found a place to sit. It's packed in here."

Mischievous cat-green eyes caught his. "My pleasure, Mr. . . . ."

"Stein, Jamie Stein. And you are?"

"Ramsey Wakefield." She extended her hand and Jamie eagerly took it.

"So, Ramsey, what brings you to the city?"

"Bachelorette party tomorrow night. My friend Margaux is getting married next month, so the bridesmaids pitched in for a fun weekend in New York." Ramsey nodded at the attractive blonde seated across the table who was involved in animated conversation with one of her girlfriends.

"Nice. And where's home?"

"Nashville."

"I thought I noticed a Southern drawl."

"More of a hick accent, you mean," she teased.

Jamie chuckled. "That's your characterization, not mine." He paused. "So is your group staying at the hotel?"

Ramsey nodded. "We are. And what brings you here?"

"I live in Greenwich, Connecticut—just up the road—and like to spend as many weekends as I can in New York. I'm not married, and the nightlife in Greenwich is pretty slow."

"Nashville's gotten a lot better in the last few years, but it's definitely not New York." Ramsey smiled and took a sip of her drink.

"So I guess your weekend is all booked up?" Jamie asked.

"Not really. We've got a dinner and some partying planned for tomorrow night, but tonight's wide open."

Jamie looked at his Audemars Piguet watch, a recent $30,000 purchase. "Let's see. It's still early. I know a great place for dinner on the Upper East Side. Interested?"

"Totally! Why don't you grab a cab and I'll give my friends a heads-up."

"I'd rather drive. I'll have my car brought around."

Ramsey's eyes widened. "Even better!"

"I'll be waiting out front."

"See you shortly."

Ten minutes later, the valet eased the Ferrari to a stop in front of the hotel.

"Well, well! Just remember I accepted your invitation before I knew you were such a big shot," Ramsey said as she gracefully accepted Jamie's hand to help her into the car.

"Noted." Jamie smiled, tipped the valet, and walked around to the driver's side.

Back in the bar, the scene had caught the eye of a man seated at a window table with his wife. They were in New York celebrating their ten-year wedding anniversary. "Honey, isn't that Jamie Stein getting into that Ferrari?"

His wife turned in her chair to get a better look. "I can't tell for sure. I only met him once, and that was at the Christmas party." She squinted her eyes. "But it sure looks like him."

"I'm curious. I'll be right back." The man got up and rushed out of the bar.

As Jamie slid behind the steering wheel, he noticed a familiar figure walking hurriedly toward the car, shouting his name. He shifted into first gear and nosed the car onto Park Avenue South.

Ramsey turned toward her date for the evening. "Who was that guy?"

"Never seen him before in my life."

CHAPTER

33

Darrin handed a legal-size envelope to Jace. The envelope was marked "Confidential," addressed to "Jace Forman, Esquire," and had no return address. "I wonder what this is. Do you need some privacy while you open it?"

"Of course not. I have no secrets from you." Jace smiled as he picked up a letter opener from the corner of his desk, sliced open the top of the envelope, and slowly pulled out a multipage document. As Jace's eyes began to scan the contents, he muttered, "I can't believe this. It appears to be a will Eugene drafted before he died."

Darrin walked around the desk so she could look over Jace's shoulder. "Turn to the last page. I notarized his signature on that affidavit we filed and am sure I would recognize it."

Jace complied.

Darrin gasped. "That's it. No doubt about it. I can tell from the way he made that funny *H*. It's identical to the one on his affidavit. So what does it say?"

"Just give me a minute." Jace flipped back to the beginning and began to read the will's provisions. Darrin did the same. Upon finishing, Jace slowly placed the document on top of his desk and looked up at Darrin, his mouth agape. "Well, I'll be damned."

"Jace, Eugene must have known—"

"That he was going to get killed on his mission to Norman, or at least had a pretty strong feeling he might."

"And he left everything to you in case that happened."

"He didn't leave anything to me. But he did make me the executor of the will."

"That's what I meant—that he left you in charge of his estate."

"He also made me the trustee of this trust he established in honor of his daughter."

"I was trying to read over your shoulder but couldn't make out that provision. What about this trust?"

"The way I read it, Eugene has directed me to sell everything he owns—his house, his car, his personal effects—and put the net proceeds into this trust named after his daughter. He also had a one-million-dollar life insurance policy, the proceeds of which will go into the trust. The trust's assets must be invested and the income used to compensate the families of those who have gone through what Eugene and Janice went through—funeral protests by the BBC."

"And what happens to the lawsuit?"

"Eugene put in a specific provision directing me to pursue it through trial, and any appeals. After deducting the fees and expenses incurred in pursuing the case, I'm instructed to deposit the net amount in the trust."

"Won't Prater move to dismiss the case since our client is dead?"

"I doubt it. He knows a motion like that wouldn't stand a chance in hell of being granted by Judge Zimmerman, for the simple reason that we do have a client—and you're looking at him. As executor, I am the representative of Eugene's estate and, as such, have legal standing to continue this lawsuit."

"Well, I've dealt with difficult clients before, but you could prove to be the most difficult," Darrin joked.

"We'll just have to see, won't we?"

Darrin picked up the envelope. "There is something else in here." She shook out the contents, and a disk in a paper cover slid out. "Jace, I'm afraid to even see what's on here, but I know we have to."

Jace took the disk from Darrin and pushed it into the drive on his computer. Their client's face appeared on the screen. After viewing the contents of the disk, Jace said, "Well, Eugene obviously wanted to make sure his wishes were followed. Not only did he sign his will but he recorded himself reading it."

"So what do we do now?" Darrin asked.

"Let me think a minute." Jace paused. "The first thing we need to do is have Kirk file an amended complaint naming me as the representative plaintiff for the estate."

Darrin grabbed a pad from the corner of Jace's desk and began to take notes. "Got it."

"You'll need to revise our discovery responses to reflect what happened up in Norman. I'll sign them as the estate's representative. Oh, be sure and have Kirk file the necessary papers to admit the will to probate. He should get that done ASAP."

Darrin nodded. "Next question. At trial, how are we going to get in Mr. Hanson's recollection about what happened at the protest? He can't testify."

"But we have his affidavit. I feel pretty sure Judge Zimmerman will overrule Prater's hearsay objection since our client is deceased."

"Maybe, but that still doesn't get us the evidence we need based upon what Judge Zimmerman wrote in her opinion."

"You're right. We need to find more evidence that the BBC intended to inflict mental anguish on our client and not just make a statement on a political issue."

"I still can't seem to find anything that would help us there. I've spent hours and hours on the Internet and have come up empty."

"Well, keep looking. In the meantime, I'll contact Jackie and see what she's turned up."

Darrin responded, "I've got to get back to work. And just remember—no more dinners by candlelight down in Austin. I'll know it if you do. You know what they say about a woman's intuition."

"You have nothing to worry about."

Darrin muttered under her breath "famous last words" as she opened the door to the hall and stepped out.

CHAPTER

34

Jackie looked at the number of the incoming call and recognized it as the number of the disposable phone she had given Leah. "Leah?"

"Jackie, hi. Listen, I've made a decision. I'm willing to do it. I just finished discussing everything with Abe. He has some concerns, just like I do, but he's on board."

"It's the right choice, I promise you."

"I hope so. So when do we put things in motion?"

"I haven't spoken with Gomez yet. I didn't want to set everything up until I had the go-ahead from you. As soon as I speak with him and get him on board, I'll let you know.

"Okay. So walk me through this one more time."

"After you hear back from me with the go-ahead, you should call Abe. Tell him you have your second source for the Cal Connors story and that you want to hibernate on Lake Travis for several days and churn it out."

"And how should he react?"

"Excited but concerned. Ultimately he should give in, on one condition."

"And that is?"

"You tell him where you will be and promise to call him if you get the least bit uneasy."

"That's exactly how he would react."

"Then wait an hour and call him back. Give him the address of where you'll be staying and assure him you will call and give him updates as the story progresses and, more importantly, that you'll call him if you feel like you're in any danger whatsoever."

"I'll plan on heading out tomorrow after lunch. I'm ready to get this over with. Jackie, are you going to catch this bastard?"

"If there's a way, we'll get him. I promise you that."

CHAPTER

35

"Mr. Stein, I assume you are curious as to why I wanted to meet with you this morning?" Andrew James, General Counsel and Ethical Compliance Officer of the Empire Risk Insurance Company, was dapperly clad in a charcoal-gray Brooks Brothers suit, starched white shirt, and yellow bow tie with navy-blue dots. His short silver hair was combed straight back, a thin mustache neatly trimmed over his pursed lips. He looked across his massive mahogany desk at his first appointment of the day.

"Yes, sir. It's not every day that I get a call from someone in the general counsel's office."

Andrew's hands formed a crude teepee as he responded. "Do you know what I do here at Empire Risk?"

"I know you are a lawyer for the company. That's about it."

Andrew smiled condescendingly. "I am, and have been since I graduated from Harvard Law almost forty years ago." He paused for a response, and Jamie nodded deferentially. "Several years ago I was given the responsibility of ensuring that Empire Risk employees—claims adjusters, actuaries, investment managers, you name it—adhere to the strictest code of ethics. Do you know why my position was created?"

"No sir, I don't."

"Because one of our officers—who will remain anonymous— was conspiring with a Wall Street stockbroker. He was receiving kickbacks for channeling a portion of Empire Risk's investment business to him." Andrew enunciated the last two words with contempt. "And so it was decided that controls should be put in place to prevent this type of conduct in the future. You following me so far?"

Jamie shifted in his chair and decided to take the offensive. "I am, but I don't see what this has to do with me."

Andrew smiled and continued. "One of your co-workers came to me on Monday morning bright and early and told me he and his wife had seen you in the City over the weekend. Were you in New York this past weekend, Mr. Stein?"

"I was, but I don't see—"

Andrew interrupted. "And were you staying at the W Hotel in Union Square?"

"I was," Jamie answered, a tinge of defiance in his voice. "Mr. James, with all due respect, I understand you have a very important role in the company, and I appreciate that. But I don't believe that what I do on my personal time should be any of your business, or any one else's at Empire Risk."

His expression stoic, Andrew hesitated a moment before responding, "You are quite right, generally speaking. But there are exceptions."

"And what might those be?"

"Patience, Mr. Stein. I'm getting there. Now, there may be nothing to what occurred over the weekend. It may be totally innocent and without consequence. But I do need to do my job. You understand that, don't you, Mr. Stein?"

"I do, but—"

"Well, I'll get right to the point. You and a young lady were seen getting into a red Ferrari in front of the W Hotel at Union Square."

Jamie shook his head and sighed. "So that's what this is all about? Yes, my date for the evening—a delightful young lady from Nashville—got into a red Ferrari 458 convertible with me."

"My research indicates an automobile like that costs around $250,000."

"I haven't researched the cost, but you are probably in the ballpark."

"So how does someone on your salary—and I have access to the compensation of everyone at Empire Risk—afford such an extravagance?" Andrew leaned back in his leather chair and stroked his mustache.

Jamie gambled. "It wasn't mine."

Andrew cleared his throat before continuing. "I see. Perhaps, then, you can tell me whose Ferrari you were driving."

Jamie smiled. "I rented it. I had always wanted to drive a Ferrari and decided last weekend to make it happen."

Undeterred, Andrew continued his interrogation. "And from whom did you rent it?"

Jamie responded quickly and with assurance, "I can't remember."

"Do you have a receipt?"

"I had no reason to keep the receipt. I wasn't going to submit it to the company for reimbursement."

"And where did you rent it?"

"Brooklyn. I rented it from this guy in Brooklyn. He rents the car out on weekends to cover his payments. I can't remember his name. It wasn't important to me."

"Let me see if I understand you correctly. You rented a $250,000 car for a weekend from someone in Brooklyn whose name you can't remember."

Jamie continued with his alibi. "Yes, sir. You can go on the Internet and find people in many of the major metropolitan areas who rent out expensive cars. Like I said, they do it to help cover their monthly payments. The guy I rented it from took a copy of my driver's license and a credit card and made me leave my car with him before he even let me take his Ferrari out of the driveway."

"Well, I assume, then, that you put this on a credit card."

"No sir, he only wanted my credit card and driver's license as security. He wouldn't take plastic. I had to pay the rental fee in cash."

"And how much did this cost you?"

"Wasn't cheap—something like $1,500 a day."

Andrew's eyes searched his guest's for any clue as to whether he was lying. Jamie didn't flinch, his stare fixed on his interrogator.

Andrew rose from behind his desk and extended his hand, which Jamie firmly grasped. "Well, thanks for coming in. I'll be back in touch if I have additional questions."

"Thank you, Mr. James. You know where to find me."

Jamie walked out the door, a look of concern on his face. Andrew James was a hard man to read. Only time would tell whether the old geezer would close his investigation or continue turning over rocks in an attempt to discover the truth.

Ten minutes after Jamie had left his office, Andrew buzzed his secretary. "Bev, would you ask Ruth Danner to come to my office?" A few moments later, a squatty, masculine-looking woman with short-cropped hair and prominent features walked into his office and stood at attention.

"You wanted to see me?"

"Yes, Ruth. Please have a seat." Andrew gestured at the chair in front of his desk. "I hear good things about your work. We are fortunate to have you here at Empire Risk."

"I feel fortunate to be here."

"I've heard through the grapevine that you are interested in going to law school."

"Yes sir, I am interested. I've already submitted my applications and am waiting to hear back."

"You should have asked me for a recommendation. I would have been delighted to give you one."

"I really appreciate that, sir."

"Let me know when you hear back."

"I certainly will."

Andrew cleared his throat and adjusted his bow tie before getting to the purpose of the meeting. "Ruth, I have a very important assignment for you, very important to Empire Risk and its culture."

"I'll be glad to help in any way I can."

"I know you will." Andrew smiled politely. "It involves a very sensitive matter. You will need to be discreet. You can't discuss your assignment with anyone but me."

Ruth nodded. "That won't be a problem."

"Good. I am concerned we may have someone on the payroll cheating the company. I say 'may' because I don't have any definitive proof, not yet anyway."

"Who do you suspect?"

"Again, 'suspect' is a strong word. Let's say I have some questions that need answers."

"I understand."

"The person's name is Jamie Stein. Do you know him?"

Ruth furrowed her brow. "Name doesn't ring a bell. What department does he work in?"

"He's in claims."

"Well, that explains it. I don't have much contact with claims people."

"That's good. You won't have any prejudices one way or the other."

"No, sir. What would you like for me to do?"

"I want to know what Stein has been working on the past six months, any cases he's settled, that type of thing. Keep your eye out for anything that seems out of the ordinary."

"How will I find that out without arousing suspicion?"

"You work in the auditing department. Is that right?"

"Yes, sir," Ruth said.

"One of your job responsibilities involves the auditing of the attorney fee statements of outside counsel, is that correct?"

"Yes, sir. I am one of many auditors in the department."

"I understand. Who's your direct supervisor?"

"George Lattimore."

"I know George well. I'm going to tell him I want some random audits done. I'll mention Stein and several other claims adjusters. You will be furnished all of the files they have worked on for the past six months."

"And the only files I should examine are Stein's?"

"Precisely."

"And what am I looking for again?"

"I am especially interested in any settlements reached in the cases Stein is handling—the amounts paid, the lawyers involved, the nature of the claims. Anything you can learn from the files."

"Yes, sir."

"And there's one other thing I would like for you to do." Andrew shifted in his chair. "You're not married, are you? I am only asking because I don't want to take you away from your family if you are."

"No, sir. I haven't found the right person yet."

"There's no rush. You've got a plenty of time. An attractive young lady like you won't have any problem finding Mr. Right," Andrew lied. "Well then. I'd like you to tail Stein on the weekends—find out where he goes, who he sees, the type of car he drives."

"Is that legal?"

"You don't think I'd ask you to do anything that wasn't, do you?"

"No, sir."

Andrew rose and extended his hand. "Thank you, Ruth. Just keep me apprised of your progress."

Ruth stood and grasped Andrew's outstretched hand. "I will, sir."

"Christine, this is Jamie Stein."

"I told you that I never wanted to talk with you again. I don't want there to be any—"

"Don't worry. I'm calling from a pay phone here in Hartford. No way for anyone to trace this call to me or you."

"So why are you calling me?"

"We've got a little problem."

"What do you mean 'we'?"

"Just what I said. I was called in this morning to meet with the head lawyer at Empire Risk."

"I'm listening."

Jamie paused. "Well, I was in New York this past weekend—"

"So?"

"And a co-worker apparently spotted me leaving the hotel where I was staying, the W in Union Square."

"And?"

"In a Ferrari convertible."

"For crying out loud! What were you thinking? Don't tell me you went out and bought a $250,000 automobile?"

"I got a really good deal—"

"Sheesh. Grow up! So what did this compliance officer ask you?"

"What do you think he asked me? He wanted to know how I could afford a brand-new Ferrari on my salary."

"And what did you tell him?"

"That I had rented it."

"And I assume he wanted a receipt, which you didn't have."

"He did, but I told him I had rented it from some guy in Brooklyn whose name I couldn't recall - for cash."

"I've at least got to give you credit for being creative with your lies. Do you think he believed you?"

"He didn't want to, but he looked pretty defeated at the end of our meeting. I don't know whether he'll close the file or continue to snoop. That's why I'm calling you."

"What do you want me to do?"

"Nothing. I just wanted to give you a heads-up."

"Did he mention anything about our settlement?"

"Not a word. This was a very preliminary meeting. I think he was just testing the waters. Hopefully we've seen the end of it."

"So where are you keeping the car?"

"In a self-rental thirty minutes from Hartford. And don't worry, I'm not going near that place until the smoke clears."

"I'd hope not. Anything else? If not, I've got to get back to work."

"Christine, hopefully this will be the last time we'll talk."

"No, this definitely will be the last time we talk."

"Well, if things get hot, I may have to get out of here."

"What do you mean?"

"I'm not going to stick around until they throw me in jail."

"Where would you go?"

"Some place that doesn't have an extradition treaty with the U.S. I've done some research, and France looks like a good candidate."

"I hope, for both of our sakes, it doesn't come to that."

"Me too, but I always like having a backup plan. And Christine, if I do have to leave the States, you know I'll expect those payments to continue month to month, just like you and I agreed. Don't think just because I'm leaving the country you can screw me."

"I wouldn't think of it, Jamie. A deal is a deal."

"Good. Because if the payments stopped, I'd rat you out in a heartbeat, you and your old man."

"You're not threatening me, are you?"

"As the old saying goes, it's not a threat, it's a promise. Just keep the money coming."

The line went dead. Christine slammed the receiver down and stared out the window of her office. She wouldn't tell her dad about the call. No need to worry him, and the fewer people who knew about this the better. Her mind raced with questions. Would this lawyer continue his investigation? She couldn't rule out the possibility. And would it lead back to the law firm of Connors & Connors? They had taken steps to cover their tracks but nothing was foolproof. She needed her own backup plan.

She would have all of the firm's physical files for the cases she had settled with Stein immediately destroyed. There was no legal obligation to keep them, and they might, just might, have something incriminating in them. She would keep the payments flowing—at least for now. She could tell Jamie's threat was not idle. Then she would wait patiently and see which cards came her way.

CHAPTER

36

The lake house rested atop a limestone outcropping overlooking the blue-green waters of Lake Travis. The surrounding landscape was barren but beautiful in a stark, primitive way, with native yucca, prickly pear, and Texas live oak dotting the rugged hills.

Leah eased her car to a stop in the circular drive in front of a chalet-like structure of native stone and cedar. She turned off the ignition and took a deep breath, wondering if she was ready for this. She looked at her watch. It was a little before six. There should be enough time to unload the groceries and mix a drink before the sun began to disappear behind the hills. Sunsets in the Texas Hill Country were awesome in the true sense of the word, and she didn't intend to miss this one. But the unloading would have to wait a few minutes until she took a quick tour of the weekend getaway that would be her home for the next two days.

She walked up the stone path that meandered toward the front porch. Upon reaching the entryway, she paused to fish for the house key Jackie had given her. Finding it, she unlocked the door and walked inside.

The entryway opened into the great room, which was rustic yet dramatic. Leah's eyes were drawn to the cathedral ceiling buttressed by dark-stained wooden beams, then to the massive stone fireplace positioned on the wall to her left, and last to the richly grained pecan-plank floors under her feet. She walked across the room to the floor-to-ceiling windows and gazed out upon Lake Travis. For a moment she wished the occasion for her visit had been different; Chip Holt's face flashed through her mind. What she wouldn't give for a carefree weekend alone with him! But that would have to wait.

Leah hurried back to the car, brought her suitcase and groceries inside, and then locked the front door; she was careful to slide the dead bolt into place before heading to the kitchen to pour a drink. Fifteen minutes later, she was in a chaise lounge on the wooden deck jutting out over a cliff, a vodka tonic in one hand, her iPad on her lap, and the disposable cell Jackie had given her on the side table to her right. She sipped her drink and watched as the sun made a slow exit, leaving a burnt-orange hue above the hills to the west.

The mood of the moment was abruptly interrupted by the unwelcome sound of her cell phone vibrating.

"Leah, just wanted you to know we have you covered. We checked the house before you arrived and have had it under surveillance ever since."

"Thanks, Jackie. That makes me feel better. I'm just watching the sunset on the deck and having a cocktail. I love this place! I only wish I were here under different circumstances."

"I hear you. I know it's easier said than done, but try not to worry. Just know we have your back. By the way, I see that you've already set up your laptop on the desk in your bedroom. I have accessed it from here and am getting a pretty good view of the room."

"Glad to hear it."

"Well, I'll let you get back to your beverage. Just wanted to make sure you knew we were here."

"I never had any doubts. Thanks, Jackie."

Jackie clicked off and maintained her position on an undeveloped hill several hundred yards to the east. She scanned the front of the house and its surroundings with military-issue, high-powered binoculars. She brought the binoculars down from her face and speed-dialed a number on her cell.

"Yeah?"

"You seen anything?"

"Nothing—all quiet from over here. I've got a pretty good view of the back of the house. Looks like your client is enjoying herself on the deck. Other than that, there has been no activity outside. This area is more deserted than I thought it would be. I guess it picks up on the weekends." Officer Gomez kept his gaze on the cabin and its surroundings. "Do you think this guy will make a move?"

"I'm counting on it. If he is looking for a chance to do something, this is it."

"I agree."

"Now don't go snoozing on me over there." Jackie chuckled.

"I've had so much coffee my eyes are brown."

"They were already brown."

Jorge ignored the quip. "Hey, how's that spyware working?"

"Pretty damn good. There are some blind spots in the room, but it's better than nothing. I plan on checking the screen intermittently, but right now I'm focused on the front of the house. You keep watching the back. We want to make sure that asshole doesn't slip by us."

Jorge took another sip of coffee. "Roger that."

Darkness began to shroud her surroundings, so Leah finished her drink and headed inside, locking the door behind her.

She made her way to the master bedroom, unzipped her overnight bag, and took out a small case holding her toiletries. As she made her way to the bathroom, an arm came out of nowhere, encircling her neck, and a handkerchief with a strange-smelling substance covered her face. Leah's mind raced as she sensed herself slipping helplessly into a bottomless crevasse of pitch-black darkness.

Ten minutes later Jackie cursed under her breath when she saw Leah blindfolded and gagged in a straight-backed chair in the bedroom. She frantically called Jorge. "Jorge, we have a problem! The son of a bitch is inside the house. Leah is bound and gagged, and her assailant is armed."

"Jackie, calm down. I'm going to call for backup. Do not, I repeat, do not attempt rescue until they get here! It's way too risky."

"I'm not going to stand by and watch while he—"

Jorge interrupted. "Has he done anything to her yet, harmed her in any way?"

"No, not that I can tell."

"Well, you can bet your ass that if we storm the place he will. He might even kill her. We just can't take the chance. Don't take your eyes off that computer screen. If things change, call me. I'm going to stay here—watch the back of the house. And Jackie, promise me you're not going to do anything rash. If you did and things went wrong, you would never forgive yourself."

Jackie sighed, her tone calmer. "You're right. How long do you think it will take backup to get here?"

Jorge fudged. "Don't know, but it shouldn't be too long."

Leah's thoughts were confused by the lingering effects of the chloroform.

Michael Randazzo sat across from her, waiting for her to regain consciousness. He was dressed in black from head to toe, his features concealed by a sleek black ski mask, his hands gloved.

"So, Ms. Rosen, it is such a pleasure to be in your company."

Leah could feel her hands begin to tremble.

"There is no need for you to be afraid. I'm not going to hurt you, not if you do exactly what I say. If you promise not to scream, I'll take that gag off. What do you say?"

Leah nodded feebly.

"If you break your promise after I take off the gag, I swear it will be the last sound you will ever make. I will slit your throat from ear to ear. Do we understand one another?"

Leah nodded again.

Randazzo rose, gently removed the gag, and returned to his seat.

"Much better, huh?"

No response.

Randazzo leaned forward and gently stroked Leah's cheek with gloved fingers. She instinctively turned her head away.

"May I call you Leah? Ms. Rosen is way too formal."

Silence.

"I'll take that as a yes. First, let's talk about that article you're working on. There are a lot of people who could get hurt if it went to print—judges who admitted Dr. Crimm's report into evidence, defense lawyers who failed to properly object to the report, injured people who received lots of well-deserved compensation from sympathetic juries, the lawyers who represented them. You get the idea."

Leah remained motionless except for her trembling hands, her lips drawn taut.

"So why do you want to drag up all that dirt months, in some cases years, after the fact? I mean, that's not in anyone's best interest, don't you agree?"

Leah remained quiet, her mind racing.

"Okay, well, enough about business. You just can't imagine how much I have enjoyed watching that video of you. You know, the one where you undress and then take a long, hot shower. I watch it every night, right before bedtime."

Leah shuddered, her bottom lip now beginning to quiver.

"You were so uninhibited—the way you washed every part of your body. You seemed to enjoy touching yourself. Did that turn you on?"

Leah began to cry, her tears absorbed by the black blindfold. Through her sobs, she uttered, "I won't write the story. I promise I won't."

"That's my girl. Just what I wanted to hear." Randazzo reached over and caressed her cheek once more. This time Leah didn't turn away. "But I'm afraid you may forget your promise once I leave. And we wouldn't want that to happen, now would we? So I'm going to give you something to think about every time you might be tempted to break your promise."

"Please don't hurt me."

"Now, what did I tell you? I'm a man of my word. I'm not going to hurt a hair on your head as long as you're a good little girl and do exactly what I say. Does that sound fair to you?"

"Please leave. You've got what you wanted."

"Not quite. Leah, I'm going to untie your hands. But if you try to escape, you know what will happen, don't you?"

Leah nodded.

Randazzo stood and walked behind her chair. He quickly untied her hands and returned to his seat. He then spoke, his tone abrupt. "Stand up."

"Why? I—"

"I said stand up! Now!"

Leah slowly rose.

"Kick off your shoes."

"I don't—"

"Do it."

Leah stepped out of her flats, revealing well-manicured toenails painted a subtle blue.

"That's better. And I love the toenail polish—very chic. And now the jeans."

"I can't—" Leah was now sobbing uncontrollably.

"I'm not going to say it again. Take off your jeans."

Leah slowly unzipped her jeans and slid them down to her ankles.

"Your legs look even better up close." Randazzo leaned over and ran his fingers up the inside of her right thigh, triggering Leah to press her legs together as tight as she could. "So soft. Just like a baby's butt."

Leah pleaded, "You've made your point. Please, I beg you, leave me alone."

Randazzo looked at his watch. "The way I figure it we have another thirty minutes or so of playtime before I have to leave. Now step out of the jeans and take off your shirt."

Leah prayed a silent prayer as she complied and began to unbutton her white blouse. After undoing the last button, she slid the shirt off one shoulder and then the other and pulled her arms out of the sleeves. She dropped the shirt to the floor, her sobs abruptly abating, controlled anger beginning to set in.

"Satisfied?"

"Very. Turn around—slowly."

Leah complied.

"Get rid of the bra. I love those little tits of yours—so firm and, I don't know, innocent-looking. If I didn't know better, I might mistake you for jailbait."

Leah grimaced as she unhooked her bra, which fell to the floor.

"And those panties."

Obediently, Leah wiggled out of her panties and then stood erect, shivering. She was now wearing nothing but the black blindfold. Randazzo stood and guided Leah toward the bathroom.

"Where are you taking me?"

"You will find out soon enough."

Once Leah felt the tile under her feet, she knew where they were. Randazzo pulled back the shower curtain and turned on the water. As he adjusted the temperature, Leah uttered a sigh of resignation.

"Now, don't you think a hot shower would feel good after your long day? Let me help you get in."

Randazzo guided Leah as she unsteadily stepped into the tub. As she stood there, he adjusted the shower nozzle so the stream bounced off her breasts. Her nipples hardened in response.

"Nice. I can see you are already getting aroused."

"Don't do this! I beg you."

"It'll be over before you know it." He put a bar of soap in Leah's right hand. "Start with those little tits of yours."

"I can't. I won't."

"Okay, then. Hand me the soap."

"No, I'll do it."

"I thought you might."

Leah slowly began to rub the bar of soap over her breasts. Her nipples remained erect.

"Now, that isn't so bad, is it?"

Leah began to sob again. Randazzo pulled a digital camcorder from his pocket, aimed the lens at Leah, and pressed the record button.

"Now move the soap down slowly. I'll tell you when to stop."

Leah slowly slid the soap down between her breasts and then over her navel. As it reached her pubic area, Michael ordered her to stop.

"Work up a nice lather. You want to be nice and clean down there." Randazzo zoomed in as Leah obeyed. "That's enough with the soap. Now, spread your legs wide."

Leah instinctively brought her legs together.

"You little bitch! I said spread your legs wide, until your feet touch the sides of the tub. Do it! Right now!" Randazzo's voice had reached a fever pitch.

Frightened, Leah slowly inched her feet toward the tub's sides.

"That's my girl." Her tormentor's tone softened. "Now play with yourself."

"I won't do that. I can't. Please don't—"

Michael interrupted, "Either you will or I will. Your choice."

Leah began to massage herself as the camera zoomed in, capturing a close-up view of every detail.

"Do it like you mean it—faster."

Leah reluctantly complied.

"And I want to hear you sigh, loudly, like you're really enjoying it."

Leah tried to obey.

"Come on. You can do better than that. You're whimpering. Act like you're about to come."

Leah closed her eyes behind the blindfold and pretended to be somewhere else. She forced out a succession of "aahs."

"Perfect! You can stop now. I have it all on tape. And you know what I'll do if you make me. I'll post it on YouTube. I promise you that."

Leah nodded.

"Well, it's time for me to go. I sure have enjoyed our little date. And it's so nice to have a little memento of our time together. I'll watch it every night and think of you." Randazzo chuckled.

"Now, no screaming. There's no need. Your investigator will be here in a matter of minutes. I promise."

Still petrified, Leah waited for what seemed like an eternity before ripping off the blindfold. She wrapped a towel around her naked body and then ran into the bedroom. She heard a loud crash. Seconds later, an out-of-breath Jackie ran into the room.

"Leah, I'm so, so sorry."

Leah hurriedly began to throw on her clothes and then screamed hysterically, "Where were you? Do you know what just happened? I thought you had all of this figured out! I thought you had my back!" She began to cry uncontrollably.

"I don't know how that son of a bitch got in here. Jorge and I went over this place with a fine-tooth comb before you got here and we haven't taken our eyes off of it since."

Between clenched teeth, Leah angrily snarled, "I trusted you. I was such a fool. You don't know what I've been through. It was horrible."

"I know it was."

"What?"

"I was watching and listening on my laptop." Jackie shook her head. "I still can't believe it."

"So you knew what was happening? Why didn't you stop it?" As tears streamed down her face, Leah delivered a barrage of blows to Jackie's chest and then buried her face in her shoulder, muttering over and over, "Why didn't you do something? Why?"

Jackie put her hand behind Leah's head and pulled her close. "I was afraid that if I tried anything he would kill you. I could see that he had a knife and a holstered revolver at his side. I couldn't take the chance."

Moments later, the house was filled with police and SWAT team members. Gomez was the first one to enter the bedroom. "Jackie, the bastard took off by boat. The lake patrol has been alerted. Hopefully they will be able to catch him. If not, at least you have him on video."

Leah looked at Jackie, her eyes again filling with tears. "On video?"

"Leah, the video is for my eyes only. I'm going to use it to catch him. I promise. Let me drive you back to Austin. You can stay at my place tonight."

Leah shook her head. "No, I'd rather you take me to Abe's. It's the only place I think I would feel safe."

Jackie followed Leah out of the bedroom and toward the front door. At least eight cop cars and two police vans were parked in front of the house, their lights flashing. "Jorge, I'm taking Leah back to town. I'll meet you at the station."

"I'll take care of everything here and get there as soon as I can," Jorge responded.

Jackie and Leah got in the car and headed back to Austin. Neither spoke as a gentle mist began to cloud the windshield.

CHAPTER

37

Jace collapsed into the chair across from Darrin's desk. "Well, that was a bust."

"Tell me about it. What was he like?"

"Cool as a cucumber. I couldn't rattle him, not one damn bit. And I tried everything." Jace grimaced and shook his head.

"Before you get into the details, how was it being back at the old firm?"

"Weird, really weird. And guess who sat in for part of the deposition?"

"Maurice Morgan."

"Yep. It was all I could do to keep myself from slapping that silly smirk off his face. He's such a prick."

"I won't argue with you on that. I never liked that guy. How was Crom?"

"He was Crom. Pompous as usual but a hell of a lot better than Maurice. You should have seen that sneer Maurice gave me when I entered the conference room. I'm sure they were trying to distract me by having Maurice there. And it worked at the very first of the deposition. But after a few minutes I just ignored him. Didn't even look his way."

"What about Shaw? Was he dressed up in his signature robe and sandals?"

"Crom got him to clean up a little. He was wearing a plain white dress shirt and blue jeans. But ol' Crom couldn't get him to chuck the sandals."

"Judge Zimmerman won't let him get away with that."

"I kinda wish she would. Underscores what a crackpot that guy is."

"Did his followers show up?"

"Yep, they were there—men and women dressed alike. They didn't say shit. I assume Shaw had told them to let him do the talking."

"So how was Shaw as a witness?"

"Like I said, he was unflappable."

"What did he say about the protest?"

"Just what we anticipated—that they were making a statement about a very important social issue, that it was nothing personal against the Hanson family, that the only reason they chose Lauren's funeral as the protest site was to garner the maximum amount of publicity for their views. According to Shaw, they have an obligation to save as many souls as they can, and time is running short."

Darrin just hung her head.

Jace added, "Shaw may be a zealot, but he is also very smart. Based on the answers he gave, there is no doubt he had read and understood every word of the Westboro opinion."

"So did you get anything helpful out of him?"

"Not really. I asked him whether he'd ever abused any of the women in his commune—mentally, physically, or sexually.

He answered all of those questions with an enthusiastic and unequivocal no."

"So after you finished with Shaw, did you question each of his followers, disciples—whatever they call themselves?"

"No, I decided it would be a waste of time. They would have just parroted what Shaw had previously testified to. I did find it interesting that Crom had one of Shaw's followers—she goes by the name of 'Sister Rebekah'—sit in while Shaw was being deposed."

"Why'd you let him do that?"

"Because under the rules the BBC is entitled to have a corporate representative at every deposition."

"Pretty smart of him, I have to admit."

"And Crom told me he was going to change the rep for each deposition. That way every witness would hear the previous witness' testimony."

"Well, at least we know what Shaw is going to say. I'll ask the court reporter to expedite the transcript. I'll read it as soon as it comes in—let you know what I think."

"Thanks, Darrin. I'll be in my office if you need me." As Jace walked down the hall, his cell rang. It was Jackie.

"Jace, I've got some great news! I just got off the phone with Gomez. He's located a young girl who ran away from Shaw's compound. She's living here in Austin and works as a waitress at County Line, a barbecue restaurant on Bee Caves Road."

"I know the place from my UT days. What's her name?"

"Maddy." Jackie glanced down at the note she had scribbled when she was talking to Jorge. "Maddy Murphy."

"How did he find her?"

"He got a hit on the APD database. Apparently a call came in several weeks ago from Maddy's roommate. She indicated Maddy had recently run away from a religious compound in West Texas run by a man named Ezekiel Shaw and was afraid

Shaw might try to hurt her. She wanted to know if the police could provide protection. I assume you want to talk with her as soon as possible."

"Absolutely. Okay, let me think for a minute." Jace looked at his watch—a little after four o'clock. "I could catch the six o'clock out of Love Field, which would get me into Bergstrom around seven. Could you pick me up?"

"Do you have to ask? Of course I'll pick you up."

"Great. I'll see you outside of baggage claim around seven."

Jace crammed a legal pad into his overstuffed briefcase and ran toward the elevator. On the way down the hall he stuck his head in Darrin's office to give her a heads-up, but she wasn't at her desk. He thought about leaving a note but punted—he didn't have time. As he waited for the elevator, he noticed Darrin coming out of the ladies' room and hollered her name. She hurried up to him.

"What's up?" Darrin asked.

"Jackie just called. Her contact at the APD has found a runaway from the compound. She's living in Austin. I'm flying down right now to go talk to her."

"That's wonderful news, Jace. I assume Ms. McLaughlin is picking you up at the airport?"

Before he answered, there was a ding and the elevator door opened. "Look, I don't have much time. I'll call you when I know more." Jace stepped onto the elevator and watched as Darrin disappeared behind the closing doors.

Jackie and Jace arrived at County Line a little before eight. Maddy was wiping down tables in her section when they approached her.

"Maddy Murphy?" Jackie asked.

Maddy glanced up at Jackie and Jace, and guardedly answered, "Yes?"

"I'm Jackie McLaughlin, a private investigator here in Austin, and this is Jace Forman, an attorney from Fort Worth. We would like to ask you a few questions."

"What is this about? Am I in trouble?"

"Not at all. We would just like to ask you a few questions. It will only take a moment, I promise."

Maddy's eyes darted back and forth between Jackie and Jace. "What about?"

"The Brimstone Bible Church."

Maddy sighed. "I don't know what you're talking about. I've never even heard of that church. And, if you'll excuse me, I've got work to do."

Maddy started to turn away, and Jackie gently caught her by the arm. "Please, Maddy. It could be very important to a lot of people that we talk with you."

"Why?"

Jackie nodded at Jace. "Jace is a lawyer. He has sued the Brimstone Bible Church and its founder Ezekiel Shaw."

Maddy's eyes widened. "What for?"

"Do you remember that protest at the funeral of Lauren Hanson, a young soldier who was killed in Afghanistan?"

Maddy nodded faintly and looked down at her hands.

Jackie took a different tack. "Maddy, how old are you?"

"Seventeen."

"Where are your parents?"

"I never knew my father. My mother is with the church."

"When was the last time you spoke with her?"

"Until several nights ago, I hadn't seen or talked with her since I left the compound."

"What happened several nights ago?"

Maddy hesitated. She looked at Jackie and Jace and then down at her hands. "She confronted me in the parking lot right after I got off work. She tried to get me to come back and I told her I wouldn't do that for anything, not in a million years." Maddy paused. "She told me I was going straight to hell and then slapped me."

"Maddy, I am so sorry," Jackie said sympathetically.

"I know it's not really her fault. She'll do anything Shaw tells her to do—anything." Maddy paused briefly before continuing. "So, now you know one of the reasons I really don't want to talk about that church, or what happened there. I just want to forget all of that."

Jace replied, "I totally understand. But please hear me out before you make any final decisions. I filed a lawsuit against the church on behalf of the parents of Lauren Hanson."

"I don't blame them for suing. What we did at that funeral, and all the other funerals, was terrible."

"You're right. So much so that, several days later, Mrs. Hanson overdosed on sleeping pills."

Maddy gasped and covered her mouth.

"Unfortunately, it gets worse. Her father drove to Norman, Oklahoma, where the BBC had scheduled another protest. He was shot by police before he could kill Savior Shaw and died at the scene."

"Oh, no!" Maddy sat down at the table in shock.

Jace and Jackie took the chairs on either side of her. Jace went on. "Eugene Hanson left a will directing me to continue the lawsuit and, if I was fortunate enough to recover anything, deposit the money in a trust for victims of the BBC's abuse."

"And I assume the reason you are here is because you want me to testify against the church."

"I'd like you to consider it."

"I just can't. I am trying to leave those memories behind, start a new life. You can't imagine the nightmares I have every single night. I just hope that someday they'll go away."

"Will you at least talk with us about what happened while you were at the commune?"

"What's the point? I'm not going to testify."

Jackie took over. "Maddy, you wanted to get out of that place in the worst kind of way. I'm sure there was a good reason for that. Do you want other young girls to continue to go through what you did?"

Maddy looked up into Jackie's eyes. "I'll think about it."

"Thank you, Maddy. That's all we can ask. I'm going to give you my card. If you want to talk, please call me." Jackie handed Maddy her card, which Maddy glanced at and then stuffed into her pocket.

"Sorry, but I've got to get back to work." Maddy pushed her chair back and rose from the table. "I really will think about it. I promise."

After Maddy was out of earshot, Jace broke the silence. "So what do you think?"

"No clue. I can't blame her if she decides not to get involved."

"Neither can I."

"So what happens to your case if she doesn't?"

"Judge Zimmerman throws it out. Shaw and his groupies continue to conduct business as usual."

"That's a depressing thought."

"I agree." Jace sighed. "Well, we'd better get a move on. I've got a plane to catch."

CHAPTER
38

Ruth Danner shifted nervously in the chair across from Andrew James, who was talking on the phone and smiling at her from behind his massive desk. He held up a finger indicating the call was about to end.

"Always good to talk with you, Riley. Keep up the good work." There was a pause and a nod. "You too. And give Margie my best."

Andrew, clad in a dark suit and striped bow tie, replaced the receiver and shook his head. "Sorry about that. Some people have trouble getting to the point. But not you and me, right Ruth?"

"That's correct, sir."

"So what have you learned about Mr. Stein?"

Ruth cleared her throat. "Well, it appears a recent settlement he agreed to may be questionable."

Andrew raised a bushy eyebrow. "Tell me more."

"I went through all of his files, and there was one group that stood out like a sore thumb."

"What group was that?"

"There were these silica cases that had been dormant for years. No trial settings, no depositions, no nothing."

"Where were the cases filed?"

"In Texas."

"I should have known. And who is plaintiff counsel?"

"A Fort Worth firm, Connors and Connors. Father-daughter team."

"Doesn't ring a bell."

"I did a little background check on the firm. I found press on them regarding a case they recently won in Brownsville, Texas. The articles referred to Mr. Connors as 'the Lone Wolf.'"

"Only in the South," Andrew chuckled.

"Connors sued Samson Pharmaceuticals and got a multimillion-dollar jury award."

Andrew shook his head in disgust. "I'm thankful the defendant wasn't one of our insureds."

"The Samson verdict is just one of many. He's chalked up a bunch of big awards over the years—that is, until Texas passed tort reform, which was a game-changer."

"You can say that again," Andrew smiled. "We lowered our reserves in Texas substantially once that legislation became effective."

"Connors, and all of the other plaintiff lawyers in Texas, are dying a slow death. They are trying to retool from medical malpractice and tort work to patent infringement and commercial cases. Some have had more success than others."

"So how has Connors fared?"

"Hard to say."

"What'd you learn about his daughter?"

"Graduated at the top of her class from Baylor undergrad and Harvard Law."

"Impressive. Any success in the courtroom?"

"Plenty. She and her dad are very accomplished trial lawyers."

"So Mr. Stein may have had good reason to settle these cases?"

"That's a possibility, but I question the timing. As I said, nothing had happened in these cases for years. And there's something else."

"What's that?"

"I called the defense lawyers who were representing our insureds. I told them I was conducting a routine audit of their bills—"

Andrew interrupted, "I bet that got their attention."

"That was my intent, and it worked like a charm. I got all the information I needed."

"Like?"

"They wouldn't have settled the cases, they had never been cut out of settlement negotiations before, they only signed the settlement docs because Stein told them to—that type of thing."

"Hmm. Why didn't they go over Stein's head?"

"He evidently told them they'd never see any more of Empire Risk's business if they did."

"I see." Andrew paused while he adjusted his bow tie. "Anything else on the settlement?"

"For obvious reasons, I didn't contact Connors or his daughter. And, by the way, his daughter Christine signed all of the settlement papers."

"Interesting. So what are your conclusions?"

"I think the settlement is dirty. I don't know what Stein got for agreeing to it, but he got something. Otherwise it just doesn't make any sense."

"I agree." Andrew sighed in disgust and then changed course. "So were you able to follow Stein?"

"Not all of the time but as much as my schedule would allow."

"Learn anything?"

"Last night I followed him to a self-rental facility just outside Hartford."

Andrew leaned forward on his desk. "And?"

"It seems he recently rented a fairly large space there, but I couldn't tell what he was keeping inside. I was parked across the street and was worried he might notice I was tailing him. At one point he glanced in my direction and then started to act funny, like he knew something was coming down. I picked up on that and left."

"Was the space large enough to house a Ferrari?"

"Without a doubt."

"Great work, Ruth."

"Thank you, Mr. James. Let me know if I can do anything else for you."

"Actually, I would like for you to follow up on one thing. Mr. Stein indicated to me that he rented a Ferrari from a man in Brooklyn. I've never heard of such an arrangement, but Stein says they are common—people buying expensive cars and then renting them out on weekends to help with their payments. Have you ever heard of that?"

"No, but I really wouldn't have reason to."

"I would like for you to find out if there's anyone in Brooklyn who is renting out a Ferrari. If there is, I want his name."

"Shouldn't be too hard to find that out."

"Can you put a rush on it?"

"I'll have an answer for you as soon as possible."

"Thank you, Ruth."

As she walked toward the door, Andrew called out, "And let me know when you hear back from those law schools you've applied to."

"You'll be the first to know." Ruth closed the door behind her.

CHAPTER

39

Jackie was sitting in front of her MacBook Pro. She leaned in to try to get a closer look as she replayed the video taken the night of Leah's assault. A figure dressed all in black lunged out of nowhere, hooked his arm around Leah's neck, and held a cloth over her face until her resistance ebbed, her body becoming a motionless mass. She reviewed every horrifying moment of the evening looking for any clue as to the identity of the assailant. Finding nothing, she replayed the video again.

She listened as Leah's assailant spoke, sensing the faint trace of a Jersey accent. She paused the video, scribbled a note, and resumed play. Suddenly, Jackie lurched forward and clicked pause. Had she missed something this important the first five times she had watched the scene? She replayed the last minute in slow motion.

Jackie watched closely as the man in black leaned over to untie Leah's wrists. She noticed the ski mask he was wearing hiked up, exposing a small portion of his massive neck. And there it was: a small tattoo. Jackie stopped the video and enlarged the screen. The tattoo was in black ink and appeared to depict two shapes intertwining.

Letters? Maybe. Jackie couldn't be sure. She made a note of the time stamp on the video and continued her review. Thirty minutes later she closed her laptop and scanned the notes she had made: male, a little under six feet, fit build, a slight Jersey accent, small black tattoo on the right side of his neck.

She Googled "Michael Randazzo." A Wikipedia site came up on the left side of the screen and two images of Randazzo on the right. She clicked on Wikipedia and began to read.

Michael Randazzo was born in Newark, New Jersey, in 1961. In 1991, he moved to Los Angeles, where he became a high-profile private investigator, with movie stars and business moguls as clients. In 2003 he was indicted for wiretapping and extortion. Two years later all of the charges were dismissed for lack of evidence. Divorced five times, he is currently married to an exotic dancer.

She exited Wikipedia and then clicked on the first image on the right of the screen. It was a frontal shot depicting a square-jawed man with a tan, wrinkled face and dark black hair. He appeared to have been in his early forties when the photograph was taken, his eyes hidden behind a pair of sleek sunglasses.

Jackie clicked on the second photo, a side view very similar to a mug shot. His nose seemed more pronounced, and he appeared to be missing the lower part of his earlobe. Jackie's eyes dropped to his neck and rested on a small black tattoo with the letters *M* and *R* artfully intertwined. She jumped up and down exclaiming, "Yes! Yes! Yes! I've got you now, you asshole!" Randazzo was definitely the man who had tormented Leah. Now she had to find him.

CHAPTER

40

Jace grabbed his laptop and settled into a chair at the small conference table in his office. He glanced at his watch: 6:25. He and Matt had agreed, via email, to Skype each other at 6:30. Jace had never Skyped before and had reluctantly enlisted Harriett's assistance in downloading the requisite app and setting up the account. He opened his laptop and clicked on the Skype icon on the right of the screen and then on Matt's account. Seconds later, he was staring at his son's face.

"Matt, how are you? How's life in the military?"

Matt smiled broadly, his face more chiseled than Jace remembered it, a faint mustache sprouting on his upper lip. "Dad, I love it! Couldn't be happier. Best decision I've ever made."

Jace forced a grin. "That's great news, Son. Tell me all about it."

"Well, they kicked our butts when we first got here. Put us through this initial physical stress test just to see if we might have what it takes to be a SEAL. And I won't lie to you—it almost killed me, but I made it through."

"Your face is a little thinner. Looks like you may have lost some weight."

Matt laughed. "Ten pounds. Lost that beer gut I had put on down at UT."

"I hear that. So what happened after they put you through the screening test?"

"They whipped us into shape—running, lifting, swimming— you name it. I was so tired every night that I couldn't wait to hit the sack."

"I bet you've toned up some."

"Don't mean to brag, but I'm pretty ripped. Even more so than when I was back playing high school football."

"Wow. That's pretty hard to believe."

"Yesterday they gave us the final physical endurance test, to see if our training had paid off."

"And?"

"I killed it."

"What did they make you do?"

"Same type of stuff, only this time it was much more intense. And they expected a lot more from us."

"Any not make the cut?"

"About half. One of my closest friends."

"That's tough."

"It is, but if someone can't cut it, it's better for everyone if they find out now rather than later."

"So what happens next?"

"I've got some more training here and then I head to Coronado, California, to learn some underwater skills. I'm not sure about all the details."

"Matt, do you miss college life at all?" Jace searched his son's eyes for clues as he waited for a response.

"Not at all. There was no real purpose to what I was doing, not like here, where I'm preparing to serve my country. Seemed like I was just wasting time in Austin."

"Well, I've done some reading about the SEALs since you enlisted. It's not just a job. It's a lifestyle that affects everything."

Matt frowned. "I know that, Dad. I did my research as well."

Jace backed off. "I'm sure you did. Do you still think you'll want to go back and get your degree from Texas?"

"Haven't given it much thought lately. But if I had to guess, I would say the chances of that happening are pretty slim. I think I've found my calling in life."

"I do worry about you, Son. This is a dangerous line of work you've chosen. I hope these wars wind down before you complete your training."

"I don't. I can't wait to see some action. Even if things settle down in Afghanistan, there will still be plenty for the SEALs to do. These terrorists want to kill us, and I want to be there to take them out before they get the chance."

Jace cleared his throat. "I hope it doesn't come to that."

"You know it will." Matt looked down for a moment. "Dad, I've got to go, but I've really enjoyed our visit."

"Me too, Son. When can we do this again?"

"I've got a pretty busy schedule. I'll email you and let you know."

"That sounds good. In the meantime, take care of yourself."

"I will."

"And remember, I love you."

"Night, Dad."

Matt's face disappeared, but Jace continued to stare at the blank screen, his mind bombarded by "what ifs." What if he had been faithful to Matt's mother? What if he and Jackie hadn't bumped into Matt outside that Austin restaurant? What if he had spent more time at home when Matt was growing up rather than travelling all over the country trying lawsuits? Would Matt still have enlisted in the SEALs?

Jace swallowed hard, packed up his briefcase and headed home.

CHAPTER

41

Darrin dialed Megan's number and waited impatiently, expecting to get her sister's voice mail. Miraculously, Megan answered. "Sis, sorry I didn't get around to calling you back yesterday, but I was running car pool and errands in between. And then Karly had a piano recital last night that ran late. By the time things settled down, it was after ten."

"No worries, Megan. I figured you got tied up. I don't know how you keep all those balls in the air."

"I drop a few from time to time." Megan laughed. "You're one to talk—always at work. You ought to get Jace to put a cot in your office."

"Things any better between you and Mark?" Darrin asked.

"Not really. He got in last night after I was asleep and was gone this morning before I got up. And I got up at six-thirty, for Pete's sake! I don't know what he does anymore."

"Megan, I've thought about what you said the other day—you know, about your comfortable lifestyle and all. I understand your reluctance to put any of that in jeopardy, but your marriage is unhealthy, and you need to do something about it."

"Like what? The thought of divorce scares me to death. Like I said the other day, I haven't worked since the girls were born and wouldn't even know where to start getting a job. And despite all his faults, Mark is a good dad. The girls simply idolize him. They would be crushed if Mark and I split."

"Megan, I'm not suggesting a divorce, but I do think the two of you should at least consider seeing a marriage counselor." Darrin juggled her cell from hand to hand as she began to change into a T-shirt and jeans.

"I've suggested that, but Mark ignores me. He says our marriage is just fine the way it is, that all couples experience the blahs after they have been married awhile, and there's no need for me to obsess about that." Megan held her hand over the phone and hollered upstairs, "Kathleen, I'll be there in a minute. I'm on the phone with Aunt Darrin. Sorry about that, Sis. Like I was saying, Mark tells me I'm getting all worked up about nothing."

"That's not what it sounds like to me. I mean, when was the last time the two of you went out to dinner by yourselves?"

There was a brief silence before Megan responded. "That's a good question. I can't tell you the last time."

"How about your sex life, Megan?"

"I could say that's none of your business, but I know you're just trying to help. The answer is it's been forever since we had sex. And believe me, it hasn't been me. I've tried to get something going on countless occasions. Mark's always too tired, got surgery early the next morning—always has some lame excuse. Finally I just gave up." Megan paused and took a deep breath before continuing. "Going back to the divorce thing, I think

236

another reason I've been so reluctant to even think about it is how we were raised—you know, being Catholic and all."

"I figured that might have something to do with it," Darrin replied.

"So how did you deal with that issue when you went through your divorce?"

"I'm not going to lie. It was very tough on me. I went on a major-league guilt trip for literally months—felt dirty, like I was this terrible sinner who had betrayed God. And that couldn't have been further from the truth. We were both so young and just had no idea what we were getting into. We made a mistake, pure and simple." Darrin sighed.

"Do you even go to church anymore?"

"I haven't set foot inside the Catholic Church, or any church for that matter, since I was reminded by the priest that I could not take communion, nor could I date or marry—at least, not without being considered an adulteress in the eyes of the church. Of course, all that would go away if I jumped through all the hoops to get an annulment. It just didn't make any sense to me—plus, it hurt like hell—so I just quit going. I got tired of getting beat up mentally when I didn't really feel I had done anything other than make a mistake."

"I remember how depressed you were. I was worried about you. I don't want to have to go through what you did. And I've got Karly and Kathleen to think about. They're already a little confused about this religion thing as it is—you know, with Mark being Jewish and me being Catholic."

"How are you handling that, anyway?" Darrin asked.

"Mark insisted that we alternate taking them to synagogue and to church and then, when they get a little older, let them decide for themselves."

"Sounds good in theory, but I—"

Megan interrupted, "It's a frigging nightmare. At Sunday school they are taught that Jesus is the Messiah and the path to heaven is only through Him and that those who don't believe that are going straight to hell. At synagogue, they are taught the Messiah has yet to come, that Jesus was a wise, good man but nothing more. I can't tell you how many questions the girls have thrown at me right before bedtime. Questions like 'Is Daddy going to hell?' 'Why doesn't Daddy believe in Jesus?' It's just awful."

"How do you answer questions like that?" Darrin asked in a troubled tone.

"I try to change the subject, but the girls are becoming more persistent as they get older. They want answers, and I simply don't have any. I mean, why does the Catholic Church teach them that their father is going to hell simply because he doesn't believe what they do?"

"Wow. I'm sure they are totally confused. I can't even wrap my head around religion anymore."

"You're not saying you're an atheist, are you?"

Darrin laughed softly before responding. "Don't worry, Megan. My faith in God is stronger now than it has ever been. I'd be lying, however, if I didn't say I have a real problem with organized religion in general, with all of its exclusionary rules, man-created dogmas, and meaningless rituals. Take this case I'm working on right now. It involves the Brimstone Bible Church and its leader, Ezekiel Shaw. They believe that women should be doormats and do whatever men tell them to. During his deposition, this Shaw guy rattled off a bunch of Scripture to support his position. When I was going through his testimony for Jace, I got out my Bible and read every passage he quoted. I was shocked. The verses say women should be submissive to men, that they shouldn't speak in church, and they should ask men if they have any religious questions."

"I don't remember any verses like that . . ."

"Trust me – they are there in black and white. But they were written literally thousands of years ago—by men, I might add—when women were considered little more than slaves. And, interestingly, not one of these verses was attributed directly to Jesus. They were mostly parts of letters written to the early Christians by Paul. And they should be interpreted in that context."

"But you do believe the Bible is the word of God, don't you?" Megan asked.

"You know, this case has really gotten me thinking. I am doing something I am ashamed to admit I have never done before. I am reading the Bible—word for word—from beginning to end. I've got these study guides I'm using as I go through it. It's hard to do, with all I've got going on at work, but I'm trying to spend an hour before going to bed studying the Bible. As far as whether I think it's the word of God, the jury's still out on that. I will let you know what I come up with once I'm finished."

"Wow, my sister, the biblical scholar," Megan joked, lightening the conversation. "Speaking of scholars, what's going on with Jace?"

"We've both been working really hard on this new case. That investigator down in Austin is still involved, but there's nothing I can really do about that right now. I have to admit—she's damn good and we need her right now. She just came up with a lead that could give us a big break in the case and—"

Megan interrupted. "You better keep an eye on her. She could be trouble."

"I'm no fool. I know that. I confronted Jace about her the other day."

"And?"

"Told me he liked her but everything was strictly professional – no hanky-panky going on."

"Did you believe him?"

"Sort of. But you know men. They sometimes let the little head do all the thinking."

Megan laughed. "No doubt about that. So why don't you give him some of his own medicine?"

"What do you mean?" Darrin asked, her interest piqued.

"Well, you could continue to work there *and* date other guys? Who knows? Making Jace a little jealous might be a good thing for your relationship – cause him to see things a little more clearly. Or you might meet someone else—"

Darrin didn't wait for her to finish. "No way I could do that. It would be torture for both of us. And no doubt the quality of my work would suffer. Besides, I don't want to go back to the dating scene."

"I don't know. If I didn't have to worry about money and going to hell," Megan laughed, "I would seriously consider taking the girls and leaving Mark. I think I would actually enjoy dating around before I get too old. I miss having some affection from the opposite sex, not to mention the fact that I'm horny as hell."

Darrin joined in the laughter. "Be careful what you wish for."

Megan interrupted, "So let's get back to ol' Jace. At some point didn't you tell me he had been fooling around with some young lawyer in the firm?"

"Yeah, there was this young associate, I can't even remember her name. They were working on a big securities case together, traveling all over the country taking depositions. I didn't put two and two together at the time. But the associate left the firm abruptly without any explanation. There was a lot of office chatter for several weeks afterwards, but then things died down."

"Didn't you tell me Jace blames himself for his wife's death?"

"He hasn't come right out and said that, but that's my sense."

"He probably feels the affair he was having caused the whole thing, and he can't get over that."

"That's a possibility but I don't think so. The associate left the firm months before his wife's accident."

"I don't get it. Then why would Jace feel responsible?"

"One night over dinner he told me that, right before she died, they had been fighting. Jace didn't tell me what it was about, and I didn't ask. I do know it was heated enough that Camille stormed out of the house, jumped into her car in a torrential downpour, and plowed into an eighteen-wheeler on the interstate. It was all over the Fort Worth Star-Telegram the next morning."

Megan shuddered. "That's awful."

"To make matters worse, Jace's son Matt was home at the time and heard the whole thing. He has never forgiven Jace."

"Not good."

"Nope, it isn't. Probably part of the reason Matt dropped out of UT and joined the SEALs."

Megan exclaimed, "For crying out loud! Well, I can't help but feel a little sympathy for ol' Jace. But it's pretty concerning, Darrin. I mean, how do you know he won't do the same thing to you?"

"I don't."

"This is a tough one. Well, we're not going to solve all of our problems tonight. And I've got to go check on the kids. If you need to talk, don't hesitate to give me a call."

After the call ended, Darrin gazed off into space, her thoughts still focused on Jace. The safe thing to do would be to help him get through this trial and then turn in her notice. She could move back to Houston, find a new job, get a new start. And there would be no more personal relationships at work – way too complicated. Too many land mines in the way. But that was a decision for another day. No need to rush it. She got up from the sofa and made her way to the kitchen for a late dinner and a glass or two of wine to dull the pain.

CHAPTER

42

Leah looked at the caller id on her office phone—"unknown."
She hesitated a moment before picking up the receiver. "Leah
Rosen."

"Ms. Rosen, my name is Berry Spitz. I am an attorney in
Topeka, Kansas, and I've been doing some legal work for Dr.
Seth Coleman. I believe you know him?" A pause.

Leah sat up straight in her chair and grabbed a pen and notepad from her desk drawer before responding. "Yes, I know Dr.
Coleman. How can I help you?"

"Dr. Coleman asked me to review some papers you gave him
during a trip you made to Topeka and to contact you regarding
my findings."

"And your client authorized you to discuss them with me?"

"He did."

"And?"

"I determined that the affidavit you gave him that Dr. Howell
Crimm filed in that Zilantin case was identical to the one the

court clerk was kind enough to fax me. Please don't take offense, but he wanted to make sure you hadn't altered the document in some way. You have to remember—he doesn't know you and is generally distrustful of the media."

"Mr. Spitz, I would never consider falsifying a document to get a story," Leah said emphatically.

"And my client never told me he thought that. He was understandably shocked when he read that affidavit you gave him. He just wanted me to make sure it was a genuine court document. He worked as the research assistant for Dr. Crimm while he was in med school and had great admiration for him. Dr. Coleman just couldn't believe Dr. Crimm might do something like that and hired me to conduct a very limited investigation to determine what happened. Dr. Coleman is a very ethical man, and the last thing he would ever want is for his research to be distorted and used in an illegal manner."

"I can understand that. And that's exactly what happened. Crimm distorted Dr. Coleman's findings and then perjured himself by filing that affidavit I gave your client."

"It appears that way. Dr. Coleman is now concerned about what repercussions this false affidavit might have for him and his practice."

"I assume you advised him that if this fraud starts to unravel, and it is only a matter of time before it does, Crimm will try to make him the fall guy."

"I can't discuss the advice I gave him, since our conversations are covered by the attorney-client privilege. That being said, he has authorized me to tell you that he will do whatever he can to help you right this wrong. He is willing to sign an affidavit or testify before a grand jury if that is what it comes to."

"Mr. Spitz, I want to be honest with you. We're dealing with some very desperate and dangerous people here, people who have a lot to lose if the truth comes out."

"What do you mean?"

"Just what I said. They will do whatever it takes to keep the lid on their scheme." Leah paused before continuing. "Several nights ago, I was assaulted and threatened. My assailant told me to lay off the story or I would be sorry—very sorry."

A gasp.

"It was the worst experience of my life—absolutely terrifying."

"Are you considering dropping the story?"

"That's certainly crossed my mind, but I haven't decided yet. Honestly, I don't know if I have the guts to finish it."

"I can certainly understand that."

"Mr. Spitz, is this the best number for me to reach you?"

"It's my cell. I keep it with me most of the time."

"Good. I should know something in the next few days after my boss and I have made a decision about the story."

"I'll be looking for your call. Thank you, Ms. Rosen."

Before Leah could replace the receiver, Jackie called.

"Leah, it's Jackie. I have great news. I know who attacked you!"

"Jackie, that's fantastic! Have the police arrested him?"

"Not yet. We've got to find him first. It was that PI out in L.A. I was telling you about. Randazzo, Michael Randazzo. I'm working with Officer Gomez on finding him. Gomez's sources have determined he is back in L.A. going about business as usual. We'll have to work with the LAPD to nab him and then move to extradite him to Travis County, where the assault occurred."

Leah shuddered. "When do you think you'll know something?"

"The next day or so. Gomez and I are all over it."

"Call me as soon as—"

Jackie interrupted. "You'll be the first to know."

Leah disconnected the call and headed to Abe's office. She knocked on his door before entering.

"Leah, come in. What's up?"

"Seth Coleman is ready to turn on Crimm."

"How do you know?"

"I just got a call from his lawyer."

"Well, there's another corroborating source for your story."

"I know, Abe. But I'm still scared."

"I would be too. Not many people have had to experience what you went through."

"I do have some good news that makes me feel a little safer. Jackie called and she thinks she knows the name of that son-of-a-bitch..." Leah's voice trailed off and her eyes began to water. Abe rose from his chair, walked quickly toward her and put his arms around her. Leah buried her face into his chest and began to sob softly.

"Everything is going to be alright, I promise. Forget that story. It's just not worth the risk."

Leah pulled away gently and looked up into his comforting eyes. "It's not that easy, Abe. These people have got to be stopped. And I may be the only one who can do it."

"This is no time to play martyr, Leah."

Leah walked toward the windows in Abe's office and, with her back to him, answered defiantly. "I'm not trying to play anything. I just want to bring down Connors and his bitch of a daughter. After what I've gone through, it's become personal. I want to see them both go to jail for the rest of their lives. If I did nothing, knowing what I know now, I could never forgive myself."

Abe was speechless.

"You and Blumenthal will definitely run the story if Coleman delivers, won't you?"

"You have my word on it," Abe replied.

"Good. Let's see if Jackie can catch that bastard. If she does, it's all over for the Connors clan."

CHAPTER

43

"Y ou've reached Security Plus. How may I direct your call?"

"Morris Weintraub."

"Who may I say is calling?"

"Jamie Stein.

"Just a moment, please."

"Jamie, so good to hear from you. How are you, my friend?"

"Not so good."

"How can I be of help?"

Jamie took a deep breath and said, "Morris, I'm getting out of here."

"Hartford weather getting to you?"

"You might say that."

"Where you going?"

"France."

"France?" Morris was unable to hide his surprise. "Well, I've always been a sucker for French women. They have a way about them. I don't mean to pry, Jamie—I mean, it's none of my business—but why France?"

"No extradition treaty."

"That's good to know. So why the sudden move?"

"Let's just say it is getting way too hot here."

"I understand. So how can I help?" Morris inquired.

"I need two things. I want you to wire one of the three payments I get to a different account, one in France. I'll call you with all the information once I get there and get it set up. On the others —just continue what you've been doing."

"Not a problem. What's the second thing?"

"Once the dust settles, I want you to sell a car for me, a Ferrari convertible."

"Nice. You have good taste, my friend. It's not hot, is it?"

"Nope, clean as a whistle."

"Where you keeping it?"

"It's parked in a rental facility nearby. I hate to give it up, but I won't be able to get it to France. I'll give you fifty percent of whatever we net on the sale. There's a bank lien against it. I can't remember exactly how much that is."

"That's a generous proposal. How will I get the keys to the car and the rental space?"

"I'll make arrangements to get them to you. And Morris, thanks for everything. You've been like a father to me. When Dad died, you took care of Mom and me. And I'll never forget that."

"Your father was a great man and a dear friend."

"I do want you to know, though, I have a little insurance to make sure you follow through for me. You taught me well. The deals we have done together, including this one—I have files on every one. And if you were to screw me, well, I wouldn't have any other choice but to send them to the feds."

"Jamie, I have taught you well. Don't worry. Nothing can destroy what we have." Morris paused. "I wish you all the luck in the world. I will miss you."

"Thanks, Morris. You'll be hearing from me about the wiring instructions and car keys sometime next week."

After the call ended, Jamie glanced around his apartment and smirked. He was glad to close this chapter of his life and open a new one. He grabbed a suitcase in each hand and headed out the door. His flight from Hartford to Paris was scheduled to depart in a little under four hours, and he couldn't afford to be late.

Michael Randazzo sat alone in one of the stark interrogation rooms of the modern headquarters of the Los Angeles Police Department. He stared blankly at the wall in front of him, his expression giving no clues as to his thoughts. The door abruptly swung open and LAPD officer Theresa Flannigan walked in, followed by Jorge and Jackie. Officer Flannigan sat down in the chair across the table from Randazzo. Jackie and Jorge remained standing.

Randazzo blurted out, "I want my lawyer. It's my constitutional right. You know, the 'one call' rule."

Officer Flannigan calmly responded, "I know, Mr. Randazzo. And you'll get your call in due time. Right now, we'd like to ask you a few preliminary questions, that's all."

Randazzo persisted. "I said I want my fucking lawyer. How hard is that to understand?"

Officer Flannigan ignored the comment. "Do you know a Mr. Cal Connors?"

Randazzo said nothing and kept staring at the wall in front of him.

Officer Flannigan continued. "After you answer a few of my preliminary questions, I will let you call your lawyer. Until you do, no dice. Now, let's try this again. Do you know a Cal Connors?"

"All right, Ms. Big Shot, we'll play it your way for a little while. I never heard of the guy."

"How about Christine Connors?"

"Same fucking answer."

"Have you been to Texas recently?"

"What business is it of yours?"

"Please answer the question, Mr. Randazzo."

"No, I haven't."

"Does the name Leah Rosen mean anything to you?"

Jackie watched Randazzo's expression closely. His vacuous, shark-like eyes gave away nothing. "Never heard of the bitch."

"Mr. Randazzo, is that a tattoo on your neck?"

"Good guess, Sherlock."

"Where and when did you get it?"

"None of your damn business. Now, either let me go or let me call my lawyer—one of the two."

"Not quite yet." Officer Flannigan pulled out her cell phone from her pocket and quickly snapped a series of close-ups of the tattoo on Randazzo's neck.

"Hey, you can't do that. You don't have a search warrant."

"I don't need a warrant. Looks like your initials, am I right?"

In response, Randazzo folded his arms defiantly and leaned back in his chair. He ignored the question and continued to stare straight ahead as Officer Flannigan and her cohorts left the room. Flannigan led the way to the observation area adjacent to the interrogation room. They could see Randazzo through the one-way window at the far side of the room.

Flannigan was the first to speak. "Well, it looks like we've got the right man."

"No doubt about it," Jorge replied. "That tattoo is a perfect match with the one on the assailant in the surveillance video. And I'd like to get a recording of your questioning today, if that's possible. We can use the voice recognition software we have back at the department to compare Randazzo's voice with the one we have on tape."

"I'll get it for you before you leave," Flannigan responded.

"And the photos you took today, could you email me copies?" Jackie asked.

"No problem." Officer Flannigan smiled. "Jackie, you and Officer Gomez wouldn't mind if I personally tell that son of a bitch he's being extradited to Texas for trial? We've been trying to nail him here for years, but he's always covered his tracks."

"Be our guest," Jackie replied, a smile creasing her lips.

Flannigan turned toward the door. "Let's not keep Mr. Randazzo waiting."

As the LAPD squad car zigzagged through traffic on its way to LAX, Jackie called Leah. "We got him! He'll be in the Austin jail in a matter of hours." She smiled as she listened to the response on the other end of the line. "You're welcome. I'll call you when he's behind bars." Jackie ended the call and turned to Jorge. "Feels damn good, doesn't it?"

"It'll feel a lot better when that jury comes back with a guilty verdict. Guys like Randazzo usually hire the best lawyers in the business. It's always tough to get a conviction."

"But our evidence is rock solid, you know that."

"I know that, and you know that. But what twelve people will do after the facts get all twisted around—well, that's anybody's guess."

"There is some peace in knowing we've done our job."

"Yeah, there is. Let's just hope the judicial system does its job as well as we did ours."

CHAPTER

44

Andrew James hit the intercom button. "Yes, Bev?"

His secretary responded. "Ruth Danner is on the line."

"I'll take it." Andrew grabbed the receiver and cradled it between his ear and shoulder while he signed the expense report in front of him. "Ruth, good to hear from you. Have you completed your research?" He swung his tasseled loafers up on the desk in front and leaned back in his swivel chair.

"I have, Mr. James."

"And what did you learn?"

"I scoured the Internet and couldn't find anyone renting Ferraris with a Brooklyn address. Stein is right, though—there are a lot of people in the business. I found people renting out Mercedes, Lamborghinis, Porsches—I could go on. Just no one that I could find in Brooklyn renting a red Ferrari convertible."

"That's what I thought you'd come up with. So Mr. Stein is lying—that's what you're telling me, isn't it?"

"That's certainly what it appears. I'm pretty confident in my research but can't be one hundred percent sure. It's always possible that the person who rented to Stein isn't doing it anymore or quit listing on the Internet. Who knows?"

"Well, I'll take that chance. Ruth, put your findings in a confidential memorandum in an envelope addressed to me and give it to my secretary."

"I'll get it done this afternoon, Mr. James."

"Perfect. And Ruth, I can't thank you enough for the excellent work you've done. I appreciate it and Empire Risk appreciates it. I will be sure and put a note in your file that I promise you will carry great weight come review time."

"Thank you, sir."

Andrew hit the disconnect button and then buzzed his secretary. "Get Weldon Trapp on the phone for me." Seconds later, he was on the line.

"Weldon, how are things at the firm?"

"Busy as always. It's good to hear from you, Andrew."

"I need your help."

"What can I do for you?"

Andrew described what his investigation had turned up about Jamie Stein. He ended by saying, "I want this guy behind bars, and I will do whatever it takes to make that happen. We need to make an example of him."

"Well, we can file a civil suit, which will break him financially and, at the same time, turn the matter over to the U.S. attorney in Hartford. He and I went to Columbia Law School together, and I have no doubt he will give the matter top priority."

"Excellent. And I want you to look into the Connors firm involvement in this. In a scheme like this one, it takes two to tango, and I want everyone who had a hand in it behind bars. I want to send a clear message that no one fucks with me, or this company."

"Understood. But it will be expensive. Remember, I'm billing out at nine hundred and fifty dollars an hour."

"That's not a problem. If my suspicions prove true, we are talking millions Stein and those shysters stole from this company. If we nail them, I'll get all of that back, plus your fees, from our fiduciary insurance carrier."

"I didn't think of that but you are right, Andrew. I'll put a team together and get right on this."

"Keep me posted every step of the way, Weldon."

"Will do."

As Andrew replaced the receiver, American flight number 2250 left the tarmac and began to gain altitude. It would land in Paris seven hours and fifty-seven minutes later. As the plane made its ascent, Jamie smiled, picturing himself on a beach in the south of France without a care in the world.

CHAPTER

45

"Megan, what a coincidence. I just walked in the door from work and was about to call you. How are you?"

"He's gone. That son of a bitch just walked out the door." Megan set her wine glass down on the kitchen counter and shuffled through the junk drawer. She found an old pack of cigarettes she was hoping was still there. With the phone between her shoulder and ear, she picked up her wineglass and walked to the stove, lit a cigarette, and chased it with a gulp of wine.

"What do you mean he's gone?"

"You were right, my marriage sucks." Megan took a drag off the cigarette and began coughing.

"Are you smoking a cigarette?"

"Cut me some slack, Darrin. I'm having a tough time here."

"I'm sorry Megan. Just tell me what's going on."

"Mark came home a little after seven. The girls are spending the night out so I thought it would be a good time for us talk. As usual, he told me he had had a rough day at work and wasn't in the mood for some heavy discussion - but I persisted. I poured us each a glass of wine and then went through, one by one, the problems with our marriage you and I talked about the other day."

"Like?" Darrin asked.

"The fact that he is never home, that we are like two ships passing in the night, that we never talk about anything but the kids, that we never go out." Megan stamped out the cigarette and took in a deep breath. "And that we hadn't had sex in months. That's when the shit hit the fan."

"What did he say?"

"He blamed everything on me. Can you believe that asshole? He told me I needed to lose some weight and make myself more attractive. I lost it, Darrin, I really did. I threw my wine right in his face."

Darrin audibly gasped.

"I know I shouldn't have, but I was just so pissed off! How could he blame everything on me? I mean, I weigh about five pounds more today than the day we were married. You know me - I play tennis every day, and do Yoga several times a week. I just couldn't believe it! It took a lot of nerve for him to say something like that to me." Megan shuddered angrily, reliving the scene.

"What did he do?"

"Without saying a word, he went into our bedroom, packed a bag, and headed toward the front door. I followed him every step of the way, trying to get him to talk to me. I remember telling him I thought he must be having an affair and he just looked at me and shook his head."

"Megan, I'm so sorry. I feel like this is partly my fault. I should have kept my mouth shut."

"No, Darrin, this needed to happen. Our marriage is in deep trouble and I need to do something. I can't just sit here, and pretend everything is alright when it isn't."

"Megan, you look awesome and you're a great mom. Mark should be scared to death of losing you. He's the one who should be scrambling to save your marriage."

"I've got the girls to think about. And I haven't had a paying job in years. Things have changed so much in the workplace, I wouldn't have a clue how to find a job. I'm not going to lie. I am scared shitless right now – for me and the girls."

"Well, you don't need to think about all that tonight. You need to get some sleep and call Mark in the morning. I'm sure he will want to talk. As I said, he's got a lot to lose here as well. Maybe what happened tonight will be a wake-up call for him. So, stop with the wine and start drinking water. And no more cigarettes – they will give you a nasty hangover. Go run a hot bath and relax."

"I don't know Darrin, you're probably right. Problems always loom large at night. Maybe Mark and I can work this out. And I know some of it's my fault. It takes two to destroy a marriage."

"Y'all have been married for a number of years now, some of the excitement is gone – although I'm no counselor, my bet is you're just going through some growing pains. It's nothing you and Mark can't work through. Now, go run that bath, and call me later if you can't sleep. Things will look a lot better in the morning, I promise."

"Thanks for being there for me, Sis. I'm going to be fine. Don't worry - I'll give you a call tomorrow. Night."

Megan hung up the phone, grabbed her purse and keys and rushed out the door leading to the garage. She was out of wine and cigarettes. She would need both to get her through the night.

CHAPTER

The receptionist at Connors & Connors buzzed in on the intercom. "Christine, there is someone here to see you."

"Who is it?"

"He wouldn't say. He just told me he was here to see you and Mr. Connors."

"Okay, we'll be right there."

Christine rose from her chair and marched out of her office toward the reception area. She stepped into her dad's office on the way. "We're wanted up front."

"What?"

"The receptionist just buzzed me. There's someone who wants to see us."

"I'm busy. Take care of it."

"She said they want to see me *and* you."

The Lone Wolf slid his boots off his desk, stood up, and sauntered toward his daughter, shaking his head as he approached her. "What in the hell for?"

"I'm not sure," Christine replied as she walked out of the office, her dad close behind.

As father and daughter entered the waiting area, a clean-cut, well-dressed young man rose to meet them. He turned first to Cal. "Are you Calvin Connors?"

"I am."

The young man handed him a document. "You've been served." He turned to Christine. "Are you Christine Connors?"

"I am."

"You've been served." The man handed a document to Christine, tipped his cowboy hat, and left.

Cal turned to his daughter. "Let's go back to my office." The two hurriedly made their way down the hall to Cal's office, closing the door behind them. "What is this shit?"

"Looks like they're subpoenas—for all of our records in the silica cases."

"I know what they are. But why in the hell did we get served with these? Christine, did you know that something like this might be coming?" Cal shook the document in his hand, threw it on his desk, and glared at his daughter.

"I didn't tell you because I didn't want to worry you. I thought it would go away."

"What in the hell are you talking about? I'm not following you." Cal turned away from Christine and walked to his office window. As he stared at the traffic below, he cautioned, "Quit beating around the bush. I want to know what's going on here, and I want to know right now!"

"Okay, okay. Here's what happened. Jamie Stein called me a few days ago. Some in-house lawyer at Empire Risk was snooping around, asking Jamie questions."

"What the hell for?"

"The idiot bought a Ferrari."

Cal shook his head in disgust. "He did *what*? That stupid bastard! I ought to wring the son-of-a-bitch's neck. This is a federal subpoena—this is serious shit!"

"It is. But we don't have anything to produce."

"What in the hell you talking about?" Cal turned back to face Christine. "I'm sure we have files on every single case we settled with that little prick."

"Did have. But they've all been destroyed—all of the files, every last piece of paper shredded."

"When did that happen?"

"Right after I got Stein's call."

A big smile crossed Cal's face. "Brilliant, my girl, absolutely brilliant. How about emails?"

"I reviewed all of them myself—nothing incriminating. But I had a tech guy in here yesterday. They've all been permanently deleted from our hard drive," Christine replied triumphantly.

"Phone records?"

"When Stein called the other day, he told me he was calling from a pay phone—untraceable to him. I double-checked to make sure."

"So what are we going to do about those," Cal cleared his throat, "payments we still owe him?"

"I haven't thought that through yet. Stein threatened to sing like a canary if we stopped making them."

"Where is the bastard now?" Cal's eyes narrowed.

"I'm not sure."

"Well, let's talk this thing through after it sinks in a little. We can't afford to be careless. No need to do anything rash."

"My sentiments exactly."

"Will you handle our response to the subpoenas?" Cal asked.

"It'll be pretty simple. How does 'ain't got none' sound?"

"I like it. Give your ol' dad a hug. Looks like we dodged a bullet." Cal put his arm around Christine's shoulders and pulled her close. "You are one smart cookie."

"I had one helluva teacher."

PART FOUR

CHAPTER

47

Leah heard a knock on her office door and, in an irritated voice, yelled, "Come in."

The door opened to a handsome man with chiseled features and salt-and-pepper hair. He was dressed casually in a plaid sports jacket, khakis, and tan Hush Puppies. Old-fashioned horn-rimmed glasses rested on his prominent nose, completing his Ivy-league appearance. "Is this a bad time?"

Leah's eyes widened in shock as she sprang from her chair. "Mr. Blumenthal, sorry, I didn't know it was you. I have this deadline—"

"No need to apologize, Leah. I know you're busy. And call me Steve, please. Let's have a seat. I would like to visit with you for a few minutes."

Leah smiled and eased back into her chair. Steve took the seat across from her.

"I have some good news for you. I've read the draft of your article on Mr. Connors. I believe the title you decided on is 'Texas Justice Gone Wrong'?"

Still in shock, Leah nodded.

"It's an excellent piece. Very well written—and meticulously documented, I might add. I carefully reviewed the affidavits you obtained from your sources. It's an understatement to say you covered all the bases. Abe has raved about your work from the time you started, and he was right in his assessment. You have a wonderful future here at *Texas Matters*."

"Thank you, Mr.— Steve." Leah laughed nervously. "Does this mean the article is going to print?"

"It does. It will be the cover story on this month's issue."

Leah gasped. "You've got to be kidding. I am so excited!"

"You should be. That's quite an achievement for someone at your experience level."

"Thank you! I've got to admit I didn't know whether *Texas Matters* would ever run the article."

"I believe Abe told you that Mr. Connors threatened me—not with violence but with a costly lawsuit."

"Yes, Abe told me."

"I imagine you thought I was caving to the pressure, but that couldn't have been further from the truth. I just wanted to make sure we had jumped through all the legal hoops so that any lawsuit this Connors fellow might file against us would be thrown out of court. And you've done that." Steve paused, his expression becoming more serious. "I know you have been through a lot lately. How are you doing?"

"Better. Much better."

"I'm glad to hear that. Even though business isn't great, this magazine will spare no expense to make sure its employees are safe."

"I appreciate that."

"One last thing. You know that, once we run the article, all hell is going to break loose. You'll be contacted by the authorities, you'll probably be sued individually, other publications may be in touch—it's going to be a wild ride."

"I know."

"Are you prepared for all that?"

"Comes with the territory."

Steve rose from his chair and re-buttoned his plaid blazer. "Congratulations, and thank you for a job well done."

"Thank you, Steve."

Leah's eyes followed as he turned and walked out the door. She picked up her cell and dialed Jackie's number.

"Leah, how are you?"

"Great! I just met with the head of *Texas Matters*. They're going to publish my article. It will be on this month's cover."

"Leah, congratulations! That is wonderful news."

"And one of the reasons I'm calling. What's the status of the Randazzo case?"

"I talked with Gomez a couple of days ago and he told me Randazzo pled not guilty. His lawyer is pushing for a quick trial. He swears there will be no plea bargain, his client is innocent."

"Is this guy grandstanding?"

"Of course. He's a lawyer, isn't he? But I don't think he's bluffing. He probably does want a quick trial. He's got a hell of a track record with juries, and the odds go up in his favor if the prosecution has less time to prepare. Plus he loves publicity—any kind of publicity."

Leah sighed. "I don't know what I'd do if that bastard walked, after what he did to me."

"I know, Leah. I've told Gomez to keep me updated. I'll let you know if I hear anything."

"Thanks, Jackie. I appreciate it."

"No problem. And congratulations again!"

"Thanks. Talk to you soon." Leah disconnected the call and shook her head. She was not going to let Randazzo ruin her day. She had finally made it! She was a real journalist, with her first byline coming out in a month. She planned to celebrate! She scrolled quickly through her contacts and made another call. "Chip, glad I caught you. You got any plans tonight?"

CHAPTER

48

Jace parked his Range Rover in a pay lot on Tenth Street in downtown Fort Worth, just blocks from the Eldon B. Mahon federal courthouse. After paying the attendant, he hurried toward the historic structure, built during the Great Depression and designed in the Art Moderne style. After entering the building and going through security, he waited impatiently for an elevator, glancing at his watch periodically. The Honorable Barbara Zimmerman had scheduled a pretrial conference for 1:30 and was a stickler about promptness. She had a busy docket and, by necessity, ran a tight ship; tardiness was taboo. She had been known to assess sanctions against late-arriving lawyers who lacked a compelling excuse. Jace walked through the doors to the ornate courtroom at precisely 1:25, breathed a sigh of relief, and took a seat at the counsel table on the right. He nodded at Crom, seated at the counsel table on the left, who responded with a snide grin.

Minutes later, the silence was broken by the bailiff announcing the entry of Judge Zimmerman. Counsel rose in deference as she stepped up to take her seat at the bench. The judge nodded, her face expressionless, and motioned for counsel to be seated. She glanced at the file in front of her and stated, "Let the record reflect that we are here today in the case styled *Jace Forman, Executor of the Estate of Eugene Hanson versus the Brimstone Bible Church and Ezekiel Shaw*. Are counsel ready to proceed?" She peered over the reading glasses perched on her nose, her dark brown eyes darting from Jace to his adversary and back again.

Both counsel rose, and Jace responded, "Plaintiff is ready, Your Honor."

Crom echoed, "Defense is ready, Your Honor."

"This case is set for trial on Monday, and I note that neither party has moved for a continuance. I take it you are ready to proceed."

Both lawyers nodded.

"All right then. I've reviewed the file and note for the record that I see no motions that have not been ruled upon, am I correct?"

"Your Honor, with all due respect," said Crom, "the defendants would like to re-urge their motion for summary judgment on First Amendment grounds. As stated in our motion, we believe the U.S. Supreme Court's decision in the Westboro case is dispositive of the plaintiff's claims in their entirety."

"Mr. Prater, I read your motion carefully and all the cases you cited. I admit, my call was a close one. But I've made it. Your motion was denied and my mind remains unchanged. Motion to reconsider overruled." Judge Zimmerman paused and turned her attention toward Jace. "Mr. Forman, you did read my opinion carefully, did you not?"

"I did, Your Honor."

"I'm very reluctant to deprive a litigant of his or her day in court, which in part explains why I denied Mr. Prater's motion.

That being said, if you don't come up with additional evidence that this protest was more personal in nature—and by that I mean directed at your clients and their deceased daughter—I will strongly, and let me repeat 'strongly,' entertain a motion for directed verdict. That's not to say I agree with the Westboro decision, but it's the law of the land and I'm obligated to follow it."

Jace swallowed before responding, "I understand, Your Honor."

"Good. Let's turn to the joint pretrial order you have filed. Either of you have any comments regarding that?"

Crom rose. "Yes, Your Honor. I have a problem with Mr. Forman's witness designations. I don't think they are specific enough."

Judge Zimmerman thumbed through the order until she found the section she was looking for. "Okay, now what's your objection?"

"Mr. Forman has designated all of the current and former members of the Brimstone Bible Church as potential witnesses. I think that is way too vague. It doesn't give me adequate notice of who he intends to call."

"Mr. Forman, he does have a point. Couldn't you be a little more specific?"

Jace stood. "Your Honor, Mr. Prater knows who the current and past members of the BBC are. I'm not hiding the ball here. And I'm not required to give opposing counsel a blueprint of my trial strategy. That's apparently what he wants this court to order me to do."

"Mr. Prater, don't you know who the current and past members of the BBC are?"

"Yes, Your Honor, but—"

"I'll overrule your objection. Any other matter you would like for me to rule on before I distribute the prospective juror lists?"

Crom was up again. "Yes, Your Honor. Mr. Forman has listed the affidavit of Eugene Hanson that was filed in opposition to my motion for summary judgment as an evidentiary exhibit."

Judge Zimmerman nodded. "Yes, I saw that."

"Well, Your Honor, Mr. Hanson's affidavit is the rankest form of hearsay."

Jace jumped up, and the judge motioned for him sit back down.

"But, Mr. Prater, his client is deceased and can't testify. I will allow its admission under several exceptions to the hearsay rule. That's Evidence 101, Mr. Prater. Anything else?"

"Your Honor, as you know, Mr. Hanson was shot by the police at a protest my client staged in Norman, Oklahoma. He had gone there to kill as many BBC members as he could, including Mr. Shaw. I believe that his actions should come into evidence."

"The court is aware of Mr. Hanson's unfortunate death. But what does that have to do with whether your clients' conduct at the protest in Hagstrom is actionable under the Westboro decision?"

Crom searched for a response. Jace came unexpectedly to his rescue. "I think the fact that my client went to the rally in Norman with the thought of possibly attacking the protesters should be admitted as evidence. It demonstrates the mental anguish my client was going through as a result of the BBC's actions, so I will not object to its introduction."

Realizing his blunder, Crom tried to backpedal. "Your Honor—"

Judge Zimmerman interrupted. "The evidence will be admitted then. Well, if there is nothing else either of you would like to bring to my attention, I would like to turn to jury selection."

She nodded to the bailiff, who rose and delivered jury lists to counsel. They eagerly began to flip through the pages.

"I have decided that, due to the publicity this case has generated, I should call up seventy-five prospective jurors. Their names and background information are on the lists my bailiff has just handed you. I will seat six jurors and two alternates from that list. Questions?"

There were none.

"I assume there is no need to admonish you about making any direct or indirect contact with any of these prospective jurors."

Both counsel shook their heads emphatically.

"We will commence jury selection promptly at nine o'clock on Monday morning." She shot a warning glare to Jace, who smiled back. "I guess there's no chance of settlement?"

Crom was the first to respond. "It would be a cold day—"

"I get it. See you gentlemen on Monday. Have a good weekend." Judge Zimmerman rose from the bench and disappeared behind the door leading to her chambers.

"Well, Jace, you ready for an old fashioned ass-whupping?" Crom grinned in Jace's direction.

"Talk is cheap, Crom. Talk is cheap." Jace grabbed his briefcase and headed toward the door.

J ace burst into the conference room. Seated at the table were Darrin; Lisa Sedgwick, their jury consultant; and Boyce Ramey, their in-house investigator. Darrin was the first to speak. "So how was Judge Zimmerman?"

"What can I say? She was Judge Zimmerman—no bullshit, right on with her rulings, fair as always. But she doesn't think much of our case, and she was pretty clear about her feelings."

"And right now we don't have anything else to give her. Any developments on getting Maddy Murphy to testify?" Darrin asked.

Lisa interrupted. "Who's Maddy Murphy?"

"She defected from the BBC and likely knows where all their skeletons are."

"So why won't she testify?" Lisa asked.

"She's afraid of the leader of this cult. And I can't say I blame her," Jace replied.

"So why is she afraid of him? He hasn't killed anyone, has he?"

"Not that we know of, but there is no telling what he's done to the female members of that group."

Lisa said, "Sure would be nice if we could get her to testify. If the head of the BBC is molesting girls, the jury will find any way they can to decide against him and award millions in damages. Maddy's testimony could be dynamite."

Jace responded, "I know, I know. But we're trying not to spook her. If we push too hard, she might disappear, and then there'd be no chance of getting her on the stand. I'll be in touch with my investigator in Austin over the weekend and find out where we are."

Boyce volunteered, "Why do we need this Austin investigator anyway? Let me talk with Ms. Murphy."

Sensing Boyce's displeasure over his territory being encroached upon, Jace tried to mollify his longtime sleuth. "I'll keep that in mind, Boyce. We just thought Maddy might be less intimidated by a female detective," Jace lied convincingly, and then pivoted to another topic. "Well, we now have the jury list." He slid copies to everyone at the table.

Lisa thumbed quickly through the pages. "Wow, there are a lot of prospective jurors. I guess the judge is concerned about the publicity."

"That's what she said. And she's probably right."

"Will we get the usual number of strikes?"

"Yep. Lisa, I would like for you to go over the list this week-end. Make notes in the margins about any problem jurors that we definitely want to get rid of. If you see a basis for a challenge for cause, write down what it is. Also, put an asterisk next to anyone you feel would be a great juror for us and detail why."

"Agreed."

"Boyce, I want you to get as much additional information on these people as you can. Drive by their houses, make notes about the cars they drive, the neighborhoods they live in, anything else you think might be helpful."

Lisa chimed in, "And see if any of their cars have bumper stickers. Research shows bumper stickers indicate a person holds firm opinions and wants the world to know about them. Typically, I don't want jurors like that unless I'm damn sure they're in my camp. If they go the other way, they tend to be very vocal in the jury room and are unlikely to change their minds."

Jace began to gather his papers. "Okay then. Let's meet in this conference room on Sunday afternoon at two. Is that good for everyone?"

Lisa responded, "Works for me."

Darrin and Boyce nodded.

"Well, we've got a lot to do between now and then. Darrin, let's meet in my office for a few minutes. I want to discuss trial logistics."

"Sure."

CHAPTER

The phone rang in Shaw's office. He put down the book he
was reading and answered, "Ezekiel Shaw."

"Ezekiel, this is Crom Prater."

"Crom, good to hear from you. What's on your mind?"

"I am on my way back from the courthouse. Judge Zimmerman
just conducted a pretrial in your case."

"I see. How did it go?"

"All right. I re-urged our motion for summary judgment."

"And?"

"The judge denied my motion, which is what I expected.
Judge Zimmerman rarely, if ever, changes her mind."

"That's too bad. I just don't see how she could do that in light
of the Supreme Court holding in the Westboro case."

"Neither do I. She did volunteer that she just doesn't like summary judgments. Bottom line, she wants juries to decide cases,
not judges."

"It's unfortunate we don't have a judge who adheres to the law. What else happened?"

"I objected to Forman's witness designation. It wasn't specific enough."

"In what respect?"

"He designated all of the current and former members of your church."

"That's preposterous. My flock won't help his case at all."

"This is a guess, but I don't think he's interested in your current flock. Have any of your sheep strayed?" Crom was proud of himself for continuing the metaphor.

Shaw cleared his throat. "That is none of your concern."

"Oh, but it is. I hate surprises. The worst thing that could happen would be for some loose cannon you haven't told me about to show up at trial and torpedo us."

"That won't happen."

"How can you be so sure?"

"Crom, are you always so distrustful of your clients?"

"It's not a question of being distrustful. You've got a lot riding on this trial, and I want to win it for you. I can't do that if you don't share everything with me, the good and the bad."

"I promise—swear, if that would make you feel more comfortable—that there will be no surprises at trial. Does that make you feel any better?"

"A little."

"When should I plan on coming to Fort Worth?"

"I need you here on Sunday afternoon. I want to prepare you for Forman's cross-examination, and I won't have time to do that once the trial gets cranked up."

"I can handle Forman. He's a lightweight."

"Don't underestimate him. He's one of the best trial lawyers in Fort Worth."

"I saw him in action at my deposition. I was unimpressed, and I'm a very good judge of character. He's easily intimidated—backs off quickly if he runs into a little resistance. Don't worry. I'll be more than ready for Mr. Forman. So tell me what's going to happen next week?"

"On Monday, we'll pick a jury. That'll probably take all day. Then on Tuesday Forman and I will give our opening statements."

"Have you prepared yours?"

"I have a good idea what I'm going to say, but since Forman goes first, I want to be flexible."

"Send me what you've prepared. I may have suggestions."

"I don't usually—"

"I don't care what you usually do. Send me a draft of your opening. I don't want you to say anything that could be contradictory to our dogma."

"It's in outline form."

"That's fine. I just want to get an idea of what you're going to say. What happens next?"

"After we open, Forman will put on his case."

"And that's when he might call me?"

"As an adverse witness."

"Of course. I look forward to it. Is there anything else you need to tell me?"

"I brought up the attempt on your life. I told the judge we wanted to put on evidence of what Hanson was up to."

"And?"

"It's coming in."

"Good. It'll show what a nutcase that guy was."

"That's what we'll argue. So can you be in my office at two on Sunday?"

"I'll move our Sunday service to Saturday, so that shouldn't be a problem. And Crom?"

"Yes?"

"Don't lose any sleep over surprise witnesses, because there won't be any. You already know everything the jury will hear."

"See you Sunday."

"Afternoon, Crom."

Ezekiel hung up the phone and picked up the Bible from his desk. He quickly flipped to a familiar passage and smiled—it should do the trick. He would meet with Sister Rebekah tonight and show her God's way. And His will would be done—the sooner, the better.

Sister Rebekah, her eyes closed and head bowed, knelt at a crude altar constructed in a corner of Shaw's bedroom. She was dressed in a white robe, her feet bare. Atop the altar was a carved wooden statue depicting Jesus' skeletal frame nailed to a crucifix, his head bowed, a crown of thorns drawing blood from his soiled forehead. Candles flickered on both sides of the statue, and incense filled the air. Shaw was standing next to Sister Rebekah, his hands clasped in front, his eyes tightly shut. After several moments of silence, he spoke. "Sister Rebekah, you may open your eyes now."

Sister Rebekah obeyed, her eyes cast downward.

"Now, look up at your true savior."

She looked up at the statue adorning the altar.

"Do you love him, Sister Rebekah?"

"I do, with all my heart and soul."

"Do you believe he has a plan for you?"

"I do."

"Do you know what that plan is?"

"To follow his word."

"That's right, Sister Rebekah. And do you know what it means to follow his word?"

"I try."

"Sister Rebekah, do you believe in revelations?"

"I do believe in revelations. They are mentioned all throughout the Bible. God speaks to people on earth."

"Sister Rebekah, look at me."

She turned her head and looked deeply into his entrancing eyes.

"I received a revelation from our Lord last night. And it was about you and how you could serve him. Do you believe that?"

"Of course I do."

"He has a mission for you, a very important mission. Will you agree to undertake it without knowing what it is?"

"I will." Her voice was firm.

"Let me read a passage from the Gospel of Matthew. I think it will make things become very clear to you."

Sister Rebekah watched intently as Shaw picked up his Bible, found a bookmark, and opened the pages to the designated chapter and verse.

"I am reading from Matthew, chapter 10, verses 34 through 39. 'Do not think that I have come to bring peace to the earth. I have not come to bring peace, but a sword.'" He paused. "Sister Rebekah, do you believe the Lord when he says that there are times when violence is necessary to do his will?"

She nodded emphatically. "Isn't that why we believe God sends our country's troops back to us in body bags? To send our nation a message that what we are doing is sinful?"

"Amen, Sister, amen. Let me continue with God's word. 'For I have come to set a man against his father, and a daughter against her mother, and a daughter-in-law against a mother-in-law. And a person's enemies will be of his own household.' I am still reading from Matthew, chapter 10. Do you understand what Jesus is telling us in these verses?"

Sister Rebekah responded, "I believe so."

"And do you, Sister, think the Lord is telling us that family members must, at times, turn against each other for his own sake?"

"That's what these verses say to me."

"And do you believe that God's word, as expressed in the Bible, should be interpreted as it is written?"

"I do, Savior Shaw. Of course I do. We are not free to disregard what God has inspired man to write. We cannot simply ignore what he tells us to do in clear language, even if it is difficult for us."

"Let me continue with the Scripture. 'And a person's enemies will be those of his own household. Whoever loves father or mother more than me is not worthy of me, and'—listen carefully, Sister Rebekah—'whoever loves son or daughter more than me is not worthy of me.' What does that mean to you?"

"That we should do God's will over and above anything else." She swallowed before continuing. "Even if that means hurting a family member."

"Good. That's what it means to me as well. I would like to conclude our reading with two more verses." He looked deeply into the eyes of his follower before continuing. "'And whoever does not take his cross and follow me is not worthy of me. Whoever finds his life will lose it, and whoever loses his life for my sake will find it.' So sayeth the Lord. Amen."

Sister Rebekah repeated, "Amen."

"You know that your daughter has lost her way, don't you?"

She nodded.

"And you went to her and tried to get her to repent, to bring her back into the fold. And she refused, isn't that correct?"

Tears began to form in the corners of Sister Rebekah's eyes. "I tried my best, but she just wouldn't listen."

Shaw frowned as he shook his head. "The Lord came to me in a dream last night. He told me that our mission would be placed in jeopardy if we did nothing when betrayed by members of our own flock. As her mother, it's up to you to set things right. Do you understand what I'm saying?"

"I don't know if . . ."

"Of course you can, with God's help. You are willing to take up his cross and follow him, aren't you?"

"I am."

"Even it means sacrificing your own daughter, a daughter who has turned against you, your church, and your Lord?"

Sister Rebekah wiped the tears from her eyes with the sleeve of her robe. She regained her composure and, in a firm voice, answered, "If that's God's will."

"It is, Sister Rebekah, it is. Now rise." As she stood, Shaw gripped her shoulders and turned her toward him, his face inches from hers. "You must not delay."

"I'll leave tomorrow at dawn."

"May God be with you. May he shine his light upon you and give you peace. Go now and do his will."

Sister Rebekah turned toward the door and, in a trancelike state, walked out of the bedroom. After he heard the front door to his house close, Shaw slyly grinned and strolled over to his bedside table. He unlocked one of the drawers, retrieved a fifth of Macallan single-malt scotch, and took a heavy hit. He licked his lips and took another. That troublesome daughter would soon be gone from this world and her mother confined to the loony bin. Nobody would remember either of them, least of all Savior Ezekiel Shaw. Mother and daughter weren't very good pieces of ass anyway. But he needed some insurance—nothing could be left to chance.

He picked up the phone from the bedside table and dialed a number, the call short and to the point. Minutes later, he heard a knock at the front door, which he hurried to open. A tall, brawny man with an unruly head of thick black hair and a bushy beard to match stood in the entryway. Dressed in a work shirt, bib overalls, and boots, Brother Isaiah resembled a mountain man from days gone by. The two men strongly embraced before Ezekiel escorted him in and the two hunkered down in the study.

"Brother Isaiah, thank you for coming." Shaw smiled at his most trusted lieutenant, now seated across from him.

"How can I be of service, Savior Shaw?"

Shaw cleared his throat before responding. "You remember Sister Mary?"

Isaiah nodded. "Unfortunately, I do. She turned her back on us and God and, according to Scripture, will suffer eternal damnation."

Shaw lowered his head and stared at the floor in feigned remorse. "I'm afraid so. It's so hard to lose one of your own, but the devil never sleeps, Brother Isaiah. He's always waiting to snatch up those who stray from the path of God. Sister Mary did just that and, as a consequence, she not only lost her own soul but is now putting our community and way of life at risk."

Brother Isaiah frowned and shook his head. "She must be stopped then."

Shaw leaned back in his chair and gripped the edge of the table. "I agree, I agree. We must get her back, where she can't speak untruths about what happens here." He searched Brother Isaiah's face for signs of recognition as to what he meant and was comforted by a knowing nod. "So I have taken steps in that direction. As you know, Sister Rebekah is Sister Mary's mother."

Brother Isaiah nodded.

"I met with Sister Rebekah just before you arrived. She is driving to Austin tomorrow to pick up her daughter and bring her back to our community," he lied.

"That's good news. It sounds like you have the situation well in hand," Brother Isaiah replied.

Shaw grimaced. "I'd like to think so. The only question I have is whether Sister Rebekah can get the job done. She made one previous attempt to bring her daughter back and was unsuccessful. I want you to follow her. We can't afford any more missteps."

"I'll do whatever you ask of me," Brother Isaiah replied obediently.

Shaw got up from the table and walked over to his desk. He opened one of the drawers, pulled out a small box, and then returned to his chair behind the table. He slid the box across the table to Brother Isaiah and said, "On the way home, put this under the car I've loaned Sister Rebekah. It's parked in front of her house. That way there will be no chance of your losing her."

Brother Isaiah opened the box and took out a small tracking device, which he carefully examined before sliding it into his pocket. He asked, "What time do you think Sister Rebekah will leave?"

"She will be leaving tomorrow at sunrise."

Brother Isaiah nodded. "Is there anything else?"

"Yes, you should take some protection with you. I don't anticipate you will need it but, as the old saying goes, it's better to be safe than sorry. Take the Browning nine-millimeter we keep in the safe in the office. I believe you have a key to that safe?"

"Yes, Savior Shaw."

"And take your cell phone with you. I want you to call me and keep me posted on what's happening every step of the way."

"I'll have it with me at all times."

"Thank you, Brother Isaiah. May God's will be done." The two men stood, and Shaw escorted Brother Isaiah to the door.

CHAPTER

50

Sister Rebekah had patiently waited in her car in the parking lot of the Austin apartment complex until she was sure her daughter would be asleep in bed and her roommate had left with her boyfriend. Getting into the apartment had been a snap. Sister Rebekah resorted to a trick she had learned when she was living hand to mouth, trying to put food on the table for herself and her young baby while scrounging desperately for enough money to keep herself plied with alcohol. That was before she met Ezekiel Shaw—before he showed her the way.

The apartment lock was cheap. It had taken only minutes to open it, with a bobby pin, no less. Before entering the apartment, Sister Rebekah surveyed her surroundings—no sign of activity anywhere. The night was dark, and it was late, almost midnight. No one was watching her—or so she thought.

After quietly easing into the apartment and noiselessly pulling the door shut, she discarded her sandals and tiptoed toward her daughter's bedroom. Once inside, she gently bound her daughter's wrists and ankles securely to the bed frame with one-hundred-pound-test fishing line. Maddy stirred only once as her mother completed the task. She now sat quietly in the cane-backed chair she had pulled up next to Maddy's bed and smiled as she gently stroked her hair. *What a beautiful young girl,* Sister Rebekah thought. *She looks so peaceful, just like she did when she was a baby.* Too bad things had turned out the way they had—too bad her Maddy had taken a wrong turn.

Sister Rebekah noticed Maddy beginning to stir, as if she were having a bad dream. Fearing she might wake, she fetched duct tape from the bag she had brought with her and placed a strip over her daughter's mouth. Maddy's eyes opened wide in horror, and then wider as she saw her mother hovering over her. She tried to speak, her words unintelligible, garbled by the tape.

"Maddy, be still! Shh!" Sister Rebekah put a finger to her lips. "Everything's going to be all right. Mommy's here."

Maddy tried to move her arms and legs. The fishing line cut into one of her wrists. She closed her eyes tightly, tears rolling down her cheeks.

"What did I do to deserve this? I tried my best to raise you right."

Maddy opened her eyes wide and tried again to speak, the words undecipherable.

"You had it so good, Maddy—living among true believers, learning God's way from Savior Shaw."

Maddy violently struggled against her bindings, breaking her delicate skin and causing blood to ooze from her wrists and ankles. She tried to speak again. This time her mother was able to make out some of the words.

"You promise not to scream?"

Maddy nodded.

"Okay, I'll take that tape off, but let me show you something first."

Sister Rebekah removed from her bag a twelve-inch, razor-sharp Bowie machete she had bought at an Army-Navy store on the outskirts of Austin. Sister Rebekah had done her research on the Internet—the knife would be perfect for her mission, silent and quick. She held the knife in front of her daughter's face.

"Do you still promise not to scream?"

Maddy nodded. Sister Rebekah removed the tape and placed the machete on the bedside table.

"So what would you like to tell me, Maddy?"

In a quivering voice, Maddy pleaded, "Don't do this, Mother. Please, please don't do this."

"Do what, dear?" Sister Rebekah smiled sinisterly.

"I know why you're here. Savior Shaw put you up to this."

Her mother's eyes turned cold. "I will not tolerate you speaking against Savior Shaw. I'll end this quicker than I want to if you say another bad thing about him."

Maddy's mind racing, she changed course. "Mother, I don't know what went wrong. I was so happy at the commune—at least, at first. I loved Savior Shaw just as much as you did."

Her mother looked confused.

"I mean, we were on the street. We were barely making it. And he took us in."

Sister Rebekah began to stroke her daughter's hair again.

"You gave up drinking."

Her mother nodded. "That I did. And I couldn't have done it without Savior Shaw showing me the way."

"I don't doubt that, not in the least. But then, there was that night."

"What night?"

"I didn't tell you about it. I didn't think you would believe me."

"You're trying to trick me. What are you talking about?"

"No tricks, Mother. You remember how Savior Shaw would pick different girls to come see him after dinner?"

Her mother didn't respond.

"On the night he picked me, I was so excited. I felt so special."

Sister Rebekah smiled. "I remember that."

"When I went to his house, he took me into his bedroom. Candles were burning. It was really beautiful." Maddy hesitated.

"Yes, it is beautiful, Maddy."

"Savior Shaw made me feel so special. We sat and talked about me and what I was doing at the commune. I really felt like he was interested, that he cared."

Sister Rebekah smiled approvingly.

Maddy swallowed before continuing. "But all of a sudden things changed. He got more serious – it was strange. Without saying anything, he got up and took me to his bedroom. And then he … he had his way with me. I'll never be able to forget that awful night – it will be with me forever." Tears streamed down Maddy's cheeks as she lifted her head and stared at her mother.

Sister Rebekah covered her ears. "Stop your lying, you little bitch! Just stop it! Do you hear me?"

Maddy's voice grew louder. "It's true, Mother. It's true. Why would I make up something like that?"

Sister Rebekah jumped out of her chair and starting pacing around the room, her hands still over her ears.

"And that was just the start. It happened over and over again. That's when I changed, Mother."

"Stop! I can't take any more!" She dropped to the floor, pulled her knees to her chest, and began sobbing, rocking back and forth, her hands still covering her ears.

"Savior Shaw used Scripture to persuade you to come here to kill me. I know he did. That's his way. He can find a verse for anything he wants to do—anything."

Her mother's sobbing continued.

"He wanted me dead because he's afraid I'll testify in that trial against him. That's why."

Her mother looked up, her sobs now sniffles, her eyes red and cheeks tearstained. "What are you talking about?"

"The trial starts Monday. They've been trying to get me to testify. But I wasn't going to. I was so scared, scared of what Savior Shaw might do to me, and to you." Maddy paused, her voice becoming softer, almost a whisper. "He was using both of us—sleeping with us, lying to us, trying to turn us against one another. Finally I couldn't take it anymore. He's no savior. He's a wolf in sheep's clothing."

Maddy's mother slowly rose from the floor and walked toward the bed. She picked up the machete from the bedside table and, grasping the hilt with both hands, hovered over her daughter. "God has directed me—"

Maddy screamed, "Mother, no!"

". . . to sacrifice you in his name. You've chosen evil over good. Savior Shaw had a vision—"

"No, Mother. There's been no vision!" Maddy screamed, her eyes flashing fear. "He's deceiving you. He's the devil."

Her mother smiled and lifted the blade high in the air. She brought it down with all of her strength. Maddy gasped and tightly shut her eyes, waiting for the blade to penetrate her chest. She felt her mother's head fall on top of her. She opened her eyes and uttered, "Mother, what have you done?" The machete blade was protruding from her mother's chest—not hers.

She heard her mother weakly whisper, "I love you, baby." And then there was silence.

As she lay there, bound and helpless, her mother's warm blood oozing its way through the sheets and onto her bare skin, Maddy screamed over and over, each time louder, and wondered if help would ever come.

Brother Isaiah was sitting in his car in the parking lot of the apartment complex. He heard screaming and reached under the seat to grab the Browning pistol. Before getting out of his car, he called Savior Shaw. "There are screams coming from the apartment that Sister Rebekah entered about a half hour ago. In your vision, did God tell you I should sacrifice one of the Sisters if need be?"

"We must do what we can to protect our way of life. Do you understand?"

"Yes, Savior Shaw. I understand." As Brother Isaiah opened his car door, he could hear sirens and see people coming out of their apartments to find out what was going on. He stayed in his car and shut the door, observing the commotion around him. The police arrived, and an ambulance was right behind. They ran up the stairs to the apartment where the screams were coming from, knocked the door off its frame, and entered. Moments later, the emergency medical workers ran out to the ambulance, pulled a stretcher out of the back, and headed back up to the apartment.

Brother Isaiah got Shaw back on the phone and explained the situation.

"Watch carefully when they bring out the stretcher. I want to know who's on it," Shaw said.

Brother Isaiah got out of his car and mingled with the crowd that had formed. He made his way to the ambulance and strained to get a better view. As the EMTs rolled the stretcher by, he saw Maddy's pale face protruding from under a sheet that covered the rest of her body. Brother Isaiah brought the phone to his ear. "It's Sister Mary."

"Are you sure?" Shaw asked.

"Positive. It's Sister Mary."

"Is she alive? Can you tell?" Shaw asked frantically.

Brother Isaiah noticed Maddy crying and talking to the medical team. "Yes, she is alive."

"Any sign of Sister Rebekah?"

"No, none. She must still be in the apartment."

"Find out where they are taking Sister Mary—what hospital. Also, see if you can get any information on Sister Rebekah."

"Will do."

After ending the call, Shaw paced back and forth in his study, plotting his next move. The trial was scheduled to start on Monday morning. His lawyer had told him it would take several days. If the little bitch was badly hurt, she might not be able to testify. But she needed to be watched around the clock, no doubt about that. And if there was any sign she was headed in the general direction of Fort Worth, she had to be stopped. Shaw poured himself a drink and threw it back. He had a good man on it. Brother Isaiah could be trusted with anything; his loyalty was unconditional. He would do what had to be done.

"Jace, I'm sorry to wake you."

"Actually, you didn't wake me. I'm up, getting ready for the trial that starts Monday. As usual, I'm having a little case of the pre-game jitters, and haven't been able to sleep. So what's going on, Jackie? What's all that noise I hear in the background?"

"I don't know where to start. I'm in the parking lot of the Cascade Apartments, in South Austin. That's where Maddy has been living."

"She's not hurt, is she?" Jace could feel his heart begin to race.

"No, thank the Lord, just in shock. She's in an ambulance on the way to Seton Hospital." Jackie paused. "But, Jace, her mother is dead. The police are still investigating, but it looks like she killed herself."

"What in the world happened?"

"Like I said, the police are trying to figure that out. Gomez is here. In fact, he's the one who called me. He's up in Maddy's apartment now, along with the investigative team."

"What was the motive? Why would Maddy's mother kill herself?"

"That's unclear right now. They couldn't interview Maddy. She was a mess, in total shock. Plus she has some pretty deep cuts on her wrists and ankles, where she had apparently been tied up."

"Jackie, you know Shaw had something to do with this, no doubt in my mind. We need to make sure Maddy is safe."

"I'm headed over to Seton right now. I just wanted to give you a heads-up."

"I'm glad you did. Will you call me after you get there—let me know how she's doing?"

"I will. And don't worry. I'll make sure no one gets near Maddy—other than the hospital staff. If I have to leave, I'll get Gomez, or someone from the Austin PD, to take my place."

"Thanks, Jackie."

Jace shook his head in anger. He had to get that bastard, and he would get his chance next week.

CHAPTER

51

The next day, Darrin, Boyce, and Lisa were all seated in the conference room when Jace walked in, his expression somber. "Sorry I'm late, but time got away from me. Before we get started, I want to share something with you that I learned early this morning. I have already discussed this with Darrin, but I thought all of you should know. It could very well affect the strategy we are about to discuss. A week or so ago, Jackie McLaughlin, our investigator down in Austin, located a young girl who had run away from the sect we are suing. Her name is Maddy Murphy, or Sister Mary, as members of the BBC knew her. Jackie and I met with Maddy—"

Lisa blurted out, "What did you learn? Will Maddy testify?"

"Lisa, please hold the comments and questions until I finish. There are a lot of moving parts here." Jace forced a polite smile, cleared his throat, and continued. "Early this morning—a little after two, to be more precise—I got a call from Jackie. She was at the Cascade Apartments, where Maddy was living. Apparently Maddy's mother broke into her apartment, bound Maddy's hands and feet, and then proceeded to kill herself." There were audible gasps as Jace continued. "Maddy is currently at Seton Hospital recovering from severe emotional trauma."

Lisa shook her head and said, "That poor girl! How old is she?"

"Seventeen."

"This sounds like something the church may be involved in," said Boyce. "Right after I get out of this meeting, I'll head down to Austin and make sure nobody lays a hand on that young girl."

"I've already taken care of that," Jace replied. "Either Jackie or someone from the Austin PD is going to be watching over Maddy twenty-four-seven. There's no chance anyone can get to her." Jace continued. "As sad as all this is, we can't let it distract us from getting ready for trial. The best way we can help Maddy right now is to take down Shaw and that church of his in Judge Zimmerman's courtroom. So, Lisa, why don't you get us started?"

"Certainly. Do you mind if I use the whiteboard?"

Jace nodded his approval.

Lisa rose and walked toward the board mounted on the conference room wall. "As you know, jury consulting is anything but an exact science. I certainly don't have all the answers and would invite each of you to weigh in as we go through this process."

She picked up a marker from the tray underneath and wrote in large purple letters "WOMEN." "First, I think we want female jurors in this case. Mrs. Hanson lost her only daughter. The maternal instinct is very strong. Jace, I think any woman who has been a mother—carried a baby—will empathize with the loss Mrs. Hanson felt. And the fact that Mrs. Hanson took her own life, well, it will be almost unbearable to them."

Jace was the first to respond. "I agree with that. But you're not saying that men would make bad jurors in a case like this?"

"Not at all. I think, generally speaking, women would make better, more sympathetic jurors than men. But that's not to say there aren't a lot of good male jurors in our pool."

"Darrin, Boyce—what do you think?" Jace looked at both.

"I'm not a mother, Jace, but I agree with Lisa. I can only imagine how a mother would feel losing her only child and then having people mock her daughter during the funeral service." Darrin shook her head, then added, "We don't know yet whether Maddy will testify, but if she does and we learn that the church played a role in her mother's death, my bet is those female jurors will come unglued. I mean, a mother loses a daughter and that church belittles her loss, then the church causes a daughter to lose her mother. Come on. What could be worse than that? Plus, I am pretty sure that most women jurors will be turned off by Shaw's views on how members of their sex should be treated."

Boyce nodded. "I wholeheartedly agree with Darrin."

Jace continued. "How many women are on the list?"

"Forty-two."

"Good."

"Don't misunderstand me, Jace. I'm not saying all of the women on the list would be good jurors for us. There are other—"

"Factors to consider. I know, Lisa. This ain't our first rodeo together."

Lisa smiled. "Just making sure we are on the same page, Jace." She turned back to the board, wrote "NO RELIGIOUS NUTS," and then swiveled to face her audience.

"There are Methodists, Presbyterians, Catholics, Jews, Episcopalians—et cetera, et cetera—on the list. I'm not talking about those people, people who come from what would be classified as traditional denominations. It's those split-off groups that scare me, groups that have left the mainstream to form their own churches. In many instances, they tend to be fanatical, and very intolerant. They believe the Bible is inerrant and should be literally interpreted. They don't like homosexuals, don't think women should be ministers, and believe that all the disciples were men for good reason. Bottom line, their beliefs are similar in many respects to those practiced by the BBC and Ezekiel Shaw. They may not be protesting at funerals but, as I said, they scare the hell out of me. For obvious reasons, I would stay away from them."

Jace responded firmly, "I agree with that. And just how many fit within that category?"

"Well, remember, we're in Texas, so there a lot more than in other parts of the country. This ain't called the Bible Belt for nothing. Hmm, let me look at my notes." Lisa walked to the conference table and rifled through her file until she found the sheet she was looking for. "Are you ready? Twenty-two of the seventy-five fall within that category."

"That doesn't surprise me one bit. We've got to keep those folks off the jury."

"We'll have to do our best to get the judge to dismiss them for cause and, if we can't get them stricken, use our peremptory challenges. But getting a potential juror dismissed for cause can be damn tough. Some people will lie when questioned about their biases. They don't want to admit they can't be fair in a case."

"You're preaching to the choir. There have been studies done on the lengths people will go to seem fair. They don't even know they're lying half of the time." Lisa raised an eyebrow. "Well, let's not get bogged down with that right now. Agree, Jace?"

"Yeah, finish your presentation and we'll see where we are."

Lisa turned back to the board and scribbled "NO ATHEISTS."

Boyce was the first to respond. "I don't get that. I mean, we're suing a bunch of religious nuts. I would have thought we'd want every atheist we could get on that jury."

Lisa responded, "A seemingly logical conclusion, but I don't think it holds water here. Atheists are very independent thinkers, very opinionated and, most importantly, fanatical supporters of free speech. The reason is the general public has tried to suppress their views for so long. So they could, and I emphasize 'could,' side with Shaw and his bunch."

Darrin interjected, "She's right. I have a girlfriend who is an atheist, agnostic, whatever, and she is always talking about how she feels discriminated against, that people don't want to hear what she thinks."

Jace volunteered, "I'm sold. Lisa, anything else?"

"There is one thing I wanted to get to but ran out of time."

"What's that?"

"I wanted to check to see which jurors had pages on Facebook and look at what they had posted for the general public to see. There might be some real nuggets there."

"I agree. Maybe Darrin could help you with that."

"I'd be glad to," Darrin offered.

"Great. I'll divide up the list and email your half to you."

Darrin nodded.

"Boyce, what did you dig up?"

"I drove by the addresses of everyone on the list. The neighborhoods run the gamut from ritzy to dilapidated. These folks live in apartments, high-rises, townhomes, mansions, modest one-story homes—you name it. I made some notes next to each juror's name, describing where he or she lived."

Lisa responded, "It would be helpful if you could get me your notes."

"Gladly. I also ran criminal background checks on everyone on the list. Nothing came up. I limited my search to Texas, so I can't be sure I caught everything."

"I believe the federal government checks that before putting them in the pool," Lisa added.

"Sometimes the feds get a little sloppy. I just wanted to make sure nothing fell through the cracks," Boyce responded.

"Good thinking."

Boyce continued. "I also noted anything else that I thought might be of interest. And yes, Lisa, I made notes as to whether any of the cars had bumper stickers and what they said."

Lisa smiled and nodded in response.

"Lisa, I'd like your thoughts on one last thing," Jace said. "We don't know yet but, as I mentioned earlier, there is a possibility Maddy might take the stand. Obviously that depends on how quickly she recovers from this horrible tragedy, as well as her willingness to testify. When Jackie and I spoke to her, she was very reluctant to get involved but didn't rule it out. If she were to testify, would that change any of the opinions you have shared with us today?" Jace kept his attention focused on Lisa as he awaited her response.

Lisa stared at Jace while contemplating her answer, and then said, "I don't think so. Of course, that depends to a large degree on her testimony. Do you know what she'd say?"

"I have no idea at this point. But my guess is she will not have anything good to say about Savior Shaw. I just don't know how bad it'll be."

"That's what I figured. Then, no, our strategy should remain the same."

"Well, this has been a productive meeting, and I thank all of you for your input. Darrin and I have some work to do tonight so, if there's nothing else, let's recess until Monday morning. How about we meet here tomorrow at eight and then head to the courthouse together. That'll give us plenty of time to make it there by nine."

Lisa and Boyce gathered their things and exited the conference room, leaving Jace and Darrin alone.

Jace looked at Darrin. "Working dinner?"

"Pizza?"

"That sounds good," Jace replied.

"Beer?"

"I don't know. I've got so much to do."

"It'll help you sleep."

"You're right. Have them bring us a six-pack of Peroni."

"Done."

J ace stared blankly at the two remaining slices of pizza in the cardboard box on the conference room table and drained the last of his third Peroni. He tossed the empty bottle into the trash can in the corner.

He felt pretty good about his opening statement. As usual, he had gone over it with Darrin, who had made critical suggestions here and there. They had reviewed their trial strategy—what witness would be called when, what they needed to get from each witness, the exhibits that would be introduced, and the objections they could anticipate. After they had finished, Darrin had retired to her office, leaving Jace to contemplate the big picture.

He grimaced as he recalled the judge's admonition at the pretrial conference: she would likely direct a verdict if Jace couldn't bring forward convincing evidence that the BBC's conduct at the Hagstrom protest amounted to more than an attention-drawing critique of the country's permissive attitude toward women—their admission into the military, their promotion to positions of authority in corporate America, their appointment to the highest court in the land, and the list went on. In the BBC's opinion, the country's conduct was blasphemous, contravening the literal meaning of not one but many passages of the Bible. After deposing Ezekiel Shaw, Jace had read the verses he had quoted from memory and had found it hard to dispute that their literal meaning was precisely what Ezekiel claimed. Women were to be submissive, subservient, silent in church, obedient—clearly, in Paul's views, it was a man's world.

So what evidence did he have to show that the BBC's actions stepped over the line and amounted to intentional and personal slurs against Lauren Hanson and her parents? Eugene's affidavit, and that was it. But Judge Zimmerman had already indicated that that would not be enough. The signs from the protest had been conveniently destroyed—no help there. Darrin had exhaustively searched the Internet with the hope of finding a YouTube video revealing a slanderous utterance on camera or an over-the-line placard but had come up empty.

Bottom line, he had nothing—nothing unless Maddy Murphy testified. And if she did, it might be a different ball game.

Jace pulled his cell out of his blue jean pocket, turned the ringer back on, and noticed Jackie had called. He punched "call back" and, seconds later, she answered.

"Has anything changed?" Jace asked as he scribbled on the legal pad in front of him.

"Not really. Maddy's still pretty doped up. She's been mumbling some things on and off but nothing that makes much sense. Maybe she'll be better tomorrow and I'll be able to talk with her. But she's been through a lot, Jace. There's obviously some real emotional damage."

"I feel so sorry for her. I only wish I could do something to help."

"You and me both. Hopefully we'll get the chance."

"Well, I've got to get back to it. Call me if anything changes."

"You know I will, Jace. And good luck tomorrow. I'm sure you'll kick ass."

"Night, Jackie."

Jace briefly reviewed the outline for his opening statement. He then stood and began to pace back and forth in front of an imaginary jury seated on the conference room wall in front of him, slowly and deliberately telling them what he expected the evidence to show.

CHAPTER

52

It was a little after six on Monday evening, and Jace's trial team was back in the conference room after a long day of picking a jury. Jace turned his attention to Lisa and began the *postmortem*.

"So what do you think of our jury?"

"Could be better, could be worse."

"Come on, Lisa. You can do better than that."

"Well, I don't particularly like that econ professor from TCU. Like I said on Friday, those ivory-tower folks are hard to predict. They like to think theoretically. They can be cold, emotionless types. I couldn't tell for sure with him, but I didn't get a warm and fuzzy feeling."

"Darrin?"

"No opinion one way or the other. Like Lisa, I watched his body language, and he wasn't giving anything away. Seemed to enjoy the process. I don't know whether that's a good thing or a bad one."

Lisa said, "Jace, I sure am glad the judge went with you on your challenge of that woman from the Charismatic Church of Saints. She was crazy!"

Jace smiled. "Yeah, and the judge knew it. She gave me a look when I stood up to object that spoke volumes, like, 'Don't worry, I've got this.' I didn't have to argue very hard."

Lisa replied, "I was really impressed with the way the judge moved through that panel. When we got there this morning and I saw all those prospective jurors, I thought we might be there for a week."

"I told you. Judge Zimmerman doesn't fool around. If she senses someone might have a bias against one side or the other, she errs on the side of caution and excuses him or her in a polite and professional way. I wish more judges did that. A lot of judges will seat just about anyone. They just want to get through the process as quickly as they can."

Lisa continued. "I love that second-grade teacher we have. She has a three year old, and I could tell by the way she was look-ing at you that she liked what you had to say. It's hard to tell this early, but that's my gut."

"I wish we could have gotten that retired colonel on the jury," Darrin added.

"You knew Prater wasn't going to miss that. And Judge Zimmerman did the right thing in excusing him without making Prater waste a challenge. Lisa, do you think I offended any of our jurors by asking all of those questions about religion?"

"I don't think so. Besides, that's what this case is about. They might as well hear it now and get used to it."

"Okay. So we've got four women and two men on the jury, with two men as alternates. Darrin, you've heard the opening argument I'll be giving tomorrow. Anything you think I should change in light of what you saw today?"

"Not that I can think of."

"Well, I appreciate all of your hard work. You heard the judge say she had an emergency motion she needed to take up at nine, so we won't start opening statements until ten or ten-thirty. Boyce, no need for you to be there tomorrow. We'll holler at you if we need something. Same for you, Lisa."

They both nodded and left the conference room, leaving Jace and Darrin alone.

"Well, it's game on, Darrin. Let's get back to work."

Once Jace was back in his office, he powered up his cell phone and waited impatiently for it to post the emails and voice mails that had built up during the day. He had turned off his phone before going to court that morning; Judge Zimmerman was more than intolerant of her proceedings being interrupted by an annoying ringtone. Her usual reaction was to have her bailiff confiscate the phone until the end of the day, or impose a small fine on the offending attorney. On occasion she had done both. Jace had made sure not to start off the trial on her bad side.

He had a series of emails, which he quickly scrolled through, nothing urgent. He would get to them when he could. He had one voice mail—Jackie. He touched the dot next to her name and put the cell to his ear.

"Jace, I know you are in court, but I wanted to give you an update. Maddy's doing much better today. They've decreased her meds and she's not nearly as groggy. The doc asked me to hold off a little longer on getting into something that might freak her out—no mention of Shaw, her mother, the BBC, that type of thing—so I haven't talked with her about any of that. The doc also told me she would probably give me the green light when she makes the rounds first thing in the morning. I'll let you know. Hope you got a good jury. I know you're super busy right now and may not have time to give me a call but, if you do, I'd love to hear how it's going. Talk to you soon." Jace called her back.

"Jackie, I just got your voice mail and thought I'd give you a ring before I got tied up preparing for tomorrow. Sounds like Maddy's making progress."

"Let me step out of the room—Maddy's dozing." A brief pause as Jackie exited the hospital room. "Now, I can talk. Yeah, Maddy's doing so much better. She has improved significantly since I left you that message. She's really coming around."

"Are you still optimistic that the doc will let you question her in the morning?" Jace asked.

"I am. And Gomez needs to question her as well. He's got to complete his investigation of Maddy's mother's death."

"There's no doubt that she killed herself, is there?"

"Not in Gomez's mind, but he needs to jump through all the hoops. He doesn't want anyone coming back later and questioning the thoroughness of his investigation."

"I get that. So when are you going to ask her about coming to Fort Worth to testify?"

"I'll have to play it by ear. I don't want to move too quickly. She's pretty coherent and all, but I'm sure she's fragile as well. How long do you think the trial will last?" Jackie asked.

"That depends on a lot of things, but my best guess right now is we'll be done by the end of the week. Again, that's just a guess."

Jackie had lost track of time and glanced down at her watch to refresh her memory. "Okay, it's Monday evening. If the doc lets me talk with Maddy in the morning, then maybe I could drive her to Fort Worth tomorrow afternoon. That assumes she is willing to testify—a big assumption."

"I'll be in court all day tomorrow and will have my cell off. Just leave me a voice mail and I'll call you back at lunch or when we break."

"Will do. Let's keep our fingers crossed. And Jace, you're going to win this. I have this feeling," Jackie added.

"Thanks for the vote of confidence. Well, I've got to get back to it. I'll talk to you tomorrow."

As she ended the call, Jackie noticed someone sitting in the reception area down the hall who she had previously seen lurking around the hospital. She decided to introduce herself and walked quickly to the area where the man was seated, his gaze focused intently on a *People* magazine. Jackie sat down in the chair diagonally across from him. He pretended not to notice. Jackie broke the silence.

"I hate hospitals, don't you? The waiting drives me crazy."

The man glanced up and forced a grin. "Not one of my favorite places." He returned to reading the magazine.

"You here for a loved one?"

"I don't want to be rude, but this has been a tough time for me. I'm not really in the mood to talk. Sorry." His dark eyes met Jackie's. "I trust you understand." He held the magazine back up. Jackie noticed it was over a year old.

"Well, I hope everything turns out well for whoever you're seeing."

The man looked up and nodded. Realizing any attempt to get information from this guy would be a waste of time, Jackie stood and made her way back to Maddy's room. Before she stepped inside, she peered back down the hall. She couldn't say for sure, but she'd have given odds it was the same man she had seen the day before.

CHAPTER

53

At precisely ten-thirty the next morning, the court bailiff, his posture erect, expression solemn, announced, "All rise. The United States District Court for the Northern District of Texas is now in session, the Honorable Barbara Zimmerman presiding."

A door in the back of the courtroom opened, and Judge Zimmerman bustled up the steps to take her seat. She positioned her half-glasses on her nose and looked first at Jace. "Mr. Forman, are you ready to proceed?"

Jace rose. "I am, Your Honor."

Judge Zimmerman turned to Jace's adversary, who was already standing.

"The defendants are ready, Your Honor," Crom answered in a booming, confident voice.

The judge turned to the bailiff. "Please bring in the jury."

Minutes later, eight jurors, four women and four men, took their seats in the jury box. They had not heard the word "alternate" during the jury selection process. As far as those eight men and women knew, they were all equals in this important process, all serving a vital role. Their emotionless expressions signaled the seriousness with which they took their sworn duty.

"Mr. Forman, please proceed with your opening statement."

Jace rose and made his way to the lectern that was situated between counsel tables. He placed an outline of his presentation on the top of the lectern, cleared his throat, and then walked slowly toward the jury box.

"Ladies and gentlemen, as we covered briefly in the jury selection process yesterday, there is a reason why my previous clients, Eugene and Janice Hanson, aren't here today—a sad reason, a tragic reason, a troubling reason and, yes, an avoidable reason. They are both no longer with us. Why? Because of the actions of the Brimstone Bible Church and its leader, Mr. Ezekiel Shaw."

Jace turned on his heels, gestured toward Shaw, and then refocused his attention on the jurors, his eyes traveling slowly from the eyes of one juror to the next until they had made contact with each.

"Janice Hanson was trying to recover from the loss of her only daughter, Second Lieutenant Lauren Hanson. And it had not been easy. From the time she was a little girl, Lauren had excelled at everything—academics, sports, you name it. She had been accepted to every university she had applied to, opting to go to West Point. Why? Because she wanted to serve her country. She wanted to give back."

Jace began to walk slowly back and forth in front of the jury. "And she did give back. She paid the ultimate price in that small village in Kandahar Province, Afghanistan. She sacrificed her very life." Jace stopped, sighed, and held the eyes of one of the female jurors. "She had been brought back to this country, to her hometown of Hagstrom, Texas, where her mother and father, Janice and Eugene Hanson—hardworking, decent people—hoped to bury her in peace. But that was not to be."

The courtroom was eerily silent, the jurors rapt with attention. Jace paused briefly to let his message sink in before resuming.

"No, that was not to be, and you know why, ladies and gentlemen? I'll tell you why. Because Ezekiel Shaw and his followers decided they didn't want the Hansons to bury their daughter in peace, and they were bound and determined to do everything in their power to see that they didn't."

Crom was on his feet. "Your Honor, I hate to object, but Mr. Forman has gone way beyond the bounds of a permissible opening statement. He is arguing his case."

Without ruling on the objection, Judge Zimmerman stated, "Move along, Mr. Forman."

"Thank you, Your Honor."

Crom shook his head and sat back down.

"So what did Mr. Shaw and his sect do to prevent this loving couple, this loving mother and father, from burying their only daughter in peace? They staged a protest at her funeral. Janice and Eugene had never done anything to that church or any of its members. They didn't even know those people, had never even seen them before—not until they showed up chanting and hoisting signs in the air at their daughter's funeral."

Crom was on his feet again. "Objection! Counsel is misstating the facts. My clients were protesting down the street from the funeral service, not on the church grounds, as Mr. Forman would have us believe."

Judge Zimmerman glared at Crom and replied, "You will have your opportunity to respond, Mr. Prater. Your objection is overruled. Please proceed, Mr. Forman."

"So why would these people protest at the funeral of someone who had done nothing to them, someone they didn't even know? I'll tell you why. Publicity. They wanted the limelight, and they didn't care what they had to do to get it. Nor did they care who they hurt in the process."

Jace surveyed the expressions of those in his jury before continuing.

"You might wonder what they were protesting against. What would make these people drive all the way from their compound near Fort Stockton to Hagstrom to protest at one of our fallen heroes' funerals? Again, it's a one-word answer: women. They believe, and preach, that women should be treated as second-class citizens. They also believe our great country is being punished for treating women as being equal to men, punished by having its soldiers sent home in body bags."

Several of the jurors frowned. One shook his head.

"Let's talk about what was written on their protest signs, in very big letters and in bright, attention-grabbing colors. Things like 'Thank God for dead women soldiers.'"

A female juror audibly gasped. Jace paused as their eyes met and then continued. "'Women are for bearing children, not arms.'"

Jace thought he noticed one of the male jurors nodding approvingly. He made a mental note before resuming.

"'A woman's place is in the home, not on the battlefield.'" Jace kept the same juror in his peripheral vision and sensed another faint nod.

"And the last one Mr. Hanson remembered seeing as the funeral procession made its way to the cemetery: 'God killed Lauren Hanson because He hates lesbians.'" Jace repeated the phrase for effect.

"So what did Eugene Hanson do when he saw that last sign while he was in the limo on his way to bury his only daughter? He did what any loving father would do. He told the driver to stop, jumped out of the limo, and jerked the sign from the protester's hands. He had to be restrained by one of the police officers present and forcibly led back to the car."

Jace's voice lowered to a whisper. All of the jurors leaned forward in their seats, waiting to hear what Jace was about to say. "And do you know what one of the female protesters yelled at Mr. Hanson? She screamed, 'Your daughter's in hell right now, and you and your wife are to blame.' Let me repeat that: 'Your daughter's in hell right now, and you and your wife are to blame.' That's what she spewed at a father who had lost his only daughter just days before."

There were gasps from several female jurors. One of the male jurors lowered his head as if in prayer.

"Can you imagine how you would have felt if that had happened to you?"

Crom jumped up, but before he could speak, the judge silenced him with a hand and glared at Jace. "Objection sustained. You're out of order, Mr. Forman. You know better. Don't let it happen again."

"I'm sorry, Your Honor. I must have gotten a little carried away." Jace had made his point with the jurors. Hopefully, his misstep would not cost him too dearly with the judge.

"To return to the question I asked at the beginning: Why is Janice Hanson not with us today? She couldn't take it anymore. The defendants' actions pushed her over the edge. She took her own life by overdosing on sleeping pills."

Jace stopped his pacing and slowly made eye contact with each juror before continuing.

"And Eugene Hanson, where is he? Why isn't he with us today? He had lost everything—his daughter and now his wife. He was distraught beyond words and, unfortunately, drove to Norman, Oklahoma, to confront the group that had caused him so much grief and despair, the defendants in this case, Ezekiel Shaw and the

Brimstone Bible Church. He had an assault rifle and two magazines with him. He tried to take justice into his own hands and lost his life in the process. And that, ladies and gentlemen, is why Eugene Hanson is not here with us today."

The jurors were visibly shaken. Jace had hit his mark.

"Ladies and gentlemen, as my mother used to say, there is a time and place for everything. And the funeral of a dead soldier is not the time or place to stage a protest. A family must be—I say must be—given an opportunity to grieve in peace, to say goodbye to a loved one without people yelling epithets in the background. As you listen to the evidence, please weigh the right we have in this country to speak our minds freely against the right of a family to have privacy and peace at a very vulnerable time. These important rights can both coexist, and I am confident you, ladies and gentlemen, will find the right balance. Thank you."

Judge Zimmerman nodded in the direction of Crom, who rose to his feet and walked confidently toward the jury box.

"As another old saying goes, there are two sides to every story. You have heard one side. We have a very different story to tell, one we are confident will be supported by the evidence and not a fable that's little more than the imaginative creation of a lawyer trying to win his case. Mr. Forman didn't mention this, but I will. Please understand that what Mr. Forman said to you today, as well as what I'm getting ready to tell you, is not evidence. The only, and I repeat 'only,' evidence you are to consider is the testimony that comes from that witness stand and the exhibits that are admitted into evidence by Judge Zimmerman. If you think that evidence is inconsistent with or contradictory to what I say, or what my worthy adversary has said, please, please disregard what we have said and go with your own recollection."

The male juror who had previously given Jace cause for concern nodded in agreement.

"Now, to the evidence my clients and I believe you will hear in this case. First, as to my clients' beliefs. They are biblically based and firmly held. You may not agree with those beliefs, and no one is saying you have to, certainly not me. The Brimstone Bible Church and its leader, Ezekiel Shaw, believe that the Bible is the inerrant word of God and should be literally interpreted. They make no apologies for this belief."

There was more nodding from the potentially troublesome juror, which prompted Jace to make a note on his legal pad.

"There are numerous passages in the Bible that speak to the role of women in society, starting with Genesis and going up to the book of Revelation. I am not going to get into those now. You will hear them read during the evidentiary phase of the trial. My clients interpret those verses in a literal sense and believe they stand for the proposition that, under God's plan, women are not to hold leadership positions in the church or in society as a whole."

Crom walked to counsel table and took a sip of water. He was not thirsty but wanted to give the jurors time to digest what he had just said.

"My clients believe this with all their heart. They really do. And they believe the Bible—again, we will cover the specific passages in the evidentiary portion of this trial—commands them to educate those who are not adhering to these scriptural tenets as to the error of their ways which, in turn, will hopefully cause them to change their behavior. My clients further believe that if their fellow countrymen do not change their errant ways, they will never experience the glory of God but will be condemned to eternal damnation. I tell you all of this so you will understand why my clients felt they had no choice but to do what they did."

Crom closed his eyes and rubbed his forehead before continuing.

"Let's turn to the protest in Hagstrom. Why picket the funeral of someone my clients didn't even know? This is one thing Mr. Forman and I agree on: my clients wanted publicity. They wanted their message to reach the maximum number of people possible. The more people who heard what they had to say and changed their ways, the better. And don't forget—my clients feel the entire country has turned its back on God. If they had protested at a park or some other obscure public venue, they would not have gotten the media exposure that they did here. And, as a result, fewer people would have heard what they had to say."

Crom walked over to counsel table once again, calmly poured water from a pitcher, and took a sip. He then returned to his position in front of the jury box.

"Now, let's talk about the protest signs. I agree. They are pretty strongly worded, but the beliefs they represent are strongly felt. And again, my clients were trying to attract attention to their views and what they consider to be God's instructions as to how we should live our lives. I emphasize—it's not important whether you agree with those views or not. Nor is it important whether you agree with the language my clients used on their signs. And that's because we have an honored tradition in this country that was written into the Constitution by our founders. It's called freedom of speech, the ability to express our views no matter how unpopular they may be. This freedom is one of the principal things that make this country so great. We have the ability to speak our minds and try to convince others as to the correctness of our views. And that is exactly what my clients were doing at the protest in Hagstrom."

Crom paused, biting his lower lip in Clintonesque style.

"One last thing before I close. It's our position that none of the statements contained on the protest signs applied to Lauren Hanson or her parents personally. They spoke to the role of women in general. Those placards no longer exist. They were discarded by my clients right after the protest. But assuming they said what Mr. Forman contends, they still constitute public commentary. Except for the alleged comment made by one of the protesters. Mr. Forman told you she screamed something to the effect that Lauren Hanson was in hell and that her parents were to blame. There is absolutely no evidence that that statement was made except Mr. Hanson's memory. The officer at the scene doesn't remember it. My clients don't remember it. We submit to you it was a figment of Mr. Hanson's imagination. I'm not saying he lied. To the contrary, he was simply confused and misremembered what had occurred."

Crom dramatically paused, letting the silence hang in the air for a couple of seconds, and then he drove home his conclusion. "Ladies and gentlemen, we are very sorry that Mr. and Mrs. Hanson are no longer with us. It's a terrible tragedy. We would, however, submit that their distress resulted from losing their only daughter and not from glancing at some homemade signs for a few minutes as the funeral procession drove to the cemetery. And remember, ladies and gentlemen, there is so much at stake here: our individual right to say what and how we feel. Stand up for that basic freedom our founders codified hundreds of years ago. Thank you."

"Thank you, Mr. Prater."

Crom returned to counsel table.

Judge Zimmerman directed her remarks to the jury: "Ladies and gentlemen, it is a little before noon. We will break until one-thirty this afternoon, at which time you will begin to hear the evidence in this case. Please do not discuss this case with each other, or with anyone, for that matter. Thank you." The bailiff escorted the jury through a door and into the jury room.

Both counsel stood as the jury exited. After they were out of earshot, the judge said, "I must say this is one of the more interesting cases I have had in a while. I'll see you both back here at one-thirty. This court is in recess."

Darrin slid into one side of the booth at the Cowtown Diner, and Jace slid into the other.

Jace was the first to speak. "So how do you think things went this morning?"

"Hard to say. The jurors were hanging on your every word—all of them except that one male juror who kept nodding his head. I'm not sure about him. But anyway, they seemed to be going with you. And then Crom got up. I hate to say it, but he did one helluva job. Bottom line, I think the score is knotted—dead even."

The waitress delivered water and took their orders—grilled chicken salad for Darrin and a Cowtown Burger for Jace.

"I agree—no question his argument was persuasive. He took a lot of the emotion out of our case. Painted his folks as sincere people trying to save everyone from hell. It was a pretty impressive theme that he came up with."

Darrin replied, "And I thought he did a good job of selling it. So what's your plan with Shaw this afternoon? He's critical. If you can destroy him, ball game's over."

"That's a lot easier said than done. I took—"

The waitress interrupted, "'Scuse me, folks." She served their lunch plates and then said, "If I can get you anything else, just holler."

Jace continued. "You read Shaw's deposition. He was a tough nut to crack—very calm and pretty damn smart as well. I've got to find a way to get under his skin, rile him up somehow."

"And just how are you planning to do that?" Darrin asked.

"This guy is a textbook narcissist. He doesn't give a rat's ass about anyone but himself. And a megalomaniac to boot—loves to lord it over other people. I've got to expose the real Ezekiel Shaw for the jury to see."

Darrin and Jace spent the rest of the lunch hour discussing how to do that.

The waitress brought the check, Jace left two twenties on the table, and they headed back to court.

"Mr. Forman, call your first witness." Judge Zimmerman eyed Jace as she awaited his response.

Jace rose and replied, "Plaintiff calls Ezekiel Shaw as an adverse witness."

Judge Zimmerman focused her gaze on the man with shoulder-length hair and a scruffy beard seated next to Crom. "Mr. Shaw, would you please come forward and be sworn?"

Shaw stood. He was dressed in a white shirt, khaki pants, and leather sandals with thick brown socks underneath. He walked to the witness stand, took the oath, and then sat down.

Jace rose and stood behind counsel table. "Please state your name, sir."

"Ezekiel Shaw."

"Has that always been your name?"

"No, sir."

"And what was your name prior to it becoming Ezekiel Shaw?"

"James Wayne Watkins."

"And did you go by Jimmy Wayne?"

Shaw took a deep breath. Forman hadn't asked him any of these questions at his deposition. Shaw wondered just what else about his past his adversary knew, causing him to feel a little unsettled—and that was just how Jace hoped he would feel.

"Sometimes."

"Did you know your father?"

"No."

"And what was your mother's name?"

"Pearl."

"Were you and your mother close?"

"What do you mean by 'close'?"

"Did you do a lot of things together? Did you love her?"

Crom jumped to his feet. "Objection, compound question."

Judge Zimmerman sustained the objection, and Jace rephrased.

"Did you love your mother, Mr. Shaw?"

Shaw squirmed in his chair. "I can't answer that. I never got to know her."

"Do you know how old your mother was when you were born?"

"Not exactly."

"Does fourteen sound about right?"

"I don't know."

"And you and your mother lived in Houston after you were born, is that correct?"

"That's right."

"But you didn't live with your mother for long, did you, Mr. Shaw?"

"I don't know what you're getting at. What's the relevance of this, anyway?"

Shaw shot a disapproving glance at his lawyer, hoping he would take the hint and object. Realizing the futility of an objection, Crom remained glued to his chair, doodling on the legal pad in front of him.

"No, I didn't," the witness finally continued. "My mother left me with my grandmother one day and never came back. That's all I can remember."

"How old were you at the time?"

"Little."

"Were you in school?"

Shaw shook his head.

"You'll need to answer out loud so the court reporter can take down your response."

"No, I wasn't, Mr. Forman." Shaw's voice was tinged with sarcasm.

Jace knew he was walking a fine line, as he sensed some of the jurors beginning to feel sorry for the witness. But he had to take that chance. It was critical to explain bit by bit how the seemingly innocent man in the witness box had become the monster he'd become.

"And how long did you live with your grandmother?"

"Until I was sixteen," Shaw responded in a defiant tone, then smiled insincerely at Jace.

"When you moved to Austin, is that correct?"

"If you knew, why did you ask me?" The witness flashed Jace another insincere smile.

"Please answer my question, Mr. Shaw."

"That's correct."

"And did you drop out of school?"

"It was a waste of my time. I wasn't learning anything. I knew more than my teachers." Shaw's narcissism was beginning to show.

"So what did you do after moving to Austin? Did you work?"

"Learned how to play the guitar, joined a band. We actually played a few gigs and made a little money. And then my life changed forever. I found Jesus."

"How old were you when that happened?"

Shaw smiled at the jury and began to turn on the charm. "Nineteen. The rest of my life might be a little foggy, but I remember that time just like yesterday. Things turned around for me."

Several of the jurors smiled back at the witness empathetically. Jace noticed but continued with his game plan.

"And where did you find religion?"

"Jesus, Mr. Forman, not religion. There's a big difference. And to answer that question, my journey started at the Fundamentalist Family Church."

"And who was the pastor of that church?"

Crom slowly rose from his chair and queried, "Your Honor, I have sat in my seat patiently, but does Mr. Forman's questioning have a point? I'll object on relevance grounds."

The judge lowered her head and peeked over her glasses. "Mr. Forman, do you have a response?"

"My response is twofold. One, this is background information which I am entitled to ask about and two, the witness's religion, which caused him to stage the protest in question, is certainly relevant to this case."

"I'll overrule the objection. You may continue, Mr. Forman."

"His name is Josiah James."

"Do you still keep in touch with Mr. James?"

"Reverend James, and the answer is no."

"And why did you leave the Fundamentalist Family Church?"

"We differed over scriptural interpretation."

"How so?"

"There were several differences, but the principal one was over the role of women in the church. Reverend James would allow some of the female congregants to preach in his absence, and I thought this was clearly forbidden by God's word."

"And what were the biblical passages that supported your position?"

"You got all day?"

"Please, Mr. Shaw, just answer my question."

"First Corinthians, chapter 14, verses 34 through 36. God's intent is clearly expressed in those verses. Also, First Timothy, chapter two, verses 11 through 15 and I quote: 'Let the women learn in silence with all subjection. But I suffer not a woman to teach, nor to usurp authority over the man, but to be in silence.' If you need more, I can give them to you."

"And did you leave alone?"

"No, there was a group of us. We left and formed the Brimstone Bible Church."

"And that is the church you lead today?"

"It is."

"And where is your church located?"

"We have some acreage in West Texas, near Fort Stockton."

"And do you have a website?"

"We do."

"And do you occasionally post opinions and comments on your website?"

"We do."

"And when did you start protesting funerals?"

"Several years ago."

"Now I want to turn to the funeral of Lauren Hanson."

"Okay."

"It was your idea to picket her funeral, wasn't it?"

"It was."

"You didn't know Second Lieutenant Hanson, did you?"

"That's not important . . ."

"It is to me, Mr. Shaw. Just answer my question, and we'll let the jury decide what is and what isn't important."

Shaw's eyes blazed back at Jace as he answered the question slowly and sarcastically, "No, I didn't know her."

"And you didn't know her parents, did you?"

"No."

"They had never done anything to you or to any of the members of your church, had they?"

"Not to my knowledge."

"You would agree that a funeral service is a solemn occasion, would you not?"

"Not necessarily. It can be, but sometimes it is more of a celebration. Check out those funerals they have down in New

Orleans—they are something else." Shaw grinned at the jurors, and several grinned back.

Sensing he was losing a little control, Jace tightened up the questioning. "But you knew that was not the kind of funeral that Mr. and Mrs. Hanson had planned for their only daughter, isn't that right, Mr. Shaw?"

"You might say that."

"I did say that. And you and your followers decided to disrupt her funeral, didn't you?"

"No, that's not accurate. We decided to stage a peaceful protest down the street in an attempt to get people to follow God's word."

"Did you see what was written on the signs used at the protest?"

"I did, but I don't remember exactly what they said. Generally they were critical of women being given positions of authority in our society, which is in direct contradiction of God's law as it is expressly laid down in the Bible."

Jace handed the witness a copy of the affidavit signed by Eugene Hanson and asked him to read it to himself. "Having read the affidavit signed by Mr. Hanson, do you agree with the portion in which he recites the writings on the signs your group had at the funeral of his daughter?"

Shaw stuck to his testimony. "I can't recall specifically what was on the signs, and they were discarded after the protest."

Changing course, Jace asked, "You don't like women, do you, Mr. Shaw?"

"That's not true."

"Okay, let me rephrase. You like them in their place, correct?"

"Objection, Your Honor. Argumentative." Crom was on his feet again.

"Overruled, Mr. Prater. This is cross-examination."

Shaw smirked and then retorted, "Could you ask the question again?"

"You like women but only in their place."

"What do you mean by 'in their place'?"

"Being submissive, subservient to men, Mr. Shaw."

"Well, that is what the Bible teaches us."

"Mr. Shaw, you have cited some verses you believe stand for that proposition, correct?"

Shaw quickly retorted, "It's not a question of what I believe. That's what those verses clearly say. You do understand English, don't you, Counselor?" He emphasized the last word, lacing it with sarcasm.

Jace ignored the slight and continued. "You believe that Jesus was the Son of God, correct?"

"Of course," Shaw sneered.

"You would then agree, would you not, that what Jesus taught us while he was here on this earth should be given great weight?" Jace halted, eyeing the witness.

The witness tilted his head and furrowed his brow. "I don't know what you're getting at, but I generally agree with your statement."

"Please cite to the jury any verse where Jesus told anyone that women should be subservient to men." Jace folded his arms and turned toward the jury box as he awaited Shaw's response.

Shaw sighed impatiently before responding. "You are missing the point, Counselor. You can't pick and choose which Bible verses you want to follow and which you do not."

Jace addressed Judge Zimmerman. "Your Honor, would you please direct the witness to answer my question?"

Without hesitation, the judge scowled at the witness and uttered, "Mr. Forman's question is pretty simple. He wants to know if Jesus ever taught his disciples, or anyone for that matter, that women should be subservient to men. Now, answer his question, Mr. Shaw."

"Your Honor, I think you and counsel are missing—"

"I'm not missing anything." Judge Zimmerman's face was crimson. "And if you don't answer his question right now, then I'll hold you in contempt of this court. Have I made myself clear?"

Shaw turned his gaze away from the judge and back to Jace. "There is no place in the Bible where Jesus specifically says that."

Jace followed up quickly, "And there is no place in the Bible where Jesus generally says that, is there?"

"No, but there are many references in Corinthians, Titus—"

Jace cut him off. "And those verses were written by Paul, formerly Saul of Tarsus, correct?"

"That's correct but—"

Jace interrupted again. "And it's true that Paul did not know Jesus, did he?"

"No, but—"

Another interruption. "In fact, Paul never, ever heard Jesus teach, did he?"

"I don't think—"

"In fact, Paul did not convert until years after Jesus had been crucified, isn't that correct?"

"Yes, but—"

"So the only verses in the New Testament that say women should be subservient to men, should be quiet in church, should ask men if they have questions, should wear their hair a certain way—all those verses were written by a man who didn't know Jesus, hadn't been taught by him in the flesh, correct?"

"That's true, but Paul—"

"Thank you, Mr. Shaw. Now, as you interpret what Paul wrote, the female members of the Brimstone Bible Church should do what you tell them to, isn't that right?"

Shaw cleared his throat. "All of the Bible is God's word, not just the four Gospels. And to answer your question, they should. But it goes without saying that I would never—never—ask them to do anything that contravenes the word of God."

"With that qualification, they should do what you tell them, correct?"

Crom jumped up. "I object to this line of questioning. It's not important whether my client's belief is correct or not. What is at issue in this case is whether he had the First Amendment right to voice that belief which, Your Honor, we submit he did."

Judge Zimmerman addressed Jace. "He has a point, Mr. Forman. Do you have a response?"

"If you will indulge me, I believe the relevance of this line of questioning will become crystal clear."

Judge Zimmerman glared at Jace. "The leash is a short one, Mr. Forman. Proceed."

"Thank you, Your Honor," Jace responded respectfully, and then quickly asked, "Have you ever told female members of your church that it was God's will for them to have sex with you?"

"Absolutely not."

Jace fired another round at the witness. "Have you ever told underage girls in the church it was God's will for them to have sex with you?"

Crom sprang to his feet. "Objection, Your Honor, irrelevant and prejudicial!"

At the same time, Shaw stood and yelled, "This is an outrage! I'll not—"

Judge Zimmerman intervened. "Sit down, Mr. Shaw. Counsel, approach."

Jace and Crom walked hurriedly to the bench and huddled close to the judge. In a whisper and out of earshot of the jury, the judge said, "Mr. Forman, do you have any evidence relative to the question you just asked?"

Jace fudged. "I believe I do, Your Honor."

"All right then, I'll allow it. Objection overruled." Judge Zimmerman motioned counsel back to their previous positions and turned to the witness. "Mr. Shaw, please answer the question."

"Absolutely not."

"Going back to the funeral protest," Jace continued, "did you ever hear one of your members yell words to the effect that Lauren Hanson was in hell and her parents were to blame? Do you recall that?"

"I recall that those words were never said by any of my people at that funeral, or anywhere else for that matter."

"Mr. Shaw, are you familiar with Matthew chapter 7, verse 12?"

"I am." The witness wiggled uncomfortably.

"That verse is known as the Golden Rule, isn't it, sir?" Without waiting for a response, Jace asked a follow-up. "If you had a son or daughter who was killed while serving this country of ours would you want some group to stage a protest at his or her funeral like you and your followers did at Lauren Hanson's?"

"In the first place, I wouldn't let my children—"

"Mr. Shaw, under your interpretation of Scripture, Her Honor shouldn't be sitting as the judge in this case, simply because she is a—"

Crom jumped up and blurted, "Objection . . ." Before he could finish, Jace withdrew the question and retook his seat at counsel table. As he did so, he looked up at Judge Zimmerman and said, "Pass the witness."

Judge Zimmerman looked at the clock hanging on the wall opposite her bench and directed her comments to the jury: "Ladies and gentlemen, it is a little after six. We have gone past the time I normally recess for the day, and I apologize for that. But I sensed counsel was nearing the end of his examination, so I let him finish. We will pick up in the morning at nine. You are excused." Judge and counsel watched as the jurors filed into the jury room. After the last juror disappeared, Judge Zimmerman smiled at counsel, stepped down from the bench, and slipped out of the courtroom.

As they drove back to the office, Darrin spoke first. "Jace, I was a little worried early on in your cross. Some of the jurors were beginning to feel sorry for Shaw. I could read it in their faces. But by the end of the day the tide began to turn. You killed him at the end. He was obviously flustered. And I could tell the jurors were sensing that. They were starting to see that other side of Ezekiel Shaw, the dark side."

Jace sighed. "I knew my strategy was a little dicey, but I had to take the chance. If I'm not able to get the jury to believe Shaw hates women because of what he went through as a child, then I've lost the case."

"Well, Crom's got all night to get Shaw ready for his questioning tomorrow. And my guess is his client's a pretty quick study."

Jace nodded. "I agree. What do you think Crom will try to bring out tomorrow?"

"He's got to stick to his theme—show that Ezekiel Shaw really believes what he says and that he practices what he preaches. I suspect he'll confront the sexual issues you raised head-on. Get Shaw to emphatically deny that he has had sex with any of the young girls in the congregation and to testify that all of the members are there of their own will and can leave whenever they want. Speaking of that, do you have any evidence that Shaw has slept with underage girls in the group?"

"Not right now."

Darrin shook her head. "I don't know, Jace. You took an awful big gamble today by throwing that out there. If you don't deliver at some point in the trial, the jurors are going to hold it against you big-time."

"I had to take that chance. I'm not going to win this case unless I can get the jurors to see Shaw for what he is. Crom's got that First Amendment argument, and somehow I've got to find a way around it." Jace pulled into the parking space next to his law office and killed the ignition. "You headed home?"

"I wish. I've got a few things to take care of in the office. Get through the mail that came today, your phone messages and mine, a few little things like that." Darrin grinned. "How about you?"

"I think I'll work from home. I'd like to get a workout in and grab some dinner and maybe a beer or two before I get back to it."

"Sounds like a good plan to me. Just call me if you need anything. I should be here for an hour or two."

"Thanks, Darrin."

Before she got out of the car, she leaned over and squeezed Jace's arm. "You were good today, Jace – real good. See you in the morning."

CHAPTER

54

Crom's eyes stayed with the jurors as he directed questions to his client. "Ezekiel, I'd like to talk about your faith in a little more detail. You drew a distinction yesterday between finding Jesus and finding religion. Would that be an accurate characterization?"

"It would." Shaw turned toward the jury and kept his voice level and instructive. "Many people call themselves religious simply because they attend a church. They spend an hour or two a week going to some type of service; they put some money in the collection plate and believe they have done all God requires of them. But if a person has really found Jesus—I mean, really found Jesus—he knows that is not nearly enough. Finding Jesus and inviting him to come into your life is transformative in the literal sense of the word and involves a full-time commitment, not just a temporary nod."

"But you're not condemning those who go to church and that's it?"

"Not at all. That's a start, and a good one. What I'm saying is they need to do more, and if they do, the rich rewards they will reap—not in a material sense but in a spiritual one—will be so worth it. You see, Jesus encouraged his followers to leave their material possessions behind and follow him. Scripture is clear on this. And that is what we try to do in our congregation."

"Let's turn to your church's teachings about the role of women—"

Shaw interrupted his lawyer. "I'm sorry to interrupt, Mr. Prater, but they are not our teachings. They are God's teachings."

Judge Zimmerman leaned toward the witness stand, her penetrating stare finding its target. Shaw returned her gaze, his eyes remaining fixed on hers as his counsel continued the questioning.

"Thank you for that clarification." Crom cleared his throat and continued. "As I recall your testimony from yesterday, you believe that, under God's plan, the woman is to be subservient to the man."

"That is what God tells us throughout the Bible, in the Old and New Testaments. There are many verses that stand for this proposition. I cited a few yesterday and could give you more, if you would like."

"Please do."

"As examples, his teaching in this regard starts in Genesis, chapter 3, verse 16 and continues through First Peter, chapter 3, verse 1, where Peter writes, 'Likewise, wives, be subject to your own husbands.' God's will on this subject is clear and is expressed over and over throughout the Bible."

Crom turned toward the jurors as he posed his next question. "Opposing counsel implied yesterday that you have used Scripture to mistreat women, is that true?"

"That couldn't be further from the truth. We have helped women get back on their feet—women who were on drugs, destitute, homeless. They have now found Jesus and are totally different people through the grace of God."

"Mr. Forman also implied that you had used Scripture to convince young female members of your congregation to have sex with older men, including yourself. Has that ever happened?"

"Never. I am appalled, and deeply insulted, that he would even make such baseless allegations. But then I guess I should have expected as much from . . ."

Jace was on his feet.

Anticipating the objection, Judge Zimmerman ruled, "Sustained. Please keep your feelings about opposing counsel to yourself, Mr. Shaw."

Shaw shot a piercing look at Jace and then muttered, "I will do my best, Your Honor."

Crom continued. "I want to address the funeral protest, which is the subject of this case."

The witness nodded.

"You have testified that you cannot recall precisely what was written on the protest signs your members carried."

"That's correct. I can only recall that they were critical of the roles our society is allowing women to fulfill—and in particular, roles in the military."

"And you didn't keep the signs. Why not?"

"They were made for this protest and for no other purpose. Once the protest was over, there was no reason to keep them."

"You weren't trying to hide anything?"

"Absolutely not. I wish we had kept them, so the jury could see exactly what they said."

Jace clenched his teeth and shook his head.

"And was there any statement on any of the signs—or any statements made by members of your church who were present at the protest—directed personally at the Hanson family or their daughter?"

"Not a one. I specifically made sure that wouldn't happen before we even went to the protest. I talked with my people about avoiding getting into any physical confrontations or verbal shouting matches. I directed them to the 'turn the other cheek' commandment."

"I have one last question for you. Why do you and your followers pick funerals to protest?"

"As I indicated yesterday, we have an obligation to reach as many errant souls as we can. We want to draw media attention to our message, and we feel this is the best way to do it."

Crom nodded at the witness and then reinforced it with an approving smile. "No further questions." He retook his seat at counsel table.

Noting it was approaching noon, Judge Zimmerman recessed the proceeding until one-thirty. As the judge disappeared into chambers, Darrin leaned over and whispered to Jace, "Not good. Prater was very effective, and the jury was buying it. We're going to have to come up with something to change the momentum— and quickly."

Jace waited until Crom and his client had exited the courtroom, then pulled out his cell and speed-dialed Jackie—voice mail. He left a message and then looked at Darrin. "We've got to take some time off the clock, stall until I hear back from Jackie."

"Well, we can call Dr. Fredericks, the psychiatrist who treated Mrs. Hanson. I talked to him last night, told him we might need him today. We can also play the videotape depositions of Lauren's fellow servicemen and women."

"Let's talk about it over lunch."

Darrin, always the pragmatist, cautioned, "If you want to call Fredericks, you need to make that decision pretty quickly. I've got to call him and—"

Jace grinned. "Darrin, I'll make a decision before our sandwiches are served."

After stuffing their files into their briefcases, Darrin and Jace hustled out of the courtroom and toward the elevators.

Maddy Murphy adjusted the height of her hospital bed and turned on the television mounted on the wall in front of her. She and Jackie silently watched as a young female reporter recounted the day's news.

"The trial against the Brimstone Bible Church and its leader, Ezekiel Shaw, continues in federal court in Fort Worth. Mr. Shaw, or Savior Shaw, as his followers call him, was on the stand again this morning and testified unequivocally that neither he nor any of the men in his congregation had abused any of its female members. Our sources tell us the trial will likely conclude later this week."

Maddy hit the power button and turned toward Jackie. "I know what I said this morning, about still not wanting to get involved. But I can't just sit here and let that monster get away with this. You heard the doctor say I could leave whenever I felt up to it. Well, I feel up to it. Can you drive me to Fort Worth this afternoon?"

"Maddy, are you sure you want to do this? You know that after Jace finishes with his questions, Shaw's lawyer is going to come after you with everything he's got. There's no telling what he'll try on you. Jace could meet with you tonight and try and prepare you but still—"

Maddy cut her off. "I'm not going to meet with Mr. Forman. I'm not going to meet with anyone. I want to tell my story one time and one time only, and that'll be from the witness stand. My memory is vivid on what he did to me. I don't need anyone coaching me. I am going to tell the truth, the whole truth—just like the oath says."

"But lawyers have a way of—"

"I know that, Jackie, and I appreciate all your concern. But I just don't want to relive those horrible memories more than one time, and I'm not going to."

"All right. I'll call Jace and let him know we'll be at the courthouse at nine in the morning. Now, let's get you dressed and out of here."

T he afternoon had been an exercise in drudgery. Over Crom's relevance objections, Judge Zimmerman had allowed Jace to play the videotaped depositions of Private First Class Wes Bartos and Staff Sergeant Shelley Crossland, both still on active duty in Afghanistan and, as a consequence, unable to testify in person. Although their testimony had been moving in substance—about Lauren's character, her courage as a soldier, and the ultimate sacrifice she had made for her country—it had lost vitality when played on the oversized screen set up in the corner of the courtroom.

Several jurors fought sleep, and even Judge Zimmerman seemed to nod off on at least one occasion. But Jace needed to buy some time. And with the deposition testimony now in the record, he could remind the jury of the critical portions during closing argument.

At the conclusion of Staff Sergeant Crossland's deposition, Judge Zimmerman glanced at the clock on the wall in the back of the courtroom and then motioned for counsel to approach the bench. In a whisper she addressed the lawyers: "Mr. Forman, it is almost five. I am thinking of recessing for the day. Is that agreeable?"

Relieved, Jace uttered, "It is, Your Honor."

The judge turned to Crom. "And you, Mr. Prater?"

"No objection, Your Honor. I would like to know who counsel plans to call tomorrow so I can prepare my cross tonight. That will make things go much more smoothly tomorrow."

Judge Zimmerman turned back to Jace. "I would like to know as well, Mr. Forman. Who do you plan to call tomorrow?"

Jace hesitated. He didn't want to mislead the judge, but he didn't want to give away his game plan either. He hedged, "I haven't decided for sure, Your Honor. My current plan is to call Dr. Fredericks at some point. My paralegal has a call in to him to determine when he could be available—you know how doctors' schedules are. I also plan on calling the Warwicks. As Your Honor may recall from the pretrial order, they were close friends of the Hansons and will testify as to the visible psychological impact the demonstration had on them."

"Mr. Forman, I still haven't heard any testimony that supports your argument that this protest was personal in nature. Right now, all I have is Mr. Hanson's affidavit. As I footnoted in my opinion denying counsel's motion for summary judgment, I don't think that's enough. Do you have anything else on this issue?"

"I'm working on it, Your Honor."

Judge Zimmerman peered over her glasses at Jace and whispered, "I hope so, Mr. Forman, because, if you don't bring me some strong, credible evidence on this issue, this case is over—I'm directing you out. Do I make myself clear?"

Jace nodded.

The judge then leaned back in her chair and turned toward the jury. Jace and Crom took the cue and scurried back to counsel table.

"Ladies and gentlemen, we are going to recess a little early today. The court is adjourned until nine o'clock in the morning."

All rose as the jurors filed out of the courtroom and the judge did her disappearing act. As the attorneys began to stuff their files into their briefcases, Crom broke the silence. "Well, I've sat through sleepers in my career, but this afternoon took the cake. I hope you have something planned for tomorrow that's a little more entertaining."

Jace ignored the comment.

"Hell, I thought about passing out NoDoz to the jurors during the middle of the second deposition. They were dying."

No response from Jace.

Shaw then piped up. "Yes, Mr. Forman. I agree with my lawyer. Everyone in the courtroom was bored to tears. I am quite surprised at your trial strategy, or lack thereof."

As Jace clutched the handle of his briefcase, he looked across the courtroom at his adversaries. "Sorry to bore the two of you. I will try to do better tomorrow." With Darrin at his side, Jace hurriedly made his way down the aisle and exited the courtroom. Once outside, he powered up his cell. There was a voice mail from Jackie. As he listened, a smile crossed his lips, followed by a frown.

"What is it, Jace?" Darrin inquired with concern.

"Maddy Murphy is going to testify."

"That's great news! So why aren't you more excited, Jace?"

"She won't tell Jackie—or anybody, for that matter—what she's going to say."

As they hurried toward the Range Rover in the corner of the parking lot, Jace called Jackie.

"Jace, I assume you got my voice mail."

"I just listened to it. Where are you?"

"Maddy and I are on the way to Fort Worth. We are on I-35, about thirty miles from Waco. We should get to Fort Worth in a couple of hours. How did it go today?"

"Not as good as I would have liked, but it's hard to know what the jurors are thinking. Maddy agreeing to testify couldn't have come at a better time. But I'm not sure I understand what you said in your message. Did you say she would not meet with me to go over her testimony before getting on the witness stand?"

"Maddy does not want to relive her experience with the BBC any more than she has to. The memories are very painful for her. So she has agreed to testify, but that is it." Jackie looked over at Maddy, who was staring straight ahead, expressionless.

"Jackie, I have never put a witness on the stand without knowing what she's going to say. It's just too dangerous."

"That may be. But do you really have a choice?"

"I guess not." Jace sighed. "Can you have Maddy outside Judge Zimmerman's court at nine?"

"We'll be there."

"I really don't have a good feeling about this."

"You're pretty quick on your feet, Counselor. You'll do just fine."

"Easy for you to say. Jackie, thanks for your help, and thank that strong young lady riding with you."

"Will do. See you in the morning."

Darrin couldn't hold back. "So what'd she say?"

"We've got our witness, but we won't know what she's going to say until she says it—from the witness stand."

"Sheesh."

"My sentiments exactly."

Jace and Darrin climbed into the Range Rover and headed back to the office for another late night.

"I'm sorry, Savior Shaw. I just never had the opportunity. There was someone in her hospital room at all times. There was nothing I could do."

"Where is she now?" Shaw responded, irritation in his tone.

"In a car about an hour or so outside of Fort Worth. Just give me the order and I'll take them both out tonight. I'll make sure it's clean—nothing that could be traced back to us."

There was silence as Shaw pondered the suggestion, scowling as he played out the scenario in his mind. If anything happened to Maddy, and that PI who was guarding her, right before Maddy was about to testify, the cops would be all over it. And all trails would lead back to him—a murder charge virtually guaranteed. No, he couldn't risk it. He would have to bank on the courtroom skills of one Cromwell Prater IV. Besides, the worst thing that could happen in that Fort Worth courtroom would be a money judgment against him and the church. And he had a backup plan for that. His decision made, at least for the moment, he responded, "I can't, and won't, ask that of you, Brother Isaiah. But God always has a way of leading us if we just ask for direction. As I was thinking about what you said, I began to pray and God answered. His message became clear to me. Brother Isaiah, he wants Sister Mary destroyed in a courtroom for all the world to see, for all to see what happens to someone who turns their back on God. We must leave it in his hands, Brother Isaiah."

"If that's God's will, then let it be done. Should I head back to the commune?"

Shaw hesitated for a moment before answering, "Not quite yet. Continue to follow them. When you find out where they are staying tonight, call me. One always needs to be prepared in the event God changes his plan."

"Consider it done, Savior Shaw."

CHAPTER

55

"All rise! The United States District Court for the Northern District of Texas is now in session, the Honorable Barbara Zimmerman presiding." Judge Zimmerman ascended to her throne and looked at Jace.

"Mr. Forman, please call your next witness."

"Plaintiff calls Madeline Murphy, Your Honor. She is waiting in the hall just outside the courtroom."

Judge Zimmerman turned to the bailiff. "Please bring Ms. Murphy in to be sworn."

Crom sprang to his feet. "I would request a conference in chambers, Your Honor."

Judge Zimmerman peered over her glasses. "Grounds?"

"The defense has an objection to this witness giving any testimony in this case and moves to strike."

"Very well then. Ladies and gentlemen, this shouldn't take long. Please remain in the jury room until the bailiff comes to get you." Judge Zimmerman rapped her gavel several times and then said, "This court is in recess for ten minutes."

In chambers, Judge Zimmerman wasted no time. "So what's this all about, Mr. Prater?"

"Your Honor, opposing counsel did not designate Ms. Murphy as a witness in the court's pretrial order."

Jace rebutted. "We've had this discussion once before at the pretrial conference. I have listed the current and—"

Crom interrupted. "I've been blindsided, Your Honor. There is no mention of Madeline Murphy anywhere in the pretrial order, and I'm not prepared to cross her. Opposing counsel knew all along he was going to call her as a witness and intentionally misled me, and this court. I object to her testimony as a flagrant violation of the rules."

"Mr. Forman, I am troubled by this. Have you been planning all along to call Ms. Murphy as a witness?" Still clad in her black robe, Judge Zimmerman leaned forward in her chair, her eyes searching Jace's for clues.

"No, Your Honor, I haven't. Ms. Murphy was just released from the hospital yesterday. I didn't know she was willing to testify until I got out of court yesterday afternoon. Moreover, opposing counsel knew there was the possibility I might call her. I listed all current and former members of the Brimstone Bible Church as potential witnesses. Ms. Murphy falls within that category. There was certainly no reason Mr. Prater could not have contacted her before trial. In fact, I have good reason to believe his client did just that."

Judge Zimmerman's eyes widened. "And what makes you think so, Mr. Forman?"

"Her mother, who went by the name Sister Rebekah and was a loyal member of Shaw's sect, paid Maddy a visit Saturday night. She tied Maddy to the bed and then killed herself."

The judge shuddered. "For goodness sake! Mr. Prater, did you know about this?"

Crom, blindsided, stammered. "No, Your Honor. And I am sorry for the witness, but it doesn't change the fact that Forman didn't list her."

"I beg to differ, Mr. Prater. As Mr. Forman points out, she was included in his catchall designation in the pretrial order. You knew she was a former member of that church. You could have contacted her. Indeed, your client might have contacted her. Your objection is overruled. Ms. Murphy will be allowed to testify. Now, if there is nothing else, the jury is waiting."

In desperation, Crom responded, "I would like to examine the witness outside the presence of the jury. I don't believe she has any relevant testimony, and unless you let me question her on voir dire, I won't have the opportunity to demonstrate that to Your Honor before the jury is poisoned."

In an impatient tone, Judge Zimmerman cautioned, "Overruled. Just be vigilant with your objections, Mr. Prater."

Sensing the judge was resolute in her ruling, Crom tried to limit the damage. "Your Honor, I would ask for a limitation on Ms. Murphy's testimony."

"And what might that be, Mr. Prater?" Judge Zimmerman asked as she rose from behind her desk.

"If Ms. Murphy's mother did in fact kill herself over the weekend, I would ask the court to exclude any testimony about that event for several reasons. One, there is no evidence the suicide is in any way connected to this case and the jurors might infer that my clients had something to do with it. Two, the jurors would undoubtedly feel great sympathy for Ms. Murphy, which in turn might cause them to give more weight to her testimony than they otherwise would."

"I agree. I'm inclined to exclude that evidence. Mr. Forman, your position?"

Ecstatic with the court's decision to allow Maddy's testimony and unwilling to press his luck, Jace conceded. "I have no objection, Your Honor."

"Well, glad you two can agree on something." Judge Zimmerman grinned as she motioned counsel toward the door.

After the jurors had taken their seats, the bailiff escorted Maddy into the courtroom. All eyes were drawn to the young girl in the simple blue dress who walked down the aisle and, after taking the oath, climbed into the witness chair. The bailiff adjusted the microphone in front of her and smiled paternally before resuming his courtroom post.

Crom stood up. "Your Honor, we would like to make sure our objections to this witness testifying are on the record. Opposing counsel did not list her in the pretrial order. Allowing her to testify would be a clear violation of this court's standing order as well as the Federal Rules of Civil Procedure. Moreover, her testimony has no relevance whatsoever to the issues to be decided by this jury."

Judge Zimmerman nodded in Crom's direction. "Your objections are noted and overruled. Please proceed with your examination, Mr. Forman."

Shaw whispered something in Crom's ear, who shook his head disgustedly in response.

"Please state your name for the record."

"Madeline Murphy." Her gaze didn't veer from Jace, her soft blue eyes locking on his.

Jace smiled. "Do you go by Madeline?"

The witness returned the smile. "My friends call me Maddy."

"Would it be okay with you if I called you Maddy?"

A nod.

"Maddy, I want to thank you for coming here today. I'm going to try and make this as painless as possible. How old are you?"

"Seventeen."

"And where do you live?"

"Austin, Texas."

"What do you do in Austin?"

"I work as a waitress at the County Line restaurant."

Jace hesitated and then continued. "Maddy, I know this will be hard for you, but I want to take you back to—"

"Objection, Your Honor. Mr. Forman is—"

Irritated, the judge responded before Crom could finish his objection. "In my court, counsel is entitled to ask his question before an objection can be lodged. Please afford Mr. Forman that courtesy."

Crom scowled and grumbled something under his breath as he sat back down.

Jace cleared his throat and then continued. "I want to talk with you about your time with the Brimstone Bible Church. Are you willing to do that?"

Maddy kept her eyes glued to Jace, purposely avoiding the piercing stare of Ezekiel Shaw.

"Yes."

Crom was again on his feet. In an attempt to spook the witness, he said, "Your Honor, would you please ask the witness to speak up? I can barely hear her."

Judge Zimmerman smiled and asked the bailiff to adjust the microphone so that it was closer to the witness. "Please continue, Mr. Forman."

"How did you come to be a member of the Brimstone Bible Church?"

"Well, my mother became a member and took me with her."

"When did your mother become a member?"

"I was young, maybe seven or eight."

"And do you have any idea why your mother joined the Brimstone Bible Church?"

"No. But I assume it was because we needed a place to live."

"And where were you living before?"

"We were living out of our car." Maddy hung her head and looked down as she testified. "My mother was drinking and didn't have a job."

"I'm sorry, Maddy." Jace briefly paused before resuming. "And did the church help you and your mother?"

"Yes, at first. We had a roof over our heads, and I had a school to go to."

"And do you know the leader of the Brimstone Bible Church?"

"Savior Shaw." Maddy held her gaze on Jace.

"Does he also go by Ezekiel?"

"I only knew him as Savior Shaw."

"So where did the Brimstone Bible Church hold its services?"

"At first in Austin. But then we moved to a compound in West Texas."

"And did you like it—your new home, that is?"

"At first I really liked it. There were lots of kids for me to play with. Mama was sober and seemed happy. Yeah, it was pretty cool."

Jace was still feeling his way. He didn't know where this was going, but he had no choice but to continue down the path. "Did your feelings ever change?"

Maddy squirmed in her seat and responded, "May I have a drink of water? My throat feels dry."

"Of course." Jace scurried back to counsel table, poured some water into a paper cup, and handed it to the witness.

Maddy took a sip and said, "Thank you."

"No problem, Maddy. We were talking about when your feelings changed. Please continue."

The witness stared down at her hands, which were tightly clasped in her lap. She took a deep breath, her eyes slowly returning to Jace. "I will never forget that night."

"Objection, Your Honor. This testimony is not relevant to any issue in this case and is highly prejudicial. I request a conference in chambers."

Judge Zimmerman shook her head and sighed. "All right, Mr. Prater. Ladies and gentlemen, we are going to take a break. I'll see you back in this courtroom in thirty minutes. And I will see counsel in chambers right now."

Jace and Crom sat patiently in the leather chairs in front of Judge Zimmerman's mahogany desk as she hung up her black robe and took her seat across from them.

"So, Mr. Prater, please enlighten the court as to how you can object when you don't even know what the witness is going to say."

"Your Honor, whether or not Ms. Murphy liked the Brimstone Bible Church has absolutely no relevance to what happened at the Hagstrom protest, which is the subject matter of this suit."

Judge Zimmerman turned to Jace. "Mr. Forman, what is Ms. Murphy going to testify to?"

"I have no idea."

"What? You didn't meet with the witness before putting her on the stand?"

"I tried to, but she wouldn't allow it. She wouldn't even talk to me on the phone. She told my investigator that she would testify in court but would not discuss her testimony beforehand. I had to make a judgment call and decided to take a chance."

"Well, I've been sitting on the bench for over fifteen years and this is a first."

"It's a first for me as well, Your Honor."

Crom interjected. "I would say Mr. Forman's explanation is hard to buy. I don't like to call fellow members of the bar—"

The judge interrupted. "Then don't. Let's hear what Ms. Murphy has to say. And Mr. Prater, if you have any further objections, you'll make them in the courtroom. No more conferences in chambers. Is that understood?"

Crom nodded.

"Good. Let's get this show on the road."

"Maddy, before we took a break, you were about to tell us when your feelings changed."

"I was twelve at the time. My mother came back to our cabin one night and told me she wanted to have a mother-daughter talk. We crawled up on her bed and she asked me how I liked Savior Shaw." Maddy hesitated.

"And what did you say?"

"I told her he seemed like a nice man."

"And how did your mother respond?"

"She went on and on about what a wonderful man he was, that he was inspired by God, that we were so lucky to have found him. I don't remember everything she said, but she praised him and was obviously very fond of him."

"Then what happened?"

"She told me Savior Shaw wanted to read a bedtime story to me. That I should immediately go to his house and, on my way, give thanks unto the Lord that Savior Shaw had picked me."

"And did you go?"

"Yes. I was happy to go. I liked Savior Shaw and had no reason to distrust him. I ran down the street to Savior Shaw's house and knocked on the door."

"What happened next?"

"Savior Shaw opened the door. He was all smiles. He ushered me in and asked if I wanted something to drink—a Coke, hot chocolate, anything. I told him I wasn't thirsty. He had baked some chocolate chip cookies. I could smell them. He must have just pulled them out of the oven. He motioned me into the kitchen where we sat down at a table. We talked for a while. I started to feel comfortable. I even ate a cookie or two. Then Savior Shaw's mood changed. He became more serious." Maddy swallowed, bit her lip, and then continued. "As always, he was dressed in his white robe. Sometimes he wore sandals but on that night he was barefooted. Without saying anything, he got up from the table and held out his hand ...." Maddy paused and was obviously having difficulty continuing with her testimony.

Judge Zimmerman leaned toward the witness. "Ms. Murphy, this must be difficult for you. Would you like to take a break?"

Maddy shook her head. "Thank you, Your Honor, but I want to get this over with." Before continuing, she flashed a cold stare at Shaw, whose eyes were fixed on the legal pad in front of him. "So I took his hand, and he led me back to his bedroom."

There were audible gasps from the jury box. The bailiff scowled at Shaw and shook his head. Judge Zimmerman took off her half-glasses, rubbed her eyes, and then returned them to the bridge of her nose.

"And what happened next?"

"There were candles burning everywhere. It was like he was trying to make it all heavenly or something. There was this altar in one of the corners. It had a wooden carving of Jesus above and a place to kneel below. He asked me to kneel and join him in prayer, so I did."

"And do you remember his prayer?"

"He read some Bible verses about women being obedient and doing what men told them to. He closed the Bible and asked me if I was willing to abide by God's word. I told him yes. He took my hand and led me toward an oversized chair – it reminded me of a throne or something like that. It was in the opposite corner of the room. He sat down . . ."

A single tear slowly meandered down one of Maddy's cheeks, and her lips began to quiver. The bailiff quickly handed her a tissue, which she brought to the corners of both eyes. She continued, her voice little more than a whisper. "He sat down and told me to take off my shoes. I sat down on the floor, untied my shoes, and pulled them off. As I sat there on the floor, Savior Shaw said something about my feet, how petite they were. He told me to stand up and take off my dress, that it was God's will. I just sat there staring at him. I was so scared. I was paralyzed with fear."

Crom was on his feet. "Your Honor—"

"Save your breath, Counselor. Overruled."

"And what happened next?"

Maddy closed her eyes and continued. "He leaned towards me, lifted me up by my arm, and then pulled the dress over my head. I have never felt so helpless—and alone—in my life. Never. I was standing there, before Savior Shaw, in my underwear. I was petrified. I had my eyes closed tight. I heard him whisper something and felt his hand between my legs. I began to cry. I remember him telling me not to be afraid, that this was God's will. And then he took me." Maddy was openly crying but continued her testimony. "After it was over, he told me to put my dress and shoes back on. He walked me to the door, gave me a hug and a kiss on the forehead, and told me to 'sleep tight.' I ran all the way home."

"Did you tell your mother what had happened?"

"I didn't say a word to her. I was afraid she wouldn't believe me. She was napping in the den when I got home. I sneaked past her to my room, closed the door and buried my face in my pillow. I cried my eyes out – soft as I could. I didn't want to wake her.

I didn't know what I would say to her if she woke up and came into my room."

Judge Zimmerman politely interrupted. "Ladies and gentlemen, we are going to take a break for lunch. We'll resume around one-thirty. I would like to see counsel in chambers."

Once in chambers, Judge Zimmerman turned to Jace. "Mr. Forman, as heartrending a tale as this is, I don't know that it has any relevance to the case at hand. Help me out here if you can."

"Your Honor, the defense theme in this case has been that Shaw and his followers protested at Lauren Hanson's funeral due to their fervent religious beliefs—their credo that God has relegated women to a position of subservience and obedience to their male counterparts. Ms. Murphy's testimony convincingly demonstrates that Shaw's beliefs are not genuinely held but constitute no more than a subterfuge to get women—and in this instance, a prepubescent girl—to do exactly what he wants them to, sexually and otherwise. If Shaw's beliefs are a fraud, then he and his 'disciples' couldn't have been protesting on a public issue."

"Creative, Mr. Forman. Response, Mr. Prater?"

"This evidence is being introduced for no other purpose than to inflame this jury, which I submit it has already done. This case now has mistrial written all over it thanks to Mr. Forman's antics. And I hereby make a motion that—"

"Okay, okay, Mr. Prater. I will give you ample opportunity to make your motion. Mr. Forman, any further response?"

"The evidence comes in on another ground—namely, impeachment. You remember when I asked Mr. Shaw if he had ever used Scripture to take advantage of women or young girls?"

The judge nodded. "I do recall that line of questioning."

"Well, he emphatically denied it. Ms. Murphy's testimony is admissible to impeach Shaw's previous testimony."

Judge Zimmerman turned to Crom. "He has a valid point, Mr. Prater. I am going to allow the witness to continue with her testimony. After we recess today, I will give you the opportunity to make your motion for mistrial on the record, outside the presence of the jury. Now let's get back to it."

"Maddy, was this the only time you had an intimate encounter with Mr. Shaw?"

"No, there were many, many others."

"Maddy, I am sorry to have to be so direct, but when you testified Mr. Shaw—the man seated at counsel table right over there—'took' you, do you mean he had intercourse with you?"

"Yes, all the time." The witness put her head in her hands and began to sob.

"And how old were you when this started?"

"From the time I was twelve until the day I ran away."

Jace paused, looked at the jury, and shook his head. He walked to counsel table and took a sip of water before continuing. He wanted to let the full impact of the testimony sink in with the jury. Moments later, he began again.

"Maddy, I would like to talk with you about the protest the BBC staged in Hagstrom. Were you there?"

"I was there. It was the first time I attended a protest. I didn't want to go, but I was ordered to by Savior Shaw."

"Were you there the entire time?"

"I was."

"Do you remember what was written on the signs that were used at the protest?"

"I do. I made them. One of them said 'A woman's place is in the bedroom, not the boardroom.' Another said 'Women are for bearing children, not arms.' There was one that said 'God hates lesbians,' or something like that."

"Did any of the signs refer to Lauren Hanson or her parents?"

The witness shook her head. "Not specifically. The signs didn't, anyway."

Jace picked up on the distinction. "Did any of the BBC members say anything at the protest that could be construed as a personal insult to Lauren Hanson or her parents?"

"One of them did, yes."

"And who was that?"

"My mother."

"And what did she say?"

"As I recall, Mr. Hanson had jumped out of the funeral car and had wrested a sign away from her. He was screaming at her when a police officer began pulling him away. With an evil look in her eye—a look I had never seen before—she hollered at that poor man, screamed at him at the top of her lungs, 'Your daughter was a lesbian whore. She deserved to die. You and your wife should be ashamed. You raised her for the devil.' I felt so sorry for him and so ashamed to be there."

"What happened next?'

"The police dragged Mr. Hanson back to the limousine he was riding in and the funeral procession drove away. We packed up our stuff and headed back to the commune."

"And did you ever have any more contact with the Hansons?"

"Not directly with the Hansons."

"What do you mean?"

"Well, after the protest, he"—Maddy nodded at Shaw—"had me post some comments about the Hanson family, and their daughter, on the BBC website. He called it a 'manifesto,' or something like that."

"Did you write this manifesto?"

"No, he did. Every word of it."

"And do you remember what it said?"

"Not verbatim."

"Do you remember generally?"

"Generally, yes."

"Tell us what you remember."

Crom leaped to his feet and blustered, "I object. The witness admitted that she could not recall what this so-called manifesto said. Any testimony as to what it might have said would be rank conjecture and nothing more."

Jace responded, "Your Honor, we asked for Mr. Prater's clients to produce any documents, broadly defined to include entries on the church's website, that related in any way to the protest that is the subject matter of this case. Nothing that fits the witness's description was produced."

Crom retorted, "That's because this document is nothing more than a figment of this young woman's imagination. There was no manifesto, or whatever Ms. Murphy called it."

Before Judge Zimmerman could rule on the objection, the witness blurted out, "Oh, yes, there was. Savior Shaw had me post it, and then he had me take it down a few days before I ran away."

Judge Zimmerman turned to the witness. "And do you recall the date you ran away?"

"I do, Your Honor. It'll be exactly six months day after tomorrow."

The judge eyed the filing date of the lawsuit contained on the cover of the file folder in front of her and continued. "Let's see. By my calculation that would have been right around the time this lawsuit was filed. Your client hasn't destroyed any important documents, has he, Mr. Prater?"

Crom glanced at his client, who shook his head vehemently. "Of course not, Your Honor. As I said, this so-called post is nothing more than the product of this young lady's imagination."

"Very well. I'll allow Ms. Murphy to testify as to what she remembers this manifesto saying. Since the actual document—the web post—does not exist, there can be no best evidence objection." Satisfied she had made the basis for her ruling crystal clear for the appellate court to consider, she turned to the witness and stated, "You may continue, Ms. Murphy."

Maddy responded, "Something like 'Lauren Hanson will burn in hell for all eternity,' that 'God will not tolerate sinners who ignore his word' and that her parents 'raised her for the devil and got just what they deserved.'"

"Thank you, Maddy. Pass the witness." Jace pivoted and retook his seat at counsel table.

Before Crom could begin his cross, the judge addressed the jurors. "Ladies and gentlemen, it's a little before five. We'll recess until nine in the morning. Ms. Murphy, you will need to be here at nine to continue your testimony. You may be excused until then." As the jurors made their way into the jury room, Maddy stepped down from the witness stand and walked through the swinging doors separating the trial's participants from its observers to a waiting Jackie McLaughlin. Jackie put her arm around Maddy's waist, and the two walked out of the courtroom.

Before leaving, Jace turned to Crom and his client, "I hope we didn't bore you this afternoon." He then grabbed his briefcase and ushered Darrin down the aisle toward the massive oak door.

Crom paced around the firm's conference room in a fever pitch, his tie loosened, shirt unbuttoned at the neck, and sleeves rolled up. His suit jacket lay crumpled in one of the conference room chairs. His client leaned forward in his chair and stared vacuously at the silk flower arrangement in the middle of the table, showing no emotion as Crom continued his tirade.

"What in the hell was that? I tell you I have to know everything—everything—to be able to properly defend you, and I don't hear this shit for the first time from the witness stand? What were you thinking? I mean, I don't know how many times I asked you if there would be any surprises at trial. 'No, Crom, I promise you there won't be. You can count on that.' Come on, Zeke! You knew about Maddy all along and made the conscious decision not to tell me about her. I can't believe this!"

Shaw took the offensive. "She's lying. Everything that little bitch said was a lie. She's trying to get back at me, that's all."

"Well, every one of those jurors was eating it up. You could have heard a pin drop in there. They bought her story hook, line, and sinker."

"Well, you've got to convince them otherwise. Isn't that what I'm paying you to do?"

"Correction. You haven't paid me a fucking nickel. Remember—our firm is representing you and that church of yours for free. So let's get that straight."

"That may be true, but you still have an obligation to represent me to the best of your ability, fee or no fee."

"How in the hell can I do that when you won't even level with me?"

"But I have leveled with you. I've told you the truth, I swear. She's the one who's lying. You've got to believe that."

"Are you saying she just made that up about you sleeping with her when she was only twelve? It sure didn't sound made up to me."

"It didn't happen. I swear it didn't."

Crom snorted sarcastically. "She sure knew a lot of details."

"And why wouldn't she? She had been in my house on countless occasions."

"For what reason?"

"Her mother, Sister Rebekah. We were romantically involved. She would come over to the house and bring her daughter. The three of us would have dinner together. We would do things together. We were like a family."

"So why would Maddy turn on you?"

Shaw hesitated before answering. "Because her mother was unstable. She must blame me for her mother's suicide."

Crom slid into the chair next to his client and leaned in close before asking his next question. "Are you telling me the truth? You'll regret the hell out of it if you're not."

"If I was lying to you, you'd be able to tell. You could see it in my eyes." Shaw stared hypnotically at Crom as he spoke. "Maddy, well, she is obviously confused and misdirected. And I find it hard to believe that Forman hadn't met with her before today, don't you? I mean, it just doesn't make any sense."

Crom leaned his head back and stared at the conference room ceiling. "I agree with you there, but that's water under the bridge. Here's the deal. I'm going to have to pull the gloves off tomorrow for us to have any chance of winning this case—go after Maddy with both barrels blazing. But it's a damn risky move and might backfire on us. If the jury doesn't buy it, not only will they decide against us, they might get mad and award millions more in damages. It's a big decision and not one for me to make. You're the client. What do you want me to do?"

"I want to win this case. My reputation—and the reputation of the church I founded—is on the line. Take your best shot."

"Well, like I said, it's damn risky, but we don't have a prayer unless we go for her jugular. Oh, and another thing. Did you send her mother to Austin?"

"Are you kidding? Why would I do that?"

"To convince Maddy not to testify."

Shaw shook his head. "I didn't even know Sister Rebekah had left the commune until one of the Brothers called me and filled me in on what had happened. Such a waste. So, no, I didn't tell her to go to Austin, and I have no idea why she went. I don't think anyone will ever know."

"One last question. Are you sure this so-called manifesto never existed?"

Shaw smirked. "Positive. And I can get every member of—"

"Forget it. I'm not going to take the risk of putting the members of your congregation on the stand and giving Forman the opportunity to go after them on cross. No way."

"I understand your concern."

Crom stepped in front of the display board on the wall of the conference room and picked up an erasable marker from its trough. "All right, let's get started. Tell me everything you can think of that I can use to destroy Maddy Murphy."

CHAPTER

"Mr. Prater, are you ready to proceed?"

Crom stood and, in a strong, deliberate voice, replied, "I am, Your Honor."

"Very well, then."

"Good morning, Ms. Murphy."

The witness meekly answered, "Good morning."

"May I call you Maddy, like Mr. Forman did?"

"I guess so."

"All right then, Maddy. Do you recall telling us yesterday that your mother and my client, Mr. Shaw, were pretty close?"

"Yes."

"Were they romantically involved?"

"I believe so."

"Did your mother stay overnight at Mr. Shaw's house from time to time?"

"Yes."

"Okay. And did you sometimes go over to Mr. Shaw's house with your mother?"

"Yes."

"Would this have happened more than once?"

"Yes."

"Isn't it true that you and your mother would regularly have dinner at Mr. Shaw's?"

The witness nodded.

"And on those occasions you would have been able to familiarize yourself with Mr. Shaw's house?"

"What do you mean?"

"Well, he didn't keep you from going throughout the house, now did he?"

"No."

"So you would have seen his bedroom upon occasion while you and your mother were there having dinner?"

"Not often."

"But on occasion you would have?"

"That's true."

"So when you described the altar in my client's bedroom yesterday, you could have been relying on your memory from one of the occasions when you and your mother were having dinner there?"

"What I testified to yesterday—about your client molesting me over and over again—that was all based upon my recollection of those horrible nights, and nothing else."

"But you knew what my client's bedroom looked like from your visits to his house with your mother, isn't that right?"

"You could say that."

Crom smiled disingenuously at the witness.

"All right. You described your time at the Brimstone Bible Church as a happy one—at least at the beginning, correct?"

"Yes."

"But that changed, didn't it?"

"Yes, when your client—"

"It changed when my client ended his relationship with your mother, isn't that true?"

"No, it changed when that man over there began to—"

"Well, your mother did have a relationship with Mr. Shaw, correct?"

"Yes."

"And you testified earlier it was a romantic relationship, correct?"

The witness nodded, then added, "But—"

Crom politely interrupted. "Please, Maddy, just answer my question. Your lawyer will have an opportunity—"

Jace rose. "Objection, Your Honor. I'm not her—"

"Sustained. Mr. Prater, do not refer to Mr. Forman as Ms. Murphy's lawyer."

"My apologies, Your Honor." As he spoke, he glanced at several of the jurors, whose expressions signaled his point had registered.

"And before you left the compound, that romantic relationship between Mr. Shaw and your mother ended, did it not?"

"I don't know if—"

"And that was not what your mother wanted, was it?"

Jace began to squirm in his chair. He didn't like where this was going.

The witness was silent.

"Your Honor, I respectfully ask that you direct the witness to answer my question."

Judge Zimmerman leaned toward the witness box. "Ms. Murphy, you must answer his question."

"I don't know the answer."

"And your mother was very unhappy after Mr. Shaw started seeing someone else, wasn't she?"

"I know what you're trying to do—"

"I'm only trying to get to the truth, Ms. Murphy. That's all."

Crom walked to the jury box and rested his arm on the ledge, his eyes connecting with those of the men and women seated there, as he asked his next question. "Now, yesterday you testified that my client repeatedly and over a number of years forced himself on you sexually. Do I recall your testimony correctly?"

The witness nodded uncertainly, not knowing what was coming next.

"But in all those years when you were allegedly being assaulted, you didn't tell a single soul, did you - not even your own mother?"

"No, but—"

"You didn't call the police?"

"I was afraid—"

"So the answer is no."

"If you would let me—"

"You didn't tell a single soul until you got on that witness stand yesterday, isn't that a fact?"

"I wanted to—"

"But you didn't, did you? And if I paraded every single member of the Brimstone Bible Church before this jury and asked each and every one of them if they had any knowledge of you and my client having sex, it wouldn't surprise you if they all answered no, would it?"

Jace jumped up from his chair. "Objection."

Before the judge could rule, Crom uttered, "Withdrawn." He was on a roll and didn't want to lose momentum.

"Now, yesterday you talked about this so-called manifesto my client had you post on the BBC website, do you recall that?"

No response.

"Well, I'm sure the jury will recall that testimony. You don't have one scrap of paper and not one witness who can corroborate your story, do you?"

"No, but it's the truth."

Crom strolled back to counsel table, but before taking his seat, he pivoted to face the witness. "Isn't it true that you have concocted this entire story—every thread of this fantastical yarn—to get back at my client because he left your mother for another woman?"

"That's not true. He—"

"Pass the witness."

Shaw smiled at his lawyer as Crom retook his seat at counsel table. In Shaw's mind, Maddy Murphy's credibility had been destroyed, his decision to leave things up to his lawyer the right one.

"Mr. Forman, redirect?"

Jace let seconds—seconds that seemed like minutes—pass before asking his final question. He remained seated, his eyes fixed on the young girl in the white dress. Silence swept over the courtroom, and then Jace spoke. "Why, Maddy, should we believe you?"

Tears wound their way down Maddy's cheeks. She turned toward the jury and said, "Because every single thing I've said here is the truth, all of it. And that man over there—he knows it."

Shaw stared impassively at the legal pad in front of him.

"No further questions, Your Honor."

"Re-cross, Mr. Prater?"

Crom shook his head.

Judge Zimmerman turned to the witness. "You may be excused."

After Maddy had left the courtroom, accompanied by Jackie, Judge Zimmerman called a short recess to meet with counsel in chambers.

"Mr. Forman, how many more witnesses do you have?"

"Your Honor, that was our last. We considered calling a psychiatrist and a couple who lived across from the Hansons to testify as to the mental anguish they suffered as a result of the defendants' conduct but decided the jury can figure that out on their own. There are some housekeeping details I need to take care of, like getting Mr. Hanson's will admitted into evidence. Other than that, I am prepared to rest."

Judge Zimmerman turned to Crom. "Mr. Prater, how long do you anticipate your case will take?"

"Your Honor, we have a motion for directed verdict we would like to present to the court. We don't think the evidence presented by opposing counsel meets the burden clearly established by the Supreme Court in the Westboro decision."

Judge Zimmerman frowned. "But how about Ms. Murphy's testimony? In my view, it took your clients' conduct out of the public realm and placed it in the private."

"I respectfully disagree. Besides, her testimony is not believable."

"But you and I both know that's for the jury to decide." Judge Zimmerman paused for a response that didn't come. "I will let you make your motion on the record, but I'm going to deny it. Last night I reread the Westboro decision and found there are significant differences between the facts of that case and the one before this court."

Crom turned white. In a desperate voice, he pleaded, "Your Honor, we are very confident in our legal position."

"And you may be right and I may be wrong. That's why we have appellate courts. Do you have any witnesses to call, Mr. Prater?"

"It's our position, and always has been, that this is a legal matter for the court to decide so, no, we don't plan on calling any witnesses."

"My inclination, then, is to release the jury for the afternoon, let Mr. Forman place his client's will into the record, and then hear your motion for directed verdict, which I'll deny. Tomorrow morning we'll have closing arguments, and I will submit the case to the jury before noon. Any objection?"

Jace shook his head, a subtle smile forming on his lips. Crom closed his eyes and mumbled his assent.

"All right then. I'll have the bailiff release the jury, and I'll see the two of you in the courtroom in fifteen minutes."

CHAPTER

57

As Darrin drove home from the office, she called Megan but got her voice mail. "Sorry we've been missing each other. I've been dying to hear all the details of what's happening with Mark. Call me when you can." Spotting a Whataburger, she turned in just as Megan returned her call.

"Darrin, finally! I've got a lot to tell you. But, first, how's that trial going?"

"We're almost done – closing arguments in the morning. Now let's talk about what's been happening between you and Mark. Tell me all about it."

"We've actually been having some civil conversations. After that horrible fight, I told him I was sorry I threw wine in his face and he told me he deserved it. He admitted I was right about the concerns I raised and apologized for saying I was fat and unattractive-"

"I hope he didn't word it like that!"

Megan laughed. "He was a little more diplomatic. And," Megan paused for effect, "out of the blue, he suggested we see a marriage counselor."

"That's great Megan! It's certainly a step in the right direction."

"I agree. I mean, at least he isn't giving up on us."

"Have the two of you decided who you're going to see?"

"Mark threw out several names during our conversation. I mean, he was like a different person. He seemed really genuine about wanting to make our marriage work. And we decided he shouldn't stay here while we are working on things."

"That's a good idea. So what did you tell the girls?"

"We sat down with them after school the next day and told them we were working through some problems and that Daddy was going to spend the night somewhere else for a few weeks. We told them we both loved them very much and that this didn't have anything to do with them, that it was between Mommy and Daddy."

"Were they upset?"

"They were very upset at first and then calmed down after we told them they would be seeing their daddy just as much as they always have."

"Wow, that sounds tough but it also sounds like you handled it well."

"We did our best," Megan glanced at the clock on the kitchen wall. "Darrin, I've got to run. It's almost eight-thirty and I have to get the girls bathed and put to bed and..."

"No problem, I understand. Keep me posted and call me if you need anything."

"I will. Hey, good luck in your trial. Let me know what happens."

"Will do." Darrin dropped the cell in her purse and pulled into the drive-thru lane. She had skimped on lunch and was starving. She could think of nothing that would taste better than a juicy Whataburger and an order of their signature fries.

372

CHAPTER

58

The next morning at nine, the jury filed into the courtroom and took their seats. Jace and Crom tried to read their expressions. Their thoughts were interrupted by Judge Zimmerman's gavel.

"Mr. Forman, are you prepared to deliver your close?"

"I am, Your Honor."

"Please proceed."

Jace walked slowly toward the jury box and stopped just in front before speaking.

"Ladies and gentlemen, I want to thank you for your time and attentiveness. I know all of you have busy schedules and it's a big sacrifice for you to be here. But your valuable time has not been wasted, I assure you of that. There are extremely important issues that are raised by this case, and those issues are for you, and you alone, to decide."

Jace slowly made eye contact with each juror before continuing.

"First, let's talk about what I'm not asking you to do in this case. I'm not—and I repeat 'not'—asking you to throw out the First Amendment right to free speech. That amendment, drafted by the founding fathers, embodies some of the most important freedoms known to man. The right to speak our minds and express our views freely sets us apart from other countries and has been one of the principal reasons we are the great nation we are. That said, the First Amendment right of free speech is not without limitation—and never has been. Let me give you some examples."

Jace began to slowly pace back and forth in front of the jurors, addressing them in a calm but deliberate voice, stopping occasionally to emphasize a point.

"No one has the right to scream 'fire' in a crowded theater. The reason is obvious. It could cause panic and harm to others. Students don't have the right to express their opinions disruptively in class, because it would interfere with the right of other students to learn. Protesters cannot protest at certain hours and in certain places, because it would interfere with the rights of others. For example, someone could not protest outside your house with a megaphone at three o'clock in the morning—it would interfere with your right to privacy. The point is there have always, always been restrictions on the right of free speech in terms of where it can be exercised, when it can be exercised, and how it can be exercised. Basically, in the examples I have cited, the courts have struck a balance between the rights of individuals to speak freely and the rights of other individuals to be free from harassment, to not be put in needless danger, and to be able to get an education. So how do these rules apply to the case before you?"

Jace briefly paused before continuing.

"There is no question that Mr. Shaw and his church had the right to speak their views, no doubt about that. But they did not have the right to express those views in a manner that harassed, insulted, and inflicted emotional pain and suffering on Eugene and Janice Hanson at one of the most vulnerable times in their lives: when they were saying their last goodbyes to their only daughter, Second Lieutenant Lauren Hanson. A young lady who was a true patriot and who, only days before, had made the ultimate sacrifice for the country she loved."

Jace paused and noticed that two of the female jurors were blotting tears from their eyes. Confident his message was resonating, he continued.

"I ask you, ladies and gentlemen, was it necessary for Shaw and his followers to choose a funeral service as the venue to voice their message that women should be submissive in every way to men? Was that the only place they could have staged their protest? Of course not. There were countless public venues where they could have made their arguments—parks, courthouse grounds, state capitols, you name it. But Mr. Shaw rejected all of those public forums for one reason and one reason only, a reason he testified to proudly and without remorse. He wanted his message to reach as many people as possible, and he didn't care who was hurt in the process. He wanted coverage—media coverage—and he knew that picketing a soldier's funeral would get him just that."

Jace paused. Before continuing, he glanced at the panel and caught the eyes of a male juror, who gave him an approving nod.

"Let's focus for a minute on the testimony of Maddy Murphy. Was she telling the truth? Or did she concoct this story to get back at Mr. Shaw? Her credibility is for you, and only you, to judge. But I submit to you this is one brave young lady, someone who under very trying circumstances came forward to do the right thing. Does her recollection of being sexually abused by Mr. Shaw not ring true? Consider the details she recounted and her demeanor on the witness stand. And her testimony about what her mother screamed at Eugene Hanson at his daughter's funeral. Why would she make up something horrific like that—and then attribute it to her mother? And how about that manifesto Shaw told her to write? Does that sound like something she just invented? Ladies and gentlemen, Maddy Murphy told you the truth, as difficult as that was, and it's a slap in that young girl's face for anyone to contend otherwise."

"So this 'free speech' issue boils down to a simple proposition. Should protesters be allowed to picket the funeral service of someone's daughter and publicly condemn her sexual orientation, whatever it might have been, say she deserved to die, claim her parents raised her for the devil, and proclaim she will burn in hell for an eternity? Is that what the founders intended when they wrote the First Amendment? The answer is an emphatic 'no'. Never in their wildest dreams did they envision that an amendment they so carefully drafted would be used to shield such vile and harmful conduct."

Jace lowered his head for a moment, as if gathering his thoughts. He then looked up and slowly made eye contact with each juror before resuming.

"And what damage resulted from the conduct of Shaw and his sect? Two loving parents are dead. The torment was so unbearable for Janice Hanson that she overdosed on sleeping pills. Eugene Hanson, without the two people he loved most in the world, drove to yet another funeral protest staged by these same defendants. He was so distraught that he drove miles to confront a man who had taken everything from him, and Eugene lost his life as a consequence."

"Ladies and gentlemen, no amount of money—no amount—will bring back my clients. No amount will erase the mental anguish and torment my clients suffered as the result of the defendants' actions. And because of those actions, they cannot tell you in their own words what they went through. But Eugene Hanson specifically indicated how any damages you might award in this case should be used. He made his intentions known in a will he signed before he died. The will provided that any damages be used to compensate past and future victims of the defendants' conduct. How much you award is entirely up to you. I only hope it will be enough to ensure that these defendants can never, ever put anyone through this again. Thank you."

Jace lingered at the jury box for a few seconds before making his way back to counsel table.

Judge Zimmerman turned to Jace's opposition.

"Mr. Prater?"

Crom, dressed solemnly in a dark blue pin-striped suit, white shirt, and silver-blue tie, a pin of the American flag adorning his lapel, spent the next hour pacing frantically back and forth in front of the jury, his voice alternating strategically from a low whisper to a controlled shout, his message enthusiastically extolling the sanctity of the First Amendment and caustically condemning opposing counsel's unabashed assault on its vitality. Unapologetically, he derided Maddy's testimony as the inept attempt of a young girl to avenge her mother's rejection by a former lover—testimony so fanciful and devoid of corroboration that no reasonable person could believe it and without which the plaintiff's case constituted nothing more than hollow allegations without factual foundation. He cited statements of numerous famous Americans as to the importance of freedom of speech in the country's heritage, as well as the words of Chief Justice Roberts in the majority opinion of the Westboro case, where he wrote, "Speech is powerful. It can stir people to action, move them to tears of both joy and sorrow, and—as it did here—inflict great pain. On the facts before us, we cannot react to that pain by punishing the speaker. As a nation, we have chosen a different course—to protect even hurtful speech on public issues to ensure that we don't stifle public debate." Crom then asked the jurors not to punish the speakers, as his opposition had exhorted them to do, but rather to follow the course charted by the Supreme Court and find for his clients. Confidently, he strode back to counsel table and took his seat next to Shaw.

At the conclusion of Crom's closing argument, Judge Zimmerman read the jurors a series of instructions, gave them their charge, and released them to begin deliberations.

Once the door to the jury room had closed, the judge addressed counsel. "If you would like to return to your offices, you are free to do so. The clerk will contact you when the jury has reached a verdict." With that, she rose and carefully made her way down from the bench and through the door to chambers.

Darrin leaned over and whispered to Jace, "You were amazing! Do you want to stay here or head back to the office?"

"I don't want to look at Prater's client any more than I have to. Let's get out of here. It could be several hours, or even days, before we know anything."

CHAPTER

59

Reginald Cowan III leaned back in his chair and gazed around at his new surroundings. He had recently been appointed interim United States Attorney for the Northern District of Texas by Attorney General Lemuel "Lem" Baxter, whose favor Reggie had carefully cultivated while an assistant district attorney in Austin. All that ass-kissing he had shamelessly engaged in at numerous cocktail parties, dinners, and other fund-raising events had paid off big-time. Now all he needed were some high-profile convictions to ensure that his interim appointment became permanent.

He picked up the most recent issue of *Texas Matters* from the top of his desk. He smiled and shook his head as he gazed at the cover. Cal Connors, dressed in his signature Stetson, bolo tie, and fringed suede jacket, glared back at him. Reginald, as he now preferred to be called, whispered under his breath, "You pompous prick! I am going to rock your fucking world," and then buzzed his secretary. "Nadine, I would like for you to place a call to a Calvin Connors for me. He's an attorney over in Fort

Worth." As he waited for his secretary to get his "old friend" on the line, Reginald thumbed through the cover feature, which was appropriately titled "Texas Justice Gone Wrong."

Seconds later, Nadine buzzed him back. "Mr. Connors is on line one."

"Thanks, Nadine." Reginald took a deep breath and cleared his throat before pressing the blinking button. "Cal, how are you, my friend?"

"Reggie, I've been meaning to call you, but, hell, I've been busier than a three-peckered goat. You know how that is." Cal laughed loudly, causing Reginald to hold the phone away from his ear. "Congratulations on your new gig! Well deserved. You're just what we need here in the Northern District. How is it to be back in Dallas?"

"Quite frankly, a big relief. Liz was constantly bitching about Austin not having any good shopping or restaurants. She just never got into that laid-back lifestyle. You know how women can be."

"Do I ever. Hell, I've been married twice, and that's it for me. Hey, I need to buy you lunch, dinner, whatever your schedule permits. You just let me know what works for you."

"That's why I was calling. I'd like to get together, the sooner the better."

Cal sensed trouble and backtracked. "Well, I know this week is out. My schedule is booked solid—depositions, hearings, you name it. It's nothing urgent, is it Reggie?"

Reginald cringed at Cal's continued use of his old nickname and then replied, "Well, have you seen the latest issue of *Texas Matters*?"

Cal lied. "I don't read that crap. In my opinion, it's no better than the *National Enquirer*. The editors are so desperate to keep that rag afloat they'll print anything."

Reginald ignored Cal's editorializing. "You made the cover."

"You've got to be shitting me."

"Nope. I'm looking at it right now."

"What in the hell are they writing about me for?"

"Well, it's a lengthy story. You might want to pick up a copy."

Silence on the other end of the line.

Reginald continued, "Cal, there are some serious allegations made against you in the article—subornation of perjury, fraud, to name a few."

Cal screamed into the receiver, "What a crock of shit! Well, I can tell you one thing. They won't get away with printing all those lies. I'll sue that rag for millions. Hell, I'll own the whole fucking magazine."

Reginald smiled at Cal's performance. "You may be right but, in the meantime, I've got to open a preliminary investigation into the matter."

"Reggie, we go way back. C'mon, you don't need to do that."

"I wish I didn't, but I don't have a choice. Hell, the local newspapers would be all over me if I did nothing. I'm new in this position, and I can't afford any negative publicity."

Cal cringed. "Like I said, my schedule is crammed the rest of this week. Let me check my calendar and get back to you."

"Fine. Why don't we meet at our offices in Fort Worth? That'll be easier for you, and I need to make a trip over there anyway. Would that work?"

"That's a little formal, isn't it?"

"I've gotta keep my distance, Cal. I am sure you can understand why. So you'll get back to me with a date?"

"Yeah, but it may take me a couple of days."

"I'll be looking for your call. And Cal, don't lose any sleep over this. I'm just going through the motions, that's all."

Cal replied coldly, "I'll be in touch," followed by a click and a dial tone.

Reginald punched in the number of one of the staff attorneys in his Fort Worth branch. "Ben, how are you?"

"Fine, Boss. How are things over in Dallas?"

"I'm settling in. Hey, listen, I'd like you to work on a case with me."

"You got it. Who's the unlucky bastard?"

"Cal Connors."

"I know Cal. Hell, everyone in Fort Worth does. What are we going after him for?"

"You obviously haven't read the latest issue of *Texas Matters*."

"Read a magazine? Are you kidding? With the caseload I've got, I don't have time to read anything but work stuff."

"I know, I know. But I need you to pick up a copy as soon as you can. Connors is on the cover. This reporter," Reginald glanced at the article, "Leah Rosen, has written some pretty serious shit about ol' Cal. She's accused him of perpetrating a huge legal fraud involving millions of dollars in manufactured jury awards—in courts all over Texas."

"Are you kidding me?"

"It's right there in black and white. And I don't think *Texas Matters* would run a story like that without having all their ducks in a row. Ms. Rosen probably had sources out the wazoo."

"Maybe I ought to fly down to Austin and have a sit-down with this Rosen woman."

"That's what I was going to suggest."

"Do you know her?"

"I met her boss, Steve Blumenthal, at some cocktail parties a while back, but I don't know Ms. Rosen."

"Well, I'll get on this immediately. This could be huge."

"I agree. And Ben, I talked with Connors a few minutes ago. I told him I wanted to meet with him at our offices in Fort Worth as soon as possible. I want you to sit in on that meeting."

"You got it. When is it scheduled?" Ben asked.

"Connors is going to get back to me with a date."

"If the allegations are as serious as you say they are, I wouldn't hold my breath." Ben chuckled.

"If I don't hear back from him in the next day or so, I'll call him."

"Just let me know."

"And Ben? Let's not leave any stone unturned in this investigation. This is a career maker."

"I'm all over it. I'll give Miss Rosen a call and set up a meeting in the morning."

Reginald opened one of his desk drawers and pulled out a cigar, which he unwrapped, sniffed, and then placed in the side of his mouth. He rocked back in his chair and propped his feet up on the desk, a satisfying image playing in his mind of a humbled Cal Connors, anxiously pacing back and forth in his office.

After ending his call with Cowan, Cal continued to glare at the phone in his office as if it were somehow at fault. He swiveled around in his chair and picked up the issue of Texas Matters from the top of his desk. There he was – big as Texas – on the cover for the whole world to see. His motto through the years had always been "there is no such thing as bad publicity." Or, as his dad had once said, "Son, I don't care if you make a good impression or a bad one – just make a damn impression." Right now he was questioning the wisdom of those sayings.

Cal had burst into Christine's office after reading the article for the first time, demanding an explanation. After all, hadn't she assured him that he had nothing to worry about with that Rosen woman? But after confronting his daughter and hearing everything she had done to kill the story, Cal had backed off. There was no use in breaking ranks now. He and Christine were in for the fight of their life. They had to stick together.

Cal slowly rose from his chair and paced back and forth in his office. This was serious shit. He could lose his law license or worse, spend time in jail. He needed a plan. Sure, he had stepped over the line here and there. But he had done it for his clients - the working people, people who counted on him, people who had been taken advantage of by Corporate America. In his mind, he and his expert, Dr. Howell Crimm, had done no more than level the playing field, making the courtroom face-offs fair fights. Cal's clients had been handsomely compensated for their losses, and Cal and Crimm had made a killing as well. So what was wrong with that? After all, wasn't this the United States of America – the land of opportunity?

Cal thought about Crimm. He would be facing the same charges – unless he cut a deal to save his own ass. No doubt that turncoat son-of-a-bitch Cowan would try and flip him. He could talk with Crimm before the feds got to him. But how would he hold up in a windowless interrogation room being double-teamed by two FBI agents, using the good-cop/bad-cop routine? Cal shook his head – not good. He needed to find a way to discredit his former expert witness and ally – undermine his credibility, punch holes in his story, raise "reasonable doubt" as to the veracity of his version of the "truth."

To put his plan into action, Cal needed the best lawyer money could buy: someone who knew how to pick the most sympathetic juries, how to cross-examine the most difficult witnesses, how to deliver a closing argument that left those twelve people sitting in the jury box spell-bound and anxious to retire to the jury room to render a verdict in his favor. But that wasn't enough. He needed a lawyer who had the respect of every federal judge in the Fort Worth division. After all, if Cal were indicted, the trial would be in his hometown. If he played his cards right, he could turn this thing around and use the publicity to get more clients than he could handle.

Cal turned and walked back to his desk. He buzzed his secretary, "Darlene, get Jace Forman on the line for me."

CHAPTER

The jury had been out for two days before the parties and counsel reassembled in the courtroom. Judge Zimmerman bustled in and asked the bailiff to bring in the jury.

"Ladies and gentlemen of the jury, have you reached a verdict?"

In a loud voice, the female juror on the front row responded, "We have, Your Honor."

"Is your verdict unanimous?"

"It is."

"Bailiff, please bring me the jury's verdict."

The courtroom was silent as a graveyard while the bailiff made his way to the jury box, received the charge from the forewoman, and then delivered it to the judge. The unsettling quiet continued as the judge slowly read through the jury's answers to the questions submitted. After she finished, she cleared her throat and began to recite from the document in front of her.

"'Do you find from a preponderance of the evidence that the defendants, Ezekiel Shaw and the Brimstone Bible Church, intentionally and recklessly engaged in extreme and outrageous conduct that caused Janice and Eugene Hanson to suffer emotional distress?'"

Judge Zimmerman paused and peered over the rims of her glasses before revealing the answer.

"To that question, the jury answered 'We do.'"

Jace closed his eyes and breathed a sigh of relief. Darrin masked a grin and looked at Jace. Crom hung his head as his client stared at the judge with a contemptuous expression.

Judge Zimmerman continued. "'What amount of money in dollars and cents do you find from a preponderance of the evidence are the actual damages suffered as a result of this extreme and outrageous conduct?'"

Another pause.

"The jury has awarded five hundred thousand dollars in actual damages."

Jace tried unsuccessfully to disguise his displeasure. Darrin bit her lip. Crom held his head a little higher. A sneer began to form on Shaw's lips.

Judge Zimmerman cleared her throat before reading the last question and answer.

"'What amount of money, in dollars and cents, do you find from a preponderance of the evidence should be awarded in punitive damages to deter extreme and outrageous conduct of this nature?'" Without pausing the judge read, "'Twenty million.'"

Out of respect, Jace and Darrin delayed their celebration until the judge had dismissed the jury and vacated the bench. As soon as judge and jury had cleared the courtroom, Darrin threw her arms around Jace's neck and pulled him close. She whispered in his ear, "I knew you could do it. I just knew it."

After walking to within feet of Darrin and Jace, Shaw shouted, "Hey, Forman. Nice work, but it's all for nothing. You won't collect a fucking dime from me." With both arms, Crom was trying to pull back his client. "Not one fucking dime. Did you hear me? It's all in trust. I don't own anything. Do you hear me? Nothing. And neither does my church."

As Crom struggled to push his client down the aisle toward the exit, Jace and Darrin began packing up their files. Darrin could hardly contain her excitement and whispered, "So where are we going to celebrate, Jace? I'm ready to blow off a little steam, and that's an understatement."

"Let's head over to the Flying Saucer, have a few drinks, and discuss where we should go to dinner."

"Perfect!"

Ten minutes later Darrin and Jace were seated at a cozy two-top at the Flying Saucer, in Sundance Square, Jace sipping on a Shiner Bock and Darrin a glass of pinot grigio.

"Well, no doubt Maddy's testimony was a game changer," Jace offered.

"Judge Zimmerman was ready to throw our case out. We dodged a bullet on that one. I hate to admit it, but Jackie really came through for us. Did you get a chance to talk to her while she was here?"

"Just briefly at the courthouse. I owe her big-time for getting Maddy here."

Darrin didn't respond but rose from the table. "I need to go to the ladies room. Would you mind ordering another glass of wine for me if the waiter comes by?"

"Sure." After Darrin left the table, Jace fished in his coat pocket for his cell. He had powered it off before entering Judge Zimmerman's courtroom and had forgotten to turn it back on afterward. There was a voicemail from Jackie. As he listened to it, a faint smile creased his lips and then morphed into a frown. The kudos were nice but her insistence on a weekend at his place problematic. He then did a couple of quick Internet searches and slipped the phone back in his coat pocket just as Darrin slid into her seat.

"So where should we go to dinner?" Darrin asked.

"How about Bayona's?"

Darrin looked puzzled. "Never heard of it."

"That's because it's in New Orleans."

"Pretty funny. Seriously, where do you want to go?"

"I was being serious." Jace glanced at his watch. "I just double-checked and there is a non-stop flight from Love to New Orleans leaving at 5:30. That would get us there in plenty of time for dinner."

"So where would we stay?"

"I made reservations at the Royal Sonesta on Bourbon Street while you were in the ladies room."

Darrin smiled. "You'd have to take me by my place so I could pack."

"That dress looks great on you – perfect for Bayona's. No need for you to pack a damn thing. So how about a 'yes' this time?"

Darrin leaned across the table and kissed him on the lips. "Does that answer your question?"

EPILOGUE

Ezekiel Shaw looked at the clock on the wall of his den and, with irritation, wondered where his latest disciple, thirteen-year-old Tammy Carnes, could be. He heard the doorbell ring and, with an expectant smile, walked hurriedly to the door and opened it. A petite redheaded girl with freckles peered up at him, her eyelids batting nervously.

"Come on in, Tammy."

She walked timidly through the threshold.

"Do you want to play some games like we did the last time?"

Tammy didn't respond.

Shaw forced a laugh. "A little shy tonight? A cat got your tongue?"

Still no response.

"Why don't we get you something to drink? Break the ice a little. Go on into the kitchen and wait for me."

Tammy walked slowly toward the kitchen while Shaw headed to the bedroom. The candles were lit. Everything was ready. He just needed to get his young disciple in the mood. He opened the door to the secret cabinet where his liquor was stored and pulled out a bottle of vodka—not much taste and no smell. He poured two ounces into a glass and returned the bottle to its hiding place.

As he entered the kitchen, he asked, "How about a little orange juice?"

Still no response.

"You really are quiet tonight." He handed the glass of orange juice and vodka to Tammy. "Bottoms up."

"I'm not thirsty."

"It'll taste good," Shaw tempted.

"I don't want any."

"All right then. Have it your way." Shaw was becoming impatient. "Okay, let's get to it then."

He took Tammy by the hand and led her to the bedroom. After positioning himself in his throne-like chair, he ordered, "Take off that dress and, while you're at it, anything you have under it. I'm waiting."

As she began to unbutton her dress, there was a loud crash, and two police officers burst into the room.

"Don't move. You're under arrest. Tom, cuff him." He smiled deeply at the young girl as he spoke. "Everything is going to be okay, honey."

"This is an outrage!" Shaw yelled.

"Yeah, it's an outrage, all right. One that's ending tonight."

"I don't know what you're talking about."

"Nice try, but nobody's buying. We've had you and your entire compound under video surveillance since the Hanson trial. The best lawyer in the world couldn't get you out of this shit. You're done, Savior Shaw or whatever they call you, you sick son-of-a-bitch. The jury will put you under the jail. I guarantee it."

As the officer led his prisoner to the patrol car, Shaw screamed, "You'll never get away with this! I'll sue your department for everything it's worth! I promise you that! It's God's will that I continue my work!"

As the officer forced Shaw's head into the squad car, he replied, "Not my God, not my God."

<u>About The Author</u>

Hubert Crouch is a graduate of Phillips Andover Academy, Vanderbilt University, and Southern Methodist University School of Law. He is a practicing trial lawyer in Texas, with over thirty-five years of experience in the courtroom. In addition to practicing law, he has taught Free Speech and the First Amendment and Legal Advocacy to undergraduates at Southern Methodist University and, during that time, was awarded the Rotunda Outstanding Professor Award. An avid rock and roll fan, he has played guitar in a Sixties "cover" band for over thirty years. He and his wife split their time between their home in Dallas, Texas and their mountain retreat near Sewanee, Tennessee. He welcomes visitors and messages at his website: www.hubertcrouch.com

CPSIA information can be obtained at www.ICGtesting.com
Printed in the USA
LVOW10s1632270415

436263LV00008B/1272/P